The Guide to Assisting Students
With Disabilities

Lisa M. Meeks, PhD, is on faculty with the University of California, San Francisco School of Medicine (UCSF-SOM). She is also the director of medical student disability services (MSDS) and provides disability services to all medical students. She is president elect and co-founder of the Coalition for Disability Access in Health Science and Medical Education and consults with private industry, other educational institutions, and government agencies on issues around disability and health care. Through her service to UCSF via the Chancellor's Committee on Disabilities, as provider for the SOM, and through her position in the Coalition, Dr. Meeks has helped shape the future of health science education for students with disabilities. Her expertise is recognized by some of the leading educational, governmental, and private institutions in the United States.

Neera R. Jain, MS, CRC, is a rehabilitation counselor by training and a passionate advocate for equal access in higher education, with a specialization in working with graduate and professional students in the health sciences. She was the first dedicated staff member to serve students with disabilities at two major health sciences institutions in the United States—the Columbia University Medical Center campus in New York City, and the University of California, San Francisco (UCSF). Formerly the director of student disability services at UCSF, she now consults for the university remotely from Auckland, New Zealand. In New Zealand, she is currently the manager of Auckland Disability Law (ADL), a specialist service that is part of the Community Law Centre movement. ADL is New Zealand's only law practice dedicated to serving the unmet legal needs of disabled Kiwis. She received her master's degree from Boston University.

The Guide to Assisting Students With Disabilities

Equal Access in Health Science and Professional Education

Lisa M. Meeks, PhD

Neera R. Jain, MS, CRC

Editors

SPRINGER PUBLISHING COMPANY
NEW YORK

Springer Publishing Company, LLC
11 West 42nd Street
New York, NY 10036
www.springerpub.com

Acquisitions Editor: Sheri W. Sussman
Composition: S4Carlisle Publishing Services

ISBN: 978-0-8261-2374-9
e-book ISBN: 978-0-8261-2379-4
Student Resource ISBN: 978-0-8261-3144-7

Student resource is available from www.springerpub.com/meeks-jain

15 16 17 18 19 / 5 4 3 2 1

The author and the publisher of this Work have made every effort to use sources believed to be reliable to provide information that is accurate and compatible with the standards generally accepted at the time of publication. The author and publisher shall not be liable for any special, consequential, or exemplary damages resulting, in whole or in part, from the readers' use of, or reliance on, the information contained in this book. The publisher has no responsibility for the persistence or accuracy of URLs for external or third-party Internet websites referred to in this publication and does not guarantee that any content on such websites is, or will remain, accurate or appropriate.

Library of Congress Cataloging-in-Publication Data

The guide to assisting students with disabilities : equal access in health science and professional education / [edited by] Lisa M. Meeks, Neera R. Jain.
    p. ; cm.
Includes bibliographical references and index.
ISBN 978-0-8261-2374-9—ISBN 978-0-8261-2379-4 (e-book)
I. Meeks, Lisa, editor. II. Jain, Neera R., editor.
[DNLM: 1. Disabled Persons—education—United States. 2. Students, Health Occupations—United States. 3. Disability Evaluation—United States. 4. Disabled Persons—legislation & jurisprudence—United States. 5. Needs Assessment—United States. 6. Schools, Health Occupations—organization & administration—United States. W 18]
HV3023.A3
362.40973—dc23
                                                                                            2015011029

Printed in the United States of America by McNaughton & Gunn.

To my children, Kate and Chris: You are my world and I love you both;
and to my amazing Cleveland and San Francisco friends who understand
when I am "in the zone."

also

To Ms. Neera Jain, my co-editor, colleague, and dear friend: You are a bright star
with a big heart. You are more brilliant and powerful than you realize.
To the faculty and staff at UCSF for their dedication to students with disabilities
and to providing an accessible and supportive environment.

To Tim and Greg: The three musketeers did it! You guys are the best!

Lisa

****

To Ronald, who makes my world go 'round, and goes with me 'round the world;
my parents, who fueled a passion for access to education; and Lisa, my partner in
crime, for giving me the courage and for making dreams real.

also

To the original Brooklyn dinner party crew, lighting the fire and fighting the
good fight, one social-justice–infused Malbec at a time; and to all the teachers and
mentors along the way, especially Dr. Dell Orto, Dr. Creasey, Dr. Brinckerhoff,
Dr. Demore-Taber, Susan Martell, and Colleen Lewis.

Most of all, to students with disabilities and their allies across the world, who are
pushing open doors, making a fuss, demanding difference, and changing the face of
health care as we know it. Thanks for letting me join you on the ride!

Kia kaha!

Neera

Contents

4.   Accommodations in Didactic, Lab,
and Clinical Settings   *59*
*Jan Serrantino, Lisa M. Meeks, Neera R. Jain, Grace C. Clifford,
    and Jane Thierfeld Brown*

5.   The Process of Requesting Accommodations on
Certification, Licensing, and Board Exams:
Assisting Students Through the Application   *89*
Neera R. Jain, Colleen Lewis, Lisa M. Meeks, and Thomas H. Tucker, II

6.   Learning in the Digital Age: Assistive Technology
and Electronic Access   *119*
*Michael J. Kenney, Neera R. Jain, Lisa M. Meeks, Elisa Laird-Metke,
    Joshua Hori, and Jonathan D. McGough*

Contributors

Shelby Acteson, MEd,   Oregon Health & Science University, Director of Student Access, Portland, Oregon

Jane Thierfeld Brown, EdD,   Assistant Clinical Professor, Yale Medical School, Child Study Center, New Haven, Connecticut; Co-Director, College Autism Spectrum

Grace C. Clifford, MAEd,   Case Western Reserve University, Associate Director for Disability Resources, Cleveland, Ohio

J. Leigh Culley, MEd,   University of Pittsburgh, Interim Director, Disability Resources and Services, Pittsburgh, Pennsylvania

Barbara L. Hammer, MEd,   University of Missouri, Director, Disability Center, Division of Student Affairs, Columbia, Missouri

Joshua Hori,   University of California, Davis, Accessible Technology Analyst, Student Disability Center, Davis, California

Neera R. Jain, MS, CRC,   Auckland Disability Law, Inc., Manager, Auckland, New Zealand; University of California, San Francisco, Disability Consultant, Student Disability Services, San Francisco, California

Michael J. Kenney, PhD,   Case Western Reserve University, Assistant Director, Faculty Support and Academic Technologies, Information Technology Services, Cleveland, Ohio

Elisa Laird-Metke, JD,   University of California, San Francisco, Associate Director, Student Disability Services, San Francisco, California

Colleen Lewis, MS,   Columbia University, Director of Disability Services, New York, New York

Jonathan D. McGough, MEd(c),   University of Washington, Assistant Director, Disability Resources for Students, Seattle, Washington

Lisa M. Meeks, PhD,   School of Medicine, University of California, San Francisco, Director, Medical Student Disability Services, San Francisco, California

Timothy Montgomery, MA,   Northwestern University, Assistant Director, AccessibleNU, Chicago, Illinois

Gregory A. Moorehead, EdD,   The University of Chicago, Director of Student Disability Services, Chicago, Illinois

Joseph F. Murray, MD,   Weill Cornell Medical College, Associate Dean of Student Affairs, New York, New York

Erin K. Phair, MA,   MGH Institute of Health Professions, Manager of Student and Disability Services, Boston, Massachusetts

Jan Serrantino, EdD,   University of California, Irvine, Director, Disability Services Center, Irvine, California

Thomas H. Tucker, II, MSPH,   A.T. Still University of Health Sciences, Director, Learning Resources, Kirksville, Missouri

Alice Wong, MS,   University of California, San Francisco, Staff Research Associate, Department of Social and Behavioral Studies, Community Living Policy Center, San Francisco, California

Foreword

If you are reading this foreword, you are probably aware of the growth in the health care sector, the demographics of disability in higher education, and the trends in medical and health sciences education. My first thought after reading the description for this guide was, "Here is much needed and practical guidance." I was not disappointed. As we approach the 25th anniversary of the Americans with Disabilities Act (ADA), I was reading the book primed to look for the broader themes that motivated this pragmatic content. For me, the theme of how far people with disabilities have come in the health sciences provides a context—a "Rosetta Stone"—for translating this guide into practice.

In September 1973, Section 504 of the Rehabilitation Act was signed into law. Concern about (resistance to) providing disability accommodations delayed implementation of the law until the spring of 1977. Two years later, the Supreme Court heard the first case under Section 504: *Southeastern Community College v. Davis.* Frances Davis, a Licensed Practical Nurse with a significant hearing loss, was denied admission to a Registered Nursing program and challenged the school's decision in court. The same issues we face today—reasonable accommodations, technical standards, fundamental alterations, and patient safety—were addressed in the decision. Although the Court ruled that the school could legally bar Ms. Davis from enrolling based solely on her hearing disability, it recognized that this may not always be the case for future students:

> We do not suggest that the line between a lawful refusal to extend affirmative action and illegal discrimination against handicapped persons always will be clear. It is possible to envision situations where an insistence on continuing past requirements and practices might arbitrarily deprive genuinely qualified handicapped persons of the opportunity to participate in a covered program. Technological advances can be expected to enhance opportunities to rehabilitate the handicapped or otherwise to qualify them for some useful employment. Such advances also may enable attainment of these goals without imposing undue financial and administrative burdens upon a State. Thus, situations may arise where a refusal to modify an existing program might become unreasonable and discriminatory.
> *Southeastern Community College v. Davis*, 442 U.S. 397 (1979)

In this case the Supreme Court predicted that improvements in technology could give students with disabilities the ability to complete educational goals that were unattainable at the time. Society has advanced as well; the ADA passed in 1990 and was refreshed with amendments and new regulations in 2008 and 2010, helping to increase disability awareness, reduce stigma, and promote the inclusion of individuals with disabilities across all aspects of society. Today, with the provision of appropriate accommodations, students who have disabilities that were once considered insurmountable barriers regularly complete demanding programs in the health sciences.

Although challenges for the disability rights movement remain 35 years later, I want to highlight a few victories following the *Davis* decision to keep in mind as you read the following chapters addressing the laws, policies, and practices that have evolved since that decision. In 1992, a profoundly Deaf student was admitted to medical school at East Carolina University—just a little over 100 miles from Southeastern Community College that denied entrance to Ms. Davis—and other schools around the country have followed suit. More recently, medical students with significant hearing loss at the University of California, Davis, and the University of California, San Francisco, entered their surgical and anesthesia rotations, made accessible with technologies that the Supreme Court could not have envisioned in 1979.

What I find most notable about these examples is that the schools' decisions to provide accommodations were based on their commitment to diversity, not on a court order. Faculty and disability resource professionals from those schools, as well as other schools, worked together to ensure a positive learning experience and a welcoming environment. To help further this interschool collaboration, in 2013, the Coalition for Disability Access in Health Science and Medical Education ("the Coalition") was established. The Coalition facilitates the exchange of innovative ideas and promotes best practices for providing disability accommodations in the health sciences, helping move forward the agenda of inclusion. And while the climate has changed for the better, the courts, the Department of Justice, and the Department of Education continue to be active and instrumental across a range of programs and disabilities. Indeed, just this year we have witnessed a number of legal challenges involving accommodations for learning disabilities, amputations, blindness, depression, and vision. Such ongoing legal challenges continue to shape and inform the work of disability services providers.

I want to share one accommodation story from my own practice working with employees, which directly relates to the Supreme Court's 1979 prediction. Health care providers, like many aging adults, may at some stage of their careers become persons with disabilities. A respiratory therapist who has worked for our medical center for a good number of years lost her hearing over time, moving from a standard stethoscope to an amplified one. The day came when the amplified stethoscope no longer did the trick. After a bit of research, we discovered that (indeed) there is an app for that! The app connects a stethoscope to a smartphone and graphs the sounds, then saves them along with a synchronized recording. When we approached the department head and proposed this equipment as a disability accommodation for the respiratory therapist, his first response was, "The technical standard is 'Must hear breath sounds.'" After I speculated that the standard was written at a time when cutting-edge technology was rolling up a tube of paper to place on the patient's chest, he agreed the intent was to *distinguish* breath sounds. With his agreement, we purchased the equipment and the therapist was able to effectively return to work. A week later, the department head called and asked if I could provide his department with another visual stethoscope—he said all the other therapists were borrowing the respiratory therapist's stethoscope so that they too could confirm their readings visually and up-load a record to their patient files. As with many accommodations, what is good for the person with a disability is often good for all.

In *Southeastern Community College v. Davis*, Frances Davis, the plaintiff, said her goal was to become a nurse in the Deaf community where, like today, both accessible medical care and professional role models are in short supply. Ms. Davis ultimately achieved her goal, albeit at a different institution—one willing to provide accommodations. The authors of this text—all members of the Coalition—are committed to helping institutions ensure their programs are accessible. With their guidance they invite you and your institution to be a part of the movement toward innovative approaches to accessibility in health science education.

L. Scott Lissner
ADA Coordinator
The Ohio State University
Past President, Association on Higher Education And Disability

Preface

The number of students with disabilities in health science programs is increasing rapidly. However, resources for assisting students, understanding accommodations, and maintaining legal compliance are scarce. This text offers a comprehensive look at how to meet and exceed the needs of students with disabilities in academic health science settings. The clear format allows the reader to use the book as a manual to help address a specific need, as a tool for training other school personnel, or as a guide to help students understand their role in the process. Legal explanations and examples of previous litigation are provided as a framework for each topic discussed. The text also provides sample forms and policies, including disability verification forms, letters of accommodation, e-mail communications, and syllabi statements. **"Professionalism in Communication: A Guide for Graduate and Professional Health Science Students With Disabilities" is also available for download from Springer Publishing Company's website: www .springerpub.com/meeks-jain.**

This comprehensive guide provides the health science program administrator, dean, faculty member, and disability services provider with a richer understanding of working with this population of students. The reader learns, through example vignettes and legal cases, about best practices for good decision making, what happens when things go awry, and how to avoid problems by implementing strong accessibility-focused policies.

Written by some of the most educated providers on the topic, at some of the most prestigious health science schools in the country, this text is backed by years of practice and expertise and is written in an easy-to-read, engaging manner that makes disability, and disability law, accessible to all. To honor our commitment to improving access in the health sciences for students with disabilities, all proceeds from this book will go directly to the Coalition for Disability Access in Health Science and Medical Education.

Acknowledgments

The editors wish to acknowledge the following individuals for their contributions to this book:

Sheri W. Sussman, Executive Editor at Springer Publishing Company, for believing in this project and supporting us through the process.

Elisa Laird-Metke, JD, for providing invaluable insight, guidance, and legal expertise on this book. We are forever indebted to you for your tireless fact-checking and editorial suggestions.

Nathaniel L. Jones, for your patience, comma corrections, and editorial expertise. Thank you for guiding the flow of each chapter and for being the first reader.

Dr. Ronald Kramer, for your keen eye and your thoughtful corrections. Thank you for the final touches and for being the last reader.

Our contributing authors, for their tireless work, for their commitment to this project, and for sharing their expertise page by page.

We also wish to acknowledge the following groups for their contributions to this book:

*The members of the **Coalition for Disability Access in Health Science and Medical Education** for their collective expertise and willingness to share their triumphs and tribulations.*

*The faculty and administration at the **University of California, San Francisco,** for their commitment to supporting students with disabilities and the development of this text.*

Students with disabilities in the health sciences: You teach us every day. You are the real experts.

Introduction

A CALL FOR EQUAL ACCESS IN HEALTH SCIENCE AND PROFESSIONAL EDUCATION

A few years ago I had to find a new primary care physician (PCP). I casually mentioned to friends and family that my new PCP is legally blind. Some people joked, "Really?! How does *that* work?" Others had serious questions about how a PCP who is legally blind would be able to perform examinations.

These kinds of comments are emblematic of the pervasive ableism in every aspect of society (Smith, Foley, & Chaney, 2008). Examples of ableism include questioning a person's competency because of perceived difference and seeing normative abilities as superior to other modes of being and activity. As a disabled Asian American woman who has a congenital disability, I experience ableism daily and such comments are not unusual. People with disabilities are easily understood as "the patient" within the health professional–patient dyad and very rarely seen as "the professional." Systemic and institutionalized ableism marginalizes people with disabilities by categorizing them as "vulnerable populations" that are "objects of care," not "professionals with expertise." The thought that a person with a disability can be a health care professional challenges, at minimum: (1) the notion of what comprises "typical" health care professionals (i.e., what they look like and how they perform their work); and (2) the low societal expectation that people with disabilities will attain a role with such authority, legitimacy, and competency.

The terms *diversity* and *cultural competency* are touted as important priorities in health science and medical education programs because having a diverse workforce is a social good that makes business sense and a way to reduce health disparities (Cohen, Gabriel, & Terrell, 2002). This is all true. However, the definition of diversity most often used leaves much to be desired. Universities aim to have diversified workforces and students by focusing outreach on women; racial, ethnic, and linguistic minorities; lesbian, gay, bisexual, transgender, queer, and other (LGBTQ+) individuals; immigrants; and veterans. With approximately 57 million Americans with disabilities in the United States—the country's largest minority at 18.7% of the general population—people with disabilities are still often excluded from diversity initiatives, practices, and policies (Brault, 2012; McKee, Smith, Barnett, & Pearson, 2013).

The Association of American Medical Colleges has included disability in its description of cultural competence for less than a decade (DeLisa & Lindenthal, 2012). One recent survey suggests that people with disabilities are vastly underrepresented in the health professions, with 2% to 10% of practicing physicians being individuals with disabilities even though such individuals make up about 20% of the overall population (DeLisa & Lindenthal, 2012). Societal attitudes, blatant discrimination, and access issues are several reasons for such low numbers, suggesting serious challenges to providing equal access to students with all types of disabilities in the health sciences and medical education.

The definition of *disability*, like that of *diversity*, has a narrow meaning for some. Having a disability is still considered by many as something purely related to health, disease, functional limitation, and impairment of the body, especially in the health sciences (Long-Bellil et al., 2011). However, there *is* a disability culture and there *are* disability communities everywhere (Robey et al., 2013). Increasing the number of culturally competent professionals with disabilities in the health sciences will broaden the knowledge base and breadth of experience within all fields, in addition to filling a critical shortage in the health care workforce. The increased presence and perspectives of people with disabilities will influence the way professionals view disability and the assumptions associated with it. Moreover, professionals with disabilities can improve patient care, impact research agendas and workplace attitudes toward disability, and reduce the significant barriers to health care, discrimination, and ableism experienced by people with disabilities (Disability Rights Education and Defense Fund, n.d.; Moreland, Latimore, Sen, Arato, & Zazove, 2013; Smeltzer, Avery, & Haynor, 2012).

An expansion of what the terms *disability* and *diversity* mean is a step in the right direction. Another critical step requires challenging the presumed abilities associated with being a student or professional in the health sciences (Association of American Medical Colleges, 2013). A student with a visual disability may need a microscope slide projected onto a screen rather than looking into the actual microscope. A student of short stature may use a step stool or an adjustable exam table to have access to a patient during rotations. These types of accommodations and adaptations do not take away from the patient experience or the student's abilities. In fact, I would argue that exposure to these different ways of doing things improves health care in general. For example, other students may discover that having images projected from a microscope to a screen can reduce eyestrain and provide easier viewing. Adjustable exam tables that are meant for a patient or health professional with a disability can suddenly become popular and used by a wide array of patients and colleagues because of their ergonomic features.

University leaders need to initiate a policy and culture shift that encourages prospective students with disabilities and communicates that they belong and are needed in the health sciences and medical education.

Students with disabilities, particularly those with visible disabilities, in the health sciences are often one in a population of several thousand. Again and again they describe the implicit messages they receive from their schools: *You are not part of this social landscape. Professional health science programs have such rigorous academic and physical requirements that it is going to be very difficult for you to succeed. People already wonder how you got into this program. Keep your head down; you already stick out enough.* In short, their disabled bodies are made to feel out of place among the student and professional body.

While people with physical or visible disabilities deal with a limited presence, there are many more students with invisible disabilities, such as psychiatric and learning disabilities, who feel uncomfortable being "out." Dr. Leana S. Wen (2014) recently wrote about her experiences in medical school:

> As I saw blatant examples of unequal and insensitive care to patients with disabilities, I felt anger, then shame and fear. I knew that the right thing to do was to speak up, but I was so afraid that I would be exposing myself and my own disability. Throughout medical training, my greatest fear was that my supervisors would find out about my stuttering and deem me unfit to fulfill my dream of becoming a doctor. There were few doctors with disabilities to serve as role models; though one or two of my professors stuttered, they never talked about it. I don't recall anyone else, not a colleague or superior, who was open about having a disability. (para. 21)

This fear and uncomfortable environment is real for students with visible and nonapparent disabilities whether they use accommodations or not.

Accommodations in educational and clinical settings are a right, not a privilege or "special advantage." They facilitate learning and work, bringing out the full potential of students with disabilities, which benefits the entire educational environment. If students see faculty and staff treat accommodations as natural parts of the workplace, it could create a ripple effect, encouraging students to be open about their identity and disability-related needs.

This ripple effect of disability acceptance can happen when institutions practice what they preach. Academic institutions can take several steps to ensure equal access for students with disabilities in the health sciences and medical education:

1. Embrace people with disabilities as a culturally diverse group in hiring, recruitment, and admission practices.
2. Create a welcoming campus climate for students with disabilities (e.g., accessible built environment, staff and faculty familiar with provision of accommodations, resources for students with disabilities such as campus organizations, and an administration that is responsive to the needs of students with disabilities).

3. Re-frame accommodations as a diversity best practice that benefits the entire student body and campus community.
4. Establish staff and programs that provide streamlined services to students with disabilities once they are enrolled, including clear policies and courses of actions for students to take in order to access needed services and appeal or file grievances, if needed.
5. Highlight the visibility of staff and faculty with disabilities (who have already disclosed this information) working on campus.
6. Support early educational programs and outreach efforts that encourage young students with disabilities to go into the health sciences, similar to current Science, Technology, Engineering, and Mathematics (STEM) initiatives for girls and people of color.
7. Integrate disability culture within cultural competency curricula. (Thomas Smith, Roth, Okoro, Kimberlin, & Odedina, 2011)

The authors in this book describe how universities can serve students with disabilities effectively and provide recommendations and solutions for complex issues related to accommodations and communication about disability-related needs. As professionals who work with students with disabilities every day, these authors demonstrate how even the most difficult or seemingly impossible case can be adequately resolved through good working relationships with students, creativity, and flexibility—while maintaining rigorous academic standards.

I did not choose my current PCP because of his disability or "in spite of" his disability. I chose him for his excellence as a doctor who listens well and actually "gets it" when I communicate my access- and disability-related needs. My PCP may do these things well as a result of his training, his education, and his lived experiences as a person with a disability—one cannot separate these elements. *And this is why diversity is so valuable.*

Diversity by disability matters beyond mere representation—it provides a critical counterbalance to the health care experience, benefiting patients, professionals, and communities. For me, it is simply an issue of power and equity.

Alice Wong, MS
University of California, San Francisco
Staff Research Associate
Department of Social and Behavioral Studies
Community Living Policy Center
San Francisco, California

REFERENCES

Association of American Medical Colleges. (2013, February). Part II: Medical students or health care professionals with disabilities. *GDI Navigator to Excellence: Summaries of Disability Articles in the* Journal of Academic Medicine 2001–2012. Retrieved from https://www.aamc.org/download/328092/data/disabilityarticlesinacademicmedicine.pdf

Brault, M. W. (2012). *Americans with disabilities: 2010.* Retrieved from http://www.census.gov/prod/2012pubs/p70-131.pdf

Cohen, J. J., Gabriel, B. A., & Terrell, C. (2002). The case for diversity in the health care workforce. *Health Affairs, 21*(5), 90–102.

DeLisa, J. A., & Lindenthal, J. J. (2012). Commentary: Reflections on diversity and inclusion in medical education. *Academic Medicine, 87*(11), 1461–1463.

Disability Rights Education and Defense Fund. (n.d.). *Welcome to healthcare stories.* Retrieved from http://dredf.org/healthcare-stories/

Long-Bellil, L. M., O'Connor, D. M., Robey, K. L., Earle Hahn, J., Minihan, P. M., Graham, C. L., & Smeltzer, S. C. (2011). Commentary: Defining disability in health education. *Academic Medicine, 86*(9), 1066–1068.

McKee, M. M., Smith, S., Barnett, S., & Pearson, T. A. (2013). Commentary: What are the benefits of training deaf and hard-of-hearing doctors? *Academic Medicine, 88*(2), 158–161.

Moreland, C. J., Latimore, D., Sen, A., Arato, N., & Zazove, P. (2013). Deafness among physicians and trainees: A national survey. *Academic Medicine, 88*(2), 224–232.

Robey, K. L., Minihan, P. M., Long-Bellil, L. M., Earle Hahn, J., Reiss, J. G., & Eddey, G. E. (2013). Teaching health care students about disability within a cultural competency context. *Disability and Health Journal, 6,* 271–279.

Smeltzer, S. C., Avery, C., & Haynor, P. (2012). Interactions of people with disabilities and nursing staff during hospitalization. *American Journal of Nursing, 112*(4), 30–37.

Smith, L., Foley, P. F., & Chaney, M. P. (2008). Addressing classism, ableism, and heterosexism in counselor education. *Journal of Counseling & Development, 86,* 303–309.

Thomas Smith, W., Roth, J. J., Okoro, O., Kimberlin, C., & Odedina, F. T. (2011). Disability in cultural competency pharmacy education. *American Journal of Pharmaceutical Education, 75*(2), article 26.

Wen, L. S. (2014, October 27). For people with disabilities, doctors are not always healers. *The Washington Post.* Retrieved from http://www.washingtonpost.com/national/health-science/for-people-with-disabilities-doctors-are-not-always-healers/2014/10/24/afb632e6-45a0-11e4-b437-1a7368204804_story.html

Know Your Campus Resources

Jonathan D. McGough and Joseph F. Murray

INTRODUCTION

This chapter discusses the role of the designated campus office for determining and implementing student accommodations, and how that office can work with other academic departments and student services. It also distinguishes the more limited role of the designated campus ADA coordinator, which is required by law, but is often entirely distinct due to its focus on managing compliance and related complaints. Finally, the authors discuss disability in the context of multiple student support programs, such as learning resources, tutoring programs, program advisors, veteran's services, first-generation initiatives, and multicultural resource programs.

In our own work and meetings with colleagues around the country, it is clear that health science and medical education programs are experiencing an increase in the number of students who self-identify as having a disability. Potential reasons for this trend include the legislative broadening of the term *disability*, which increased early interventions in primary and secondary education, as well as changes in the climate or stigma around having a disability. The increasing number of students with disabilities studying the health professions adds to the diversity of our student bodies and to a diverse workforce in the health sciences.

Despite the increasing number of students with disabilities, many institutions identify one university official responsible for coordinating services and accommodations for these students. Oftentimes this individual has multiple roles within the institution, instead of a dedicated role as a disability provider. Given the multitude of settings in which accommodations are needed and the nuances of clinical health science and professional education, it is difficult for one individual to support students with disabilities from admissions through graduation. Therefore, support for this growing population of students must be a shared effort, especially for schools with a one-person disability services (DS) office. This chapter explores how disability providers can build effective campus partnerships that pave the way toward a more accessible, inclusive environment, and identify those offices that provide additional supports for students with disabilities.

THE ROLE OF DISABILITY SERVICES

The office responsible for services for students with disabilities falls under a variety of names (e.g., disability resources, disability services, access services). Regardless of the name, each institution identifies a department (or person) that serves students with disabilities. The role of this office (or individual) in supporting students is three-fold: (1) determining and coordinating academic adjustments, reasonable modifications, and auxiliary aids; (2) ensuring students have equal access to all aspects of the university experience; and (3) helping students understand their civil rights as members of a protected class. Of equal importance is the office's support for faculty and staff in understanding the rights of students with disabilities and preserving the integrity of a professional program by recommending reasonable adjustments that do not fundamentally alter the nature of a program or challenge academic rigor. This multifaceted role requires DS staff to have a thorough understanding of state and federal laws, professional and technical standards in health science programs, and best practices.

It is important to acknowledge that despite the best efforts of faculty and administration, many students simply are not aware that DS resources exist. Faculty, staff, and administrators can be excellent referral sources, but often feel unqualified to answer detailed questions and are often uncomfortable with the term *disability* or the legal definition, which uses the word *impairment*. Furthermore, many administrators may not recognize their students as having a disability, given that students may be quite accomplished, especially those enrolled in graduate programs. Although talking about "disability" carries negative connotations for some, disability is an integral and positive aspect of identity for others. When referring a student to the DS office, administrators and faculty should focus on the barrier the student is facing, not the student's disability or presumed disability (see also Chapter 7, Professionalism and Communication About Disabilities and Accommodations). Faculty and staff can also work to normalize the DS office by including it as one of many resources available to students on campus. As this chapter illustrates, the DS office is *a support* for students with disabilities; it is not, however, *the only* one.

LEGAL COMPLIANCE RESPONSIBILITY

Numerous offices in each school oversee implementation of policies in accord with disability laws and regulations. DS providers work with these offices and their representatives to support students with disabilities and prevent

• TABLE 1.1 Compliance, Grievances, and Formal Complaints Offices/Officers and Their Roles

Institutional Office/Officer	Role in the Process
Americans with Disabilities Act (ADA) coordinator	Oversees planning, compliance, and implementation regarding the ADA as well as Sections 503 and 504 of the Rehabilitation Act of 1973, in addition to other federal and state regulations.
Equal Employment Opportunity (EEO) office	Charged with ensuring that the school does not discriminate in employment against anyone with regard to race, color, religion, sex (including pregnancy), national origin, age, disability, or genetic information, or as retaliation for a complaint of discrimination in any of the former categories.
Title IX coordinator	Oversees university compliance with Title IX, which deals with claims of gender-based discrimination, including sexual misconduct (harassment, discrimination, and assault), misconduct against someone who is pregnant or parenting, and misconduct against someone because of sexual orientation or gender identity. This covers employees and students.
Risk management office	Reviews policies and practices to ensure adherence to relevant laws and regulations and offers guidance to decrease the likelihood of an adverse outcome (e.g., litigation or harm).
General counsel office	The university's legal department. Works with all relevant offices to provide legal advice and represent the university in any administrative or legal proceeding.

discrimination (see Table 1.1). In some institutions, one or two administrative officials fill these roles; on other campuses, a wider range of officials or a staff is charged with these tasks.

ADA Coordinator

Any institution with 15 employees or more that receives federal funds is required to designate an employee whose responsibilities include coordinating compliance with disability discrimination laws.[1] This person is typically referred to as the Americans with Disabilities Act (ADA) coordinator,

---

[1] 28 C.F.R. § 35.107(a); 34 C.F.R. §104.7.

although the individual's job title may vary, and he or she may have other duties beyond ensuring disability compliance. The ADA coordinator is responsible for coordinating an institution's compliance with its obligations under Section 504 of the Rehabilitation Act of 1973 and the ADA through planning, assessments, and trainings. The ADA, Section 504, and their regulations outline an institution's responsibilities to its multiple constituencies (e.g., students, employees) and in multiple environments (e.g., buildings, stadiums, websites). ADA coordinators often advise administrators on multiple aspects of an institution's business, ranging from construction to event ticketing to website design. The ADA coordinator also is required to manage the investigation of complaints alleging discrimination on the basis of disability or failure to comply with disability law. The ADA coordinator's name, office address, and telephone number must be made available to the public.[2]

Equal Employment Opportunity Office

Like all large employers, universities typically have an Equal Employment Opportunity (EEO) office charged with overseeing nondiscrimination in hiring and employment. This office, which may be part of the human resources department, ensures that the school, as an employer, will not discriminate on the basis of race, color, religion, national origin, age, or genetic information, or retaliate against any individual who makes a complaint. This office also oversees nondiscrimination on the basis of sex (including pregnancy) and disability. The duties of the EEO office and the DS office often parallel one another, with the DS office assisting students with disability accommodations, and the EEO office assisting employees and job applicants. Because of this parallel, there are inherent benefits in developing a relationship with the EEO office. A strong relationship will ensure that both offices are aware of, and have shared access to, new developments in best practices, the latest in technology, and campus resources.

Title IX Coordinator

Title IX of the Education Amendments of 1972 (Title IX)[3] prohibits discrimination on the basis of sex, including sexual harassment of or discrimination against individuals who are pregnant, parenting, or nursing. This law applies to employees (including faculty) and students. Every school that receives federal funding is required to designate a Title IX coordinator who is responsible for coordinating the school's legal responsibilities, including investigating allegations of gender discrimination.[4] Frequently, the Title IX

---

[2] 28 C.F.R. § 35.107(a).
[3] 20 U.S.C. §1681, et seq.
[4] 34 C.F.R. § 106.8.

coordinator is also tasked with educating the campus community about Title IX responsibilities and facilitating broader compliance with Title IX through formal training. Because discrimination may occur based on multiple aspects of identity (gender, race, disability, etc.), resolving discrimination complaints on a campus often requires collaboration between the ADA coordinator, EEO office, and Title IX coordinator.

Risk Management

Larger campuses often have a risk management office that identifies and assesses liability risks to the institution; its duties include crafting policies and procedures, reviewing contracts, and participating in key decision making to protect the school from litigation where possible. On some campuses, the risk management office can be a critical partner in working toward changing the culture around disability in an effort to reduce the incidence of disability-related litigation.

Legal Counsel

All colleges and universities have some form of legal representation in place. Larger schools usually have a legal department or general counsel's office consisting of attorneys, paralegals, and other colleagues who stay abreast of all regulations applicable to postsecondary education. Smaller schools may have a lawyer or law firm on retainer to provide legal counsel as needed. As these firms and individuals have the ultimate responsibility of defending the university in any legal proceeding, legal counsel should work closely with the DS office to review cases that might later become subject to an Office for Civil Rights (OCR) complaint or litigation. Heeding the advice of legal counsel can prevent contentious situations from moving toward formal complaints and litigation. Schools that use outside counsel should establish a protocol for when these individuals should be brought in to consult on a DS issue; paying for a small amount of an attorney's time early on can help avoid an expensive legal issue down the road.

STUDENT SUPPORT OFFICES ON CAMPUS

Although understanding the available resources on campus is important for any student, it is of particular importance for a student with a disability. DS providers should familiarize themselves with the resources available and be able to refer students to the appropriate offices for assistance as needed. As well, DS providers should ensure that other support offices are familiar with the DS office's role in supporting students and encourage these colleagues to refer students to the DS office as appropriate.

Such collaborations can take many forms. For example, consider the case of a first-year medical student with attention deficit hyperactivity disorder (ADHD; see Example 1.1).

EXAMPLE 1.1 • Multioffice Collaboration to Support a Medical Student With Attention Deficit Hyperactivity Disorder

A first-year medical student arrives at school with documentation of her disability and recommendations for testing accommodations. She reports that those accommodations worked very well in her undergraduate education, and the institution approves and implements these accommodations in her first-year courses. After failing the first two quizzes in one of her classes, the student returns to the DS office. She is upset and feels overwhelmed by the volume of material in medical school, and reports difficulty in organizing and prioritizing her studies.

Potential Collaborations for Example 1.1

In this case the DS provider has the opportunity to refer the student to multiple campus resources:

1. A learning specialist or academic support center to explore alternate study strategies
2. A peer-tutoring program that can help the student prioritize material
3. A psychiatrist in the student health or counseling center, who can discuss the use of psychotropic medications to mitigate symptoms of inattention
4. A therapist in the student counseling or wellness center to help the student work on executive functioning skills and identify ways to reduce any anxiety

The referral process works both ways to benefit students—when the DS office is a known resource, colleagues in other offices will feel comfortable referring students there (see Example 1.2).

EXAMPLE 1.2 • Student Referral From the Counseling Center

A student visits the campus counseling center and shares concerns about the behavior of faculty and perceived concerns about access. The student is unaware that the DS office exists. The staff counselor, who understands the DS office and its mission, refers the student to DS and informs the student that assistance regarding disability access is available from this office.

The DS office should take special care to collaborate with other campus resources that support students from marginalized groups. It is important to ensure that students' multiple identities are respected and supported (see Example 1.3).

EXAMPLE 1.3 • Working to Support Students With Multiple, Diverse Identities

An African American student with a disability shares feelings of stress about adjusting to the health sciences environment. He states that he has not found a community of students who understand where he is coming from, and feels that all of his time is focused on academic achievement and addressing accommodation needs. The student laments that his social support group is lacking and that he has not found a comfortable and supportive community.

Potential Collaborations for Example 1.3

It is important to remember that students have identities outside of being students with disabilities. In fact, their identities as students with disabilities may be the identity that least affects their academic success. The case in Example 1.3 affords the DS provider an opportunity to connect the student to other university resources, for example:

1. Referral to the multicultural resource center to meet and network with students from all programs on campus
2. Referral to the student activities office to learn more about campus groups and activities available to connect with other students outside the academic environment
3. Referral to program-specific diversity initiatives both internal and external (e.g., Association of American Medical Colleges [AAMC], American Association of Colleges of Nursing [AACN])
4. Referral to mentorship programs on campus or other specialized programs (e.g., First Generation to College, Veterans Affairs)
5. Referral to the counseling center to address feelings of loneliness, depression, or anxiety

Ensuring Effective Support

Partnerships with other support offices on campus (see Table 1.2) will not only benefit students already registered with the DS office, but will help other offices identify students with disabilities not yet registered with the DS office who might otherwise fall through the cracks. A collaborative approach to supporting students with disabilities ensures that issues such as accessibility and universal design continue to be a part of the conversation, and eventually the campus culture.

SUPPORTING STUDENTS EXPERIENCING DIFFICULTY

Helping students identify effective resources and ensuring that they have appropriate disability accommodations can go a long way toward preempting

• **TABLE 1.2 Student Support Offices on Campus**

Office	Services
Tutoring/writing center	• Assistance in keeping up with course work • Individually focused attention • Support for editing and the writing process
Learning specialists and academic coaching	• Assessment of learning styles and current study habits • Design of individual learning strategies for the student • Suggestion of multiple ancillary study materials and approaches • May refer for more specific neurocognitive testing
Career services	• Assistance with job applications and résumés • Practice interviews for clinical placements or employment
Student health center	• Provide medical care • Refer to specialist care when necessary • Knowledge of campus medical resources
Counseling center/ wellness center	• Support for students • Assess and sometimes treat psychiatric conditions • Refer to or provide mental health care • Foster wellness • Mindfulness/meditation education
Veterans support office	• Familiarity with military-service–related disabilities • Benefits and programs • Scholarships and financial assistance • Community building and peer support
Financial aid	• Individualize a financial aid plan to account for expenses associated with disability • Knowledge of scholarships or other financial assistance
Diversity offices, including: • Multicultural/minority resource centers • Lesbian, gay, bisexual, transgender, queer, and others (LGBTQ+) resource center • First generation to college support office	• Peer support and community building • Networking • Advocacy • Safe space to discuss multiple identities

(continued)

• **TABLE 1.2 Student Support Offices on Campus (*continued*)**

Office	Services
Campus ombudsperson	• Confidential office • Takes a neutral stance in mediating difficult situations • Linkage to campus supports • Identifying university policy and procedure • Often empowered to facilitate change and improvements across campus

academic difficulties. We must remember, though, that many students will experience academic difficulty at some point in their education, regardless of their disability status. The DS office can assist students with identifying the appropriate resources for a given issue. When working with students who are experiencing academic difficulties, there are several key points to consider:

1. Do the difficulties relate to the disability?
2. Is the student receiving appropriate accommodations?
3. Does the student have the appropriate resources to study (including time)?
4. Who else on campus might have the expertise to assist?

Identifying the Issue

When a student encounters academic difficulties, it is often helpful to have the student "walk" the DS provider through the course or clerkship activities, describing his or her experiences and challenges, in order to isolate the problems or barriers that the student is experiencing. The DS provider's knowledge of the health sciences curriculum is especially important when working through these issues. In addition to the student's self-described difficulties, it is often necessary to elicit the expert assistance of a faculty member from within the department or to see the environment firsthand in order to determine whether reasonable accommodations might address the student's difficulties.

Working as a Team

Although DS providers mainly focus on classroom and clerkship environments, it is important to remember that students' disabilities do not impact them in a vacuum. Their disabilities may affect them outside of school, or the functional limitations may come as a result of other life issues—not the disability. For students studying the health professions, time is a precious resource. The DS provider, alongside other campus resources (e.g., learning specialist, academic coach, mental health services), can help a student strategize regarding time management and practicing good self-care. When academic difficulties are the result of another aspect of students' lives or identities, connecting them with the appropriate support on campus can be a crucial link, particularly if students have a good relationship with DS providers and trust their recommendations.

Effective collaboration allows DS providers to garner the expertise of campus partners in order to ensure students have equal access to all aspects of their university experience. The result brings together existing resources to ensure effective and high-quality services for students. Although each student is different, Figures 1.1 and 1.2 offer examples of how multiple campus offices can come together to meet student needs.

Academic Standing

In the health sciences, a student who continues to experience academic difficulty, or failure, is typically brought before a review committee to determine the student's academic future (e.g., placed on probation, suspended, dismissed). Each school within the institution has a committee that reviews the student's academic progress and fitness for promotion to the next level of study (e.g., promotion committee, fitness committee, student review committee). DS providers do not sit on these committees as a matter of standard practice; however, it may be beneficial to include DS providers in an annual meeting in order to inform them about the academic review process. Observing the process will expand the provider's understanding of the types of concerns raised about student performance, as well as general barriers students experience and how they are managed. It can also help to highlight the understanding (or lack of understanding) faculty might have about

• **FIGURE 1.1 Example of Collaborations: Deaf or Hard-of-Hearing Students**

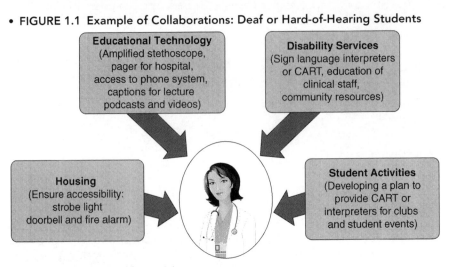

CART, communication access real-time translation.

• FIGURE 1.2 Example of Collaborations: Student With a Learning Disability

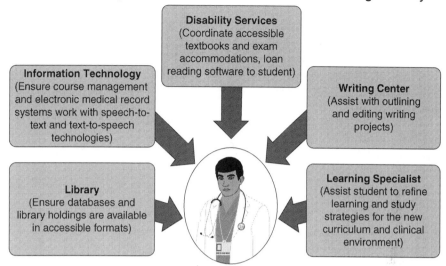

disabilities and accommodations, and inform future training to build the skills and understanding of faculty.

Disability Claims in Response to Academic Sanctions

In some cases students might disclose a disability at the last minute as a means of staving off an academic sanction or dismissal. These students should enter the DS office's registration process and be evaluated in the same manner as a student who enters without impending sanctions. The information about the disability as assessed by the DS provider may not change the academic outcome, but can help the committee members to incorporate any relevant disability information—along with all other information—into their decision-making process. It is also a show of good faith to examine disability claims immediately and in line with published procedures, should the situation later result in a grievance or complaint.

Above all, it is important to inform all students *early* and *often* about the process for declaring a disability, requesting accommodations, and determining eligibility for disability services (see Chapter 2, Disability Law and the Process for Determining Whether a Student Has a Disability).

GRIEVANCES AND FORMAL COMPLAINTS

Internal Complaints

Institutions of higher education that receive federal funds are legally obligated to "adopt grievance procedures that incorporate appropriate due process standards and that provide for the prompt and equitable resolution of complaints."[5] The designated ADA coordinator is obligated to receive and process disability discrimination complaints,[6] but the school can designate any other campus offices or individuals it would like to be part of the grievance procedure, and can determine the process it would like to use, as long as due-process standards are maintained. Public universities that employ more than 50 people are also legally obligated to publicize the grievance procedure;[7] most schools post the grievance procedure on the school's website.

It is important for DS providers, and the university as a whole, to objectively evaluate a grievance, viewing it as an opportunity to evaluate the institution's practices and make improvements that lead to positive changes for students and the school. Grievances can serve as opportunities to grow or change a practice, or they can confirm that existing practices are effective and legally sound.

In the case of a grievance, DS providers should enlist the assistance of the risk management office and/or the institution's legal counsel, as they can be tremendous assets when reviewing relevant laws, regulations, and guidelines. Risk management and legal personnel can ensure that the university is appropriately evaluating risk and possible outcomes of a specific grievance and provide pressure to address matters when issues become stagnated.

Complaints Outside the School

OCR Complaints—What to Expect

In addition to the internal complaint processes, students with a grievance have the right to make a formal complaint to the federal Office for Civil Rights (OCR) in the Department of Education within 180 days of any alleged discrimination on the basis of disability or within 60 days of the conclusion of an internal grievance procedure, if one was filed with the institution (OCR, 2010). The OCR is the office responsible for investigating complaints alleging discrimination on the basis of disability in education, in accordance with the Rehabilitation Act of 1973 and the ADA. In the event of an OCR investigation, the university's counsel, working with the director of student disabilities and sometimes with the assistance of additional outside counsel, will represent the school in the proceedings. Disability services documentation will become critical in these procedures. A timeline of events including dates of requests, contact, responses, and additional information about decision making concerning accommodations should be made available to legal counsel. It is always best to resolve any complaints quickly and in a manner that supports the student while upholding academic and technical standards.

---

[5] 34 C.F.R. §104.7; 28 C.F.R § 35.107(a).
[6] 28 C.F.R § 35.107(a).
[7] 28 C.F.R § 35.107(b).

If both parties are amenable to resolving the complaint without the OCR conducting a full investigation, the parties will likely pursue the OCR's Early Complaint Resolution (ECR) process.[8] This process allows the OCR to identify terms that are agreeable to the complainant and the institution, thereby settling the grievance. If all parties agree to the terms of a resolution, the OCR will cease its investigation. However, if the university fails to comply with the agreed-upon terms, the student can file another complaint within 180 days of the date of the original incident or within 60 days of the date the student learns of failed compliance—whichever is longer.

In the event of a full OCR investigation, a letter is sent to the head of the institution describing the basis of the discrimination complaint. Institutions are asked to provide all pertinent policies, procedures, and guidelines, as well as communications and files that apply to the student's complaint. OCR investigations seek to determine if the institution was violating the law. If the result of an investigation concludes that an institution was discriminatory in its behavior or policies, the OCR can, for example, order that the institution refund tuition, readmit the complainant (i.e., student), or award damages to the student. Investigations also frequently result in mandated training, clarification of policies and procedures, as well as strict timelines to resolve barriers to accessibility—even if the findings do not conclude that the institution was wholly in violation of the law.

The OCR retains, at its discretion, the ability to broaden an investigation to become or include a complete compliance review.[9] For example, the OCR may consider a complaint filed against a college a "compliance review" if a school is part of a larger system of colleges or universities and the OCR determines that it would be worthwhile to assess compliance in the broader system.

Similarly, the OCR might take a complaint alleging noncompliance in one sector of the institution and decide to conduct a compliance review in light of information gained during an investigation. For example, a student might file a complaint alleging discrimination in admissions procedures, but the OCR could decide to conduct a compliance review of the accessibility of all website materials. Because of the potentially broad scope of a compliance review, many institutional legal services act swiftly to engage in the ECR process.

Private Litigation

Although it is less common, students may sue a school if they believe they were discriminated against on the basis of disability. The designated legal counsel will represent the school to defend the lawsuit (see previous Legal Counsel section). Once a lawsuit has been filed, the DS office should carefully

---

[8] OCR Case Processing Manual, Article II.
[9] OCR Case Processing Manual, Article V, Section 501-2.

follow any instructions from the school's counsel, including instructions about communications with the student and retaining documents.

Disability and Diversity

Administrators are wise to be aware of compliance concerns in serving students with disabilities, but "disability" is *not reducible to a compliance issue*—it's an aspect of identity for many students, and an aspect of diversity on college campuses. In common with other marginalized populations, many students with disabilities identify with a culture rooted in a civil rights struggle. On many campuses there are groups that work to build community for broad disability activism, Deaf culture, and students on the autism spectrum, to name a few. These groups celebrate the culture around disability and disability identities, thereby working to promote awareness, inclusion, and protection of their civil rights.

Since the 1970s, Section 504 has required institutions receiving federal funds to provide notice that they do not discriminate on the basis of disability.[10] Recently, many institutions and employers have gone further by actively seeking applicants with disabilities. As of March 24, 2014, changes to Section 503 of the Rehabilitation Act of 1973[11] require nearly all federal contractors to recruit and hire a workforce of employees of which 7% identify as having a disability. This should translate to hospitals and other federal medical facilities intentionally seeking out applicants with disabilities. Similarly, the National Institutes of Health is providing supplemental funding in its grants to support research conducted by students, post-doctoral students, and investigators with disabilities (National Institutes of Health, n.d.).

Students with disabilities are an underrepresented minority in higher education, research, and the workforce. There are reasons to be hopeful that increased awareness and revised legislation can play a role in correcting this. People with disabilities want and deserve empathic health care professionals with disabilities. By working together, departments in health science programs can support students in achieving this goal.

REFERENCES

National Institutes of Health, U.S. Department of Health and Human Services. (n.d.). *Research supplements to promote diversity in health-related research.* Retrieved from http://www.nidcd.nih.gov/funding/types/pages/minority_disability.aspx

Office for Civil Rights, U.S. Department of Education. (2010, September). *How to file a discrimination complaint with the Office for Civil Rights.* Retrieved from http://www2.ed.gov/about/offices/list/ocr/docs/howto.pdf

---

[10] 34 C.F.R. §104.8(a).
[11] 41 C.F.R. § 60–741, et seq.

Disability Law and the Process for Determining Whether a Student Has a Disability

Elisa Laird-Metke and Gregory A. Moorehead

INTRODUCTION

This chapter first addresses what a disability is and how to determine whether someone meets the legal definition of a person with a disability. It contains a diagram to guide the decision-making process for determining a student's disability status. It then offers an explanation of the Americans with Disabilities Act and other applicable laws, to help administrators and disability services personnel understand their obligations to students. Specific examples from the health sciences are provided.

A BRIEF HISTORY OF DISABILITY RIGHTS LAWS

Societal perceptions of disability have changed over time. The **medical model** of disability was based on the notion that disabilities are a physical or mental deficiency, and that the individual with disabilities should be "fixed" or otherwise conform to society's definition of normal. This model also assumed that people with disabilities would never be full participants in society. This model was prevalent throughout much of human history, in fact, until very recently. In contrast, the **social model** of disability, developed in the 1970s and 1980s, asserts that it is *society's* environmental, cultural, and attitudinal barriers, as opposed to the disability itself, that prohibit people with disabilities from participating fully in all aspects of society. The social model encourages society to accept disability as another form of human diversity, and to develop societal structures and programs that accommodate and include all forms of disability, thus reducing the need for individualized

15

accommodations. The introduction of the social model helped inform the development of civil rights laws for individuals with disabilities.

The passage of Section 504 of the Rehabilitation Act of 1973[1] and the Americans with Disabilities Act (ADA) in 1990[2] created broad protections for individuals with disabilities, including mandating that postsecondary education institutions remove barriers for, eliminate discrimination against, and facilitate inclusion of students with disabilities. The laws also provide individuals with the right to sue if they are discriminated or retaliated against on the basis of their disability or perceived disability. The ADA Amendments Act was passed in 2008, largely to address the effects of a series of court decisions that had increasingly limited the law's scope since its enactment, particularly with regard to what constitutes a disability. The result of the 2008 amendments to the ADA was a substantial increase in the number of individuals eligible for disability protections under the law, and therefore more students in higher education qualifying for disability accommodations than ever before.

THE UNIVERSITY'S LEGAL OBLIGATIONS TO STUDENTS WITH DISABILITIES

The ADA states, "No qualified individual with a disability shall, by reason of such disability, be excluded from participation in or be denied the benefits of the services, programs, or activities of a public entity, or be subjected to discrimination by any such entity."[3] It has a similar provision applying to private colleges.[4] It requires that institutions of higher education make modifications to their policies, practices, and procedures that would otherwise deny equal access to students with disabilities, unless doing so would result in a fundamental alteration of the services provided.[5] This means that the law does not ask schools to lower their educational standards, but rather to provide for reasonable flexibility to allow students with disabilities alternative modes of accessing the campus environment and demonstrating competency. Most campuses have designated a disability services (DS) office or individual to provide these reasonable accommodations to students with disabilities (see Chapter 1, Know Your Campus Resources).

WHAT IS A DISABILITY UNDER THE ADA?

The ADA defines a disability as a physical or mental impairment that substantially limits one or more major life activities, a record of such an impairment, or being regarded as having such an impairment.[6] The law expressly

---

[1] 29 U.S.C. § 794, et seq.
[2] 42 U.S.C. § 12101, et seq.
[3] 42 U.S.C. § 12132.
[4] 42 U.S.C. § 12182(a).
[5] 42 U.S.C. § 12182(b)(2)(A)(ii); 28 C.F.R. § 36.302(a).
[6] 42 U.S.C. § 12102(1).

states, "An impairment that is episodic or in remission is a disability if it would substantially limit a major life activity when active."[7] To qualify as a disability, a disabling impairment does not need to be a permanent condition, but must last a substantial amount of time.[8] Further, a condition might substantially limit a major life activity, and therefore constitute a disability, even if the individual uses "mitigating measures," such as auxiliary aids or medication.[9] For example, a person who is able to walk, but only with the assistance of a cane, is still a person with a disability because the major life activity of walking is affected.

The law requires not only that a person have a medical condition, but that this condition "substantially limits" a major life activity. The limitation must go beyond a nuisance to rise to the level of being a disabling condition. "Major life activities" include breathing, walking, talking, hearing, seeing, eating, learning, reading, concentrating, and thinking.[10] The ADA Amendments Act also expressly includes impairments of major bodily functions and systems (e.g., digestive, neurological, endocrine), making clear that individuals with chronic health conditions or diseases, such as diabetes or cancer, are covered by the ADA's disability protections. To be considered a disability requiring accommodations in the college environment, the medical condition must not only substantially limit a major life activity, but the affected activity must be related to the student's functioning in the campus environment, including all aspects of that environment (e.g., academics, housing, transportation, parking, extracurricular activities, and dining services).

As mentioned, the ADA's definition of disability also includes those who "have a record of" or are "regarded as" an individual with a disability.[11] A student with "a record of" having a disability is one who has a history of having a disability, even if it is no longer present or does not substantially limit a major life activity. For example, the Office for Civil Rights (OCR) has asserted that students with hepatitis B are individuals with disabilities who should be allowed full participation without restriction in most dental and medical programs.[12] An individual who is "regarded as" a person with a disability is someone who does not have a condition that substantially limits a major life activity, but due to appearance (e.g., visible surgery scars or very short stature) is assumed by others to have a disability. In either case, the individual is typically not entitled to disability accommodations on the basis of that condition alone, because it does not substantially limit a major life

---

[7]42 U.S.C. § 12102(4)(D).
[8]42 U.S.C. § 12102(3)(B).
[9]42 U.S.C. § 12102(4)(E)(i).
[10]42 U.S.C. § 12102(2)(A).
[11]42 U.S.C. § 12102(1).
[12]Joint Dear Colleague Letter from Acting Assistant Secretary for the Office for Civil Rights Seth Galanter, Principal Deputy Assistant Attorney General for the Civil Rights Division Jocelyn Samuels, and Director of the Office for Civil Rights Leon Rodriguez, U.S. Departments of Education, Justice, and Health and Human Services, June 12, 2013.

activity. However, an individual who has a past record of disability, or who is regarded as having a disability, could sue for discrimination under the ADA if he or she was treated in a discriminatory manner because someone assumed a disabling condition was present (see Example 2.1).

EXAMPLE 2.1 • "Regarded as" an Individual With a Disability

A student has extensive burn scars on her face and arms, but the scars do not impose any functional limitations, nor has the student requested any accommodations with regard to that condition. Although the student can perform all of the required tasks at the same level as her peers, the clinical director assigns her to a less desirable clinical rotation because she believes that the student's appearance will make her less effective and therefore negatively reflect on the school, and the director wants to avoid harming the school's relationship with the more prestigious clinical locations. This student may win a lawsuit against the school under the Americans with Disabilities Act (ADA) for disability discrimination, even though she is not a student with a disability who required accommodations in the clinical setting.

Because of the complexity of the law and its associated protections, it is important not to allow accommodations to be determined and provided by faculty or others—even those with the best of intentions—in the absence of a student request, careful review of medical documentation, and approval of appropriate accommodations by a trained disability professional. This will be discussed in detail in Chapter 3, The Process for Determining Disability Accommodations, and Chapter 4, Accommodations in Didactic, Lab, and Clinical Settings.

Definitions of a Disability in State Law Versus Federal Law

It is important to note that some states have their own disability laws and may have a definition of *disability* that differs from the federal ADA definition just described. For example, whereas the federal government defines a disability as a "substantial limitation" of a major life activity, California state law states that a disability must merely "limit"—not "substantially limit"—a major life activity, making more individuals eligible for disability accommodations in the state.[13] Likewise, although federal law limits service animals to dogs or miniature horses, in Washington State, service animals can be any type of animal.[14] Although these states and others may have disability laws

---

[13]Cal. Gov't Code § 12926.1(c).
[14]RCW 49.60.040.

that allow broader disability accommodations than the federal government, other states may have more restrictive—or no—state law governing disability accommodations. In states with their own disability rights laws, the law that provides the most protection for individuals with disabilities—whether federal or state law—provides decision making in the state. Where there is no state disability rights law, the ADA is the relevant law to follow.

Due to the variations in laws at the state level, this book will refer only to federal law, with which residents of all states must be familiar. Faculty and DS staff should consult with their school's legal counsel to ensure appropriate compliance with federal, state, and local disability laws.

DISABILITY DETERMINATION PROCESS: GATHERING INFORMATION

To determine whether a condition substantially limits a major life activity that affects the student in the academic environment—and therefore requires disability accommodations in the educational setting—the DS provider must review the student's relevant documentation and gather subjective information from the student about past experiences with the disability and any prior accommodations received. This information will help the school evaluate whether a student's condition rises to the level of a disability under the law.

Type of Documentation Required

The type of documentation sufficient to establish the presence of a disability depends on the disability type. A health care provider who has a relationship with the student and is sufficiently trained to provide an expert opinion on the diagnosis, as well as details about the student's functional limitations, should provide documentation. Documentation should clearly describe how the student's condition limits a major life activity related to the educational environment. It should include a description not only of symptoms directly related to the underlying condition, but also the side effects of any necessary medication.

The documentation verifying a student's disability should be in writing. Most schools have a standard form for health care providers to complete, and will also accept a letter on the provider's letterhead if it provides all of the relevant information. One exception is the documentation necessary for learning disabilities. Learning disabilities require extensive testing, and schools should request a full neuropsychological or psychoeducational assessment.

The documentation requirements of each school may vary. For example, some schools require psychoeducational testing results to verify a diagnosis of attention deficit hyperactivity disorder (ADHD), whereas some will accept a psychologist's or psychiatrist's written assertion that ADHD is present, based solely on the professional's clinical judgment or student self-report. Each institution should clearly define documentation requirements and apply those standards equally to all students.

• TABLE 2.1 Disability Categories and Typical Documentation

Disability Category	Documentation Typically Necessary
Learning disability	Psychoeducational testing report written by a qualified professional with expertise in learning disabilities, training in administering the tests used, and experience working with adults, such as a licensed educational psychologist, clinical psychologist, or learning disabilities specialist
Hearing disability	Audiology report or letter from an audiologist verifying the extent of hearing loss
Vision disability	Form or letter provided by a treating physician describing the type and extent of the vision limitations
Attention deficit hyperactivity disorder (ADHD)	Psychoeducational testing report (see learning disability requirements), form, or written assessment from a treating professional (generally a psychologist or psychiatrist) verifying the diagnosis and describing how the symptoms substantially limit a major life activity
Psychological disability	Form or letter from a treating professional verifying the diagnosis and describing how the symptoms substantially limit a major life activity
Physical/mobility disability	Form or letter from a treating professional verifying the diagnosis and describing how the symptoms substantially limit a major life activity

See Table 2.1 for general descriptions of the documentation most commonly required for the broad categories of disability.

Readily Apparent Disabilities

If a disability can be clearly observed, there is no need to require documentation verifying the disability. However, if a student with an observable disability is requesting accommodations for any nonobservable aspect of the disability, then it is appropriate to request documentation verifying the functional limitations imposed by the disability.

The Need for Current Documentation

Documentation should not be so old that it fails to reflect the student's *current* level of functioning. This typically means that the documentation should be recent enough to reflect the student's functioning as an adult, using adult-normed measurements. There are limited situations in which older documentation may be acceptable, such as when the condition has been stable for a significant period of time. In that case, a recent note from the student's health care professional verifying that the older documentation still reflects current functioning may be requested. Students relying on older documentation should be made aware that although the school may accept it, certain licensing or certification boards may require more recent documentation before providing accommodations on their exams (see also Chapter 5, The Process of Requesting Accommodations on Certification, Licensing, and Board Exams: Assisting Students Through the Application).

Cost of Obtaining Documentation

Students can legally be made responsible for bearing the cost of any medical appointment or evaluation necessary to document the existence of a disability. Some schools offer evaluations or testing to students free of charge or at a reduced rate. This may be facilitated by the school's insurance plans for student health, through available student health services, or through available stipends intended to cover the expense of obtaining an evaluation outside the institution. There is, however, no legal obligation for the school to cover the cost of obtaining documentation.

Disability Verification Form

Most schools have a verification form available for treating professionals to use for documenting a student's disability. This form provides guidance regarding the information deemed necessary by the institution (see Appendix 2.1 for a sample form). Generally, such a form includes the following elements:

- Credentials of the person completing the form and relationship to the student
- Student's diagnosis(es), including severity and predicted course
- Procedures/assessments used to diagnose the condition
- The extent and degree to which the condition interferes with a major life activity;
- How the condition (and/or current treatment) impacts the student's ability to function in the school environment
- Any accommodations that the health care professional believes are necessary to provide the student access to the institution's programs, activities, and services (a school is not obligated to do what the professional recommends, but this step can help identify potential needs)
- Permission from the student for DS personnel to speak directly to the person who provided the documentation to clarify the disability-related needs, if necessary

Disability Documentation Must Be Sufficient, But Cannot Be Burdensome to Obtain

If the documentation initially provided by a student does not contain sufficient information to adequately assess the student's disability-related needs, it is appropriate to request additional documentation (see Case Example 2.1). However, a school cannot request that a student provide documentation of disability beyond an amount that is reasonable (see Case Example 2.2).

CASE EXAMPLE 2.1 • *Kaltenberger v. Ohio College of Podiatric Medicine*[15]

A student struggling in classes underwent testing at her university to determine if attention deficit hyperactivity disorder (ADHD) was present; the testing concluded that there was no clear evidence that the student had ADHD. A few months later, she provided the university with a short, handwritten note from a physician stating that she had been under an MD's care for ADHD for the last 3 weeks and together they were "trying different medications." The note did not include information regarding the basis for the diagnosis, nor did it indicate the doctor's credentials for diagnosing ADHD; therefore, the university informed the student the note was insufficient to establish that she has a disability. The student sued the university for disability discrimination after she was ultimately dismissed from the school due to low grades. The court held that it was reasonable for the university to have required more documentation than one short doctor's note to establish the presence of ADHD and the need for accommodations.

CASE EXAMPLE 2.2 • *Abdo v. University of Vermont*[16]

A student provided letters from doctors confirming that she had been in automobile accidents and detailing the physical limitations that resulted. The university said that it needed more documentation because the letters did not state a particular *diagnosis*, and refused to provide the disability accommodations requested by the student and recommended by the student's physicians in the letters. The student sued the school, alleging disability discrimination, and the court agreed with the student that the university's requirement that students obtain and present to the university a formal diagnosis in order to receive accommodations was not legal because it was unnecessarily burdensome. The court held that the thorough descriptions of the physical limitations included in the student's medical documentation constituted sufficient evidence of disability, even without the label a diagnosis provides.

Intake Interview With the Student

The review of the student's documentation is just an initial step. Although some verification and information from a qualified health care professional

---

[15] Kaltenberger v. Ohio College of Podiatric Medicine, 162 F. 3d 432 (6th Cir. 1998).
[16] Abdo v. University of Vermont, 263 F.Supp.2d 772 (D.Vt. 2003).

is needed to substantiate the need for accommodations, specific information about the *effects* of an individual's disability on educational activities must be obtained from the student. During the process of determining reasonable accommodations, students should be invited to describe:

- How the condition affects them in and out of the classroom;
- Personal history of academic difficulties;
- Personal history of receiving accommodations, if any; and
- Any strategies used to facilitate participation and functioning in and out of the classroom.

MAKING THE DISABILITY DETERMINATION

On its own, a diagnosis does not automatically mean a disability is present. Once all of the relevant information from health care providers and the student has been gathered, the DS office must determine whether the condition interferes with a major life activity. If not, it is not a disability, and no accommodations are needed. It is good practice to include a question on the form completed by the treating professional that asks whether the condition interferes with a major life activity, and, if yes, to explain the activity and how it is affected. This assists the school personnel in making that determination.

It is also important for the DS personnel making the determination regarding whether the student has a disability to make sufficient notes documenting the decision-making process. That way, if the decision is later questioned, the DS provider's reasoning is clear. See Flowchart 2.1 for a description of the process of reviewing documentation and determining whether a student has a disability as defined by the ADA.

OBLIGATIONS OF THE STUDENT AND THE SCHOOL

Notification of Disability and Accommodation Request Process

It is the student's obligation to follow the school's published procedures for submitting and requesting accommodations. Students cannot expect that accommodations will be provided if they do not comply with the procedure for requesting accommodations. The OCR has repeatedly agreed, finding in favor of the school in cases in which a student did not follow the steps required to obtain accommodations.[17]

However, the school must make reasonable efforts to make students aware of the disability services procedures (see Best Practice 2.1). If students are not sufficiently informed about the process for requesting accommodations, the OCR has held that the student is not accountable for failing to fulfill them.[18]

---

[17]College of Saint Rose, Case No. 02-00-2055 (OCR Region II 2001); Texas Woman's University, Case No. 06-00-2038 (OCR Region VI 2000); Western Michigan University, Case No. 15-99-2016 (OCR Region XV 2000); A.T. Still University, Case No. 07-09-2017 (OCR Region VII 2009).
[18]Concord Career Institute, Case No. 09-05-2022 (OCR Region IX 2005).

• **FLOWCHART 2.1 Process of Reviewing Documentation and Determining Whether a Student Has a Disability as Defined by the ADA**

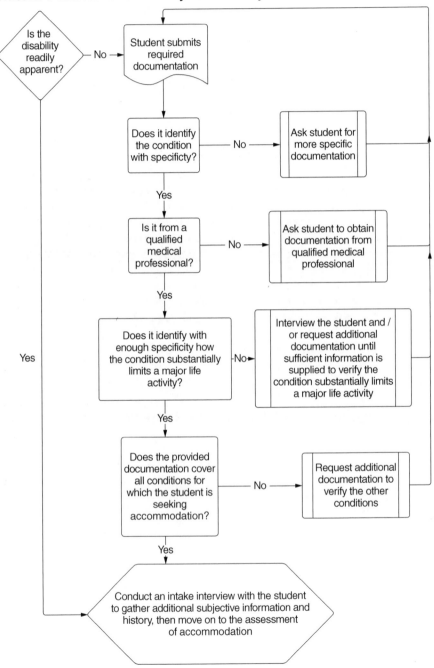

Continue to Flowchart 3.1, Determining Appropriate Accommodations, in Chapter 3.

BEST PRACTICE 2.1
Ensuring Visibility of the Disability Services (DS) Office

Make sure students at your school know about the student disability services office by ensuring each of the following:

- Your school's DS registration procedures and forms are readily available online.
- Students are informed about the office and what it does during orientations in each department (a short presentation by DS staff allows new students to get to know service providers).
- Written information about the DS office is included in the acceptance or registration documents sent to students prior to attending.
- Faculty members are provided with standard language to include on their syllabi that describes how to obtain accommodations and encourages any students who think they may have a disability to visit the DS office.

Making these practices standard not only helps ensure that no student can ever say, "I didn't register my disability because I didn't know there was a disability office for students on campus," but it also has the effect of normalizing the presence of disabilities on campus by making nondisabled students aware that students with disabilities are in their midst, even if the disabilities are not readily visible.

Confidentiality of Students' Documentation

Health science students are frequently concerned about who will know about their disability and who will have access to their records. As future medical professionals, students understandably want to know whether their documentation could be used against them in a future career (e.g., inability to get malpractice insurance, inability to get licensed, concern with malpractice suits having access to documentation), and also have general concerns regarding the privacy of their sensitive information.

The Family Educational Rights and Privacy Act (FERPA) is a federal law that requires schools to protect students' educational records, including the documentation that students submit to verify a disability, as well as the other portions of a student's disability file.[19] Generally, schools must have written permission from the student in order to release any information from a student's educational records beyond what would be considered directory information, such as name and contact information. However, FERPA lists a few categories of employees who may be privy to students' private academic records—even without written consent—in limited circumstances, including school officials and faculty with legitimate educational interest or in health and safety emergencies.[20]

---

[19]20 U.S.C. § 1232g.
[20]34 C.F.R. § 99.31.

It is important to emphasize that because the DS office is not a health care provider, any documentation of a student's disability that is maintained by the DS office is considered an educational record and is therefore *not* afforded protection under the Health Insurance Portability and Accountability Act of 1996 (HIPAA).[21] (See also, Chapter 7, Tip 7.3, Ensuring Confidentiality of Student Information.)

Although they are not legally required to do so, many DS offices opt to maintain stricter confidentiality than is legally required, and do not release information to faculty without written permission from the student. However, a DS office should *not guarantee* complete confidentiality to students; DS providers could be required to disclose a student's disability information in some limited circumstances, such as in the case of an emergency or if compelled in the course of litigation (see Case Example 2.3). The office should make its policy regarding when disability-related information may be released *very clear*, and then stick to the published policy uniformly. See Best Practice 2.2 for tips on maintaining the confidentiality of documents.

CASE EXAMPLE 2.3 • *Tecza v. University of San Francisco*[22]

A school's Disability Services Handbook promised students complete confidentiality regarding all information pertaining to disability. Later, other students were accidentally permitted to see information about a disabled student's accommodations, and the student sued the university for, among other reasons, breach of contract for violating the promise of confidentiality contained in the DS handbook. The court held that a student may sue for breach of contract when a school fails to uphold the level of confidentiality promised.

BEST PRACTICE 2.2
Maintaining Confidentiality of Documents

- Shred any paper created in the office on which private information—even just a student name—is written, including sticky notes or phone message slips. Never put those in trash or recycling bins.
- If the institution has a mechanism for encrypting e-mail or electronic records, use it for electronic communications that contain student names or disability information.

(continued)

---

[21] 42 U.S.C. § 1320d-5 & 6; 45 C.F.R. §§ 160 & 164.
[22] Tecza v. University of San Francisco, 532 Fed. Appx. 667 (9th Cir. 2013).

BEST PRACTICE 2.2 (*continued*)

- Keep student names and disability information out of e-mail subject lines, which are not included in encrypted or secure systems and may be viewed on a computer screen by visitors to an office.
- Keep the office fax machine in a place where others cannot access it.
- Keep paper files locked when not immediately using them.
- Do not transport paper files to insecure locations.
- Password protect electronic records, and limit the access only to necessary staff.
- Keep electronic records "walled off" from access by other campus departments that may share the server or other online access.

Readmission Requirements and Limitations

The ADA prevents schools from imposing eligibility or screening requirements that "screen out or tend to screen out an individual with a disability or any class of individuals with disabilities from fully and equally enjoying any goods, services, facilities, privileges, advantages, or accommodations, unless such criteria can be shown to be necessary for the provision of the goods, services, facilities, privileges, advantages, or accommodations being offered."[23] Accordingly, a college may only legally require a mental health assessment as a prerequisite to allow a student to attend if there is a valid, realistic threat posed by the student. The OCR has held that a school cannot ask a student who was suspended for a drug violation to undergo a psychiatric assessment before allowing the student back on campus, unless the school first conducts a direct-threat analysis and concludes that the student poses a significant risk to the health and safety of others on campus.[24]

Wellness contracts are another matter that requires caution. The courts have held that requiring students to enter into a behavior or wellness contract as a condition of returning to school following a hospitalization may be a violation of their rights. For example, one school's contract required that a student get a certain amount of sleep, not cry during class, and no longer serve as student body vice president, among other requirements. The student filed a complaint with the OCR, which held that the school must stop requiring students to abide by such "wellness contracts." After the school failed to abide by the OCR's decision, the student filed a lawsuit and the court allowed the disability discrimination lawsuit to go forward.[25] However, if a student exhibits behavior that legitimately threatens the health or safety of others, the OCR has held that a school may require that a student undergo a mental health evaluation before

---

[23]42 U.S.C. § 12182(b)(2)(A)(i).
[24]Letter to Keystone College, Case No. 03-09-2027 (OCR Region III 2009).
[25]Larson v. Snow College, 115 F. Supp. 2d 1296 (D.Utah 2000).

readmission is allowed.[26] It is important to remember that schools can only require a mental health evaluation before readmission in cases where a student shows a direct threat to others—otherwise readmission policies for students with disabilities must be the same as for nondisabled students.[27]

TEMPORARY DISABILITIES

The ADA Amendments Act (ADAAA), passed in 2008, expanded the ADA's legal obligation for a university to accommodate students with temporary disabilities, although it is not specific about how long a disability must last to qualify. Courts have begun to rule in accordance, holding that an individual with a temporary disability is not necessarily excluded from the ADA's protections.[28] Although this is a fairly recent legal obligation, it has long been common for schools to provide temporary accommodations to students who acquire a short-term disabling condition, often due to injury or surgery, even if not mandated by law.

Documenting Temporary Disabilities

The documentation requirements for a temporary disability may be less rigorous—a note from a health care professional verifying the injury or surgery is usually sufficient. The verification for a temporary disability should include an anticipated end date, so that a student does not continue to receive accommodations beyond the time they are no longer needed. If the anticipated recovery date is later postponed due to a change in the student's recovery prognosis, an updated note from the provider should be requested and kept on file.

Pregnancy

Pregnancy is not typically considered a disability under the ADA; however, if medical complications from pregnancy arise, the student might become eligible for services under disability law. In either case, Title IX protections apply to women who are pregnant or who recently gave birth.[29] Whether the DS office or the Title IX office (or another campus office) oversees pregnancy accommodations varies by school. Each school should identify a particular office and establish how it will evaluate and accommodate needs related to pregnancy and/or complications arising from pregnancy.

CONCLUSION

Understanding the relevant laws, and staying abreast of recent cases, will ensure that DS providers, faculty, and staff conduct their work in a manner

---

[26] Regent University, Case No. 11-03-2022 (OCR Region XI 2003).
[27] Western Michigan University, Case No. 05-13-2038 (OCR Region V 2013).
[28] Summers v. Altarium Institute, 730 F.3d 325 (4th Cir. 2014).
[29] Title IX of the Education Amendments of 1972, 20 U.S.C. §1681, et seq.

that upholds the academic standards of the institution while honoring the spirit and intention of the legislation—to ensure the full participation of people with disabilities in the educational environment. Once the responsible administrator has determined that the student meets criteria for being recognized as a student with a disability, the next step is to determine what, if any, accommodations are needed. Chapter 3 reviews the interactive process for determining accommodations once disability eligibility is met.

Sample Verification of Disability Form

Student Name: _____ Birthdate: _____

> I am requesting disability support services through the Student Disability Services (SDS) at [NAME OF SCHOOL/UNIVERSITY]. The SDS requires current and comprehensive documentation of my disability/medical condition as one of the criteria used to evaluate my eligibility for disability-related accommodations or services. Please respond to the following questions as soon as possible and return to me or send to SDS by mail or fax. I authorize the Student Disability Services office to contact you if clarification is needed.
>
> Student Signature: _____ Date: _____

Health care provider name (print): _____

Title: _____ Phone: _____ Fax: _____

Organization and address: _____

The following area must be completed by the health care professional listed on this page.

1. Diagnosis(es) and date(s): _____
   _____

2. Current status of condition(s) (e.g., active, progressing, controlled, in remission): _____

3. Current level of severity (choose one):   Mild   Moderate   Severe

4. How long is this condition(s) likely to persist (be as specific as possible—e.g., lifetime; 1 academic year; duration of academic program enrollment; 1 month): _____

5. Please list procedures/assessments used to diagnose this student's condition: _____ _____
   _____
   _____
   _____

6. What are the functional limitations or symptoms of this condition(s)?

   _____

   _____

   _____

   _____

7. What exacerbates this student's specific disability(ies)? (Please be as specific and detailed as possible) _____

   _____

   _____

   _____

8. How does the condition (and/or current treatment) impact the student's ability to learn or meet the demands of the university setting, clinical requirements, and/or ability to live in university housing? _____

   _____

   _____

   _____

9. Identify any accommodations you believe may be necessary in order for the student to participate in the university's programs, activities, and services: _____

   _____

   _____

   _____

This information is current and accurate to the best of my knowledge based on my recent evaluation of this patient or my review of records of a recent evaluation by a qualified health care provider.

Signature of Treatment Provider _____

License # _____

Date _____

Thank you for your cooperation. You may fax or e-mail your report to the Student Disability Services at _____. Please call _____ if you require additional information. Please attach any additional reports or relevant information. All information on this form will remain confidential in accordance with the Family Educational Rights and Privacy Act (FERPA).

The Process for Determining Disability Accommodations

Elisa Laird-Metke, Jan Serrantino, and J. Leigh Culley

INTRODUCTION

Those outside the designated disability services (DS) office often wonder how accommodations are determined. This chapter outlines the process by focusing on the review of documentation. It then considers the interactive process that occurs between DS provider, faculty, staff, and student in determining what accommodations are appropriate for the academic and clinical environment. It outlines the considerations that can and cannot be made in determining accommodations, and how to proceed when a potential accommodation could affect the integrity of the learning outcomes or challenge technical standards. Finally, it discusses methods for implementing accommodations once these are determined.

As described in Chapter 2, once the DS provider determines that a student is a qualified individual with a disability, the next step is to determine whether accommodations are needed and, if so, what accommodations are reasonable for this student. This determination is made as part of an interactive process between the student and the DS office, and sometimes includes faculty or other experts within the relevant department or school. This chapter describes the steps in that process and provides guidance about what can and cannot be considered when determining reasonable accommodations.

GATHERING INFORMATION
FOR THE DETERMINATION PROCESS

What Is an Accommodation?

A *disability accommodation* refers to academic adjustments and auxiliary aids provided to enable students with disabilities to have access to education equivalent to that of their peers. Accommodations typically take the form of modifications to policies, practices, and procedures and the provision of auxiliary aids and services. The purpose of accommodations is not to ensure that a student with a disability succeeds in school; rather, it is to ensure that all students—with or without disabilities—have an equal opportunity for success. To use a football metaphor, disability accommodations ensure that all students begin their education at the 50-yard line; whether the students carry the ball into the end zone is up to them.

Are Accommodations Necessary?

The first question to ask when determining whether an accommodation is needed is "Does the disability affect the student in the educational environment?" Accommodations in a higher education setting are meant to provide a student with access to the school's programs and facilities equal to that of the nondisabled students. However, the presence of a disability alone does not automatically mean that accommodations are necessary for that student. If the student's disability does not prohibit access to the program, then no accommodations are necessary. The Office for Civil Rights (OCR) has agreed, holding that a student who had a documented disability but did not prove a need for academic accommodations was not eligible to participate in the DS office's academic support program.[1] However, even if a student does not need accommodations now, disability-related needs could change, creating the need for accommodations in the future (see Example 3.1).

EXAMPLE 3.1 • When Are Accommodations Necessary?

> A student with type I diabetes has been managing the disability for her whole life and has never needed disability accommodations. Although the student is certainly an individual with a disability, the diabetes is stable and well managed. However, faced with a scheduling conflict, the student now needs to request accommodations. Her condition requires that blood glucose levels be checked daily at specific intervals, including at 3:00 p.m. A required lab course is only offered from 1 to 4 p.m. In this scenario, the student who previously did not need accommodations should now be granted an accommodation to leave the lab each day for a few minutes at 3 p.m. to check and manage blood glucose levels.

---

[1] University of Idaho, Case No. 10-99-2044 (OCR Region X 1999).

Changes in demands and expectations throughout a student's education are to be expected. As such, some students with disabilities, particularly those with chronic health conditions that may worsen unpredictably, register with the DS office "just in case" they need accommodations in the future. In these cases, students provide the medical documentation that verifies their disability, but do not request or receive accommodations. If the disability later begins to affect the student in the academic arena, the DS provider can quickly proceed to the process of determining reasonable accommodations, avoiding unnecessary delays.

An Individualized Analysis of Student Needs

Once it has been determined that a student has a disability and qualifies for disability-related accommodations (see Chapter 2, Disability Law and the Process for Determining Whether a Student Has a Disability), it is the responsibility of the DS provider to conduct an individualized assessment of the particular needs of the student in order to determine what, if any, academic adjustments and/or auxiliary aids are reasonable. Some information necessary for this analysis will come from the documentation; however, much of the information should also come from the student's self-report. During the intake process, the student and the DS provider should meet to discuss the unique needs of the student, including any difficulties or barriers, history of accommodations, and current level of functioning.

The information obtained from a student will vary depending on the student's past disability experience and level of self-awareness. Students with a history of receiving academic accommodations often have a clear understanding of what accommodations to request when arriving at a new institution. For example, a student with a reading-based learning disability may know to request textbooks in an audio format and extended time on classroom exams, as these were effective accommodations in previous educational experiences. Similarly, a student with a visual impairment may know to request course-related print materials in an electronic format in order to effectively access the information using assistive technology. Students who have never received academic accommodations before often are not aware of what accommodations may be available or what they might request, and therefore look to the DS provider to provide guidance about what accommodations they should receive.

For some students, particularly those who have never had academic accommodations before, disclosing a disability and requesting disability accommodations can be a difficult process. Self-advocacy skills may still be emerging, and many students fear disclosing in such high-stakes environments. It is therefore important that the DS provider draw out information regarding the effect of the disability or functional limitations experienced by the student. This can be done during the intake process, and is an opportunity for the DS provider to build rapport with the student.

Regardless of students' knowledge of effective accommodations, the health science academic environment is often new, making predicting necessary accommodations more difficult. Students may not be able to anticipate how the class structure and requirements impact their disabilities, or be able to anticipate barriers to their participation. It is important for the DS provider to have a good understanding of the curriculum and the required activities in order to provide educated predictions about the types of adjustments and supports needed. It is also helpful for DS staff to develop a repertoire of detailed, open-ended questions to inform their understanding of students' needs. A list of relevant questions to guide the DS provider and inform a rich conversation during the accommodation determination process can be found in Appendix 3.1. DS providers should develop tailored questions depending on the unique structure and requirements of the programs on their campuses.

DETERMINING ACADEMIC ACCOMMODATIONS

The process for determining the appropriate accommodations for each individual student is to first determine what educational, programmatic, and/or physical barriers are present, then the DS provider and the student—and sometimes faculty—collaborate to develop potential accommodations. In some situations, the process is not complicated—especially if a student requires standard accommodations, such as extended time or alternate-format materials. However, because health sciences education is increasingly moving toward collaborative and experiential learning, DS professionals are challenged to find new and novel ways to include students with disabilities in this environment, while ensuring that rigorous academic and technical standards are upheld.

Nonacademic Accommodations

Some disabilities may affect a student in a nonacademic setting, such as housing (e.g., need for wheelchair accessibility, a service or assistance animal, to live alone, for visual fire alarms in the living space), dining (e.g., food allergies, prescribed diets), or transportation and parking (e.g., need access to a particular parking lot, shuttle vans that are wheelchair accessible). Those are accommodations the DS office would coordinate with the relevant campus office (such as housing or dining services) to ensure that the student has equal access to all campus programs.

Providing Effective, Reasonable Accommodations

When considering a student's disability-related needs, the Americans with Disabilities Act (ADA) mandates that the accommodations provided must be "reasonable."[2] This means two things: (1) the institution cannot provide

---

[2]42 U.S.C. § 12182(b)(2)(A)(ii).

accommodations that do not sufficiently address the student's needs; but (2) it does not have to provide the exact accommodations requested by a student, as long as the accommodations that are provided are equally effective, adequate, and appropriate. Accommodations provided must allow a student to get an opportunity to benefit from the educational program equal to that of nondisabled students.[3] Compare Case Examples 3.1 and 3.2, in each of which a student rejected the offered accommodations from a school and later sued the school, with different results.

CASE EXAMPLE 3.1 • *Darian v. University of Massachusetts*[4]

A nursing student who experienced complications in her pregnancy that rendered her unable to complete a clinical rotation requiring patient home visits was offered an approved accommodation reducing her clinical load to one patient per day in locations without stairs, per the doctor's recommendation. The school also offered the student the option of taking an incomplete in the rotation, which could be made up at a later date.

The student rejected the school's offer of taking an incomplete, instead requesting to be excused from a substantial amount of patient care, and to take patient records home to review, in lieu of seeing patients face to face. The school determined that the student's further accommodation requests were unreasonable, and denied those requests. Despite the approved accommodations, the student did not complete the course requirements, received a failing grade in the course, and sued the university for failing to provide her with reasonable accommodations.

The court held that the student's requested accommodations were not reasonable, saying the school "certainly had no obligation to permit [the student] to forego providing patient care, forego half of the required clinical assignments, and still receive credit for the course."

CASE EXAMPLE 3.2 • *Argenyi v. Creighton University*[5]

A medical student with a hearing impairment requested communication access real-time translation (CART) services, cued speech interpreters, and a frequency modulation (FM) assistive listening system as accommodations. The university granted him the FM system, but denied his requests for CART and interpreting services, despite the fact that his physician

(continued)

---

[3] Argenyi v. Creighton University, 703 F.3d 441 (8th Cir. 2013).
[4] Darian v. University of Massachusetts, 980 F. Supp. 77 (D. Mass. 1997).
[5] Argenyi v. Creighton University, Case No. 8:09CV341 (D. Neb., Dec. 19, 2013); Argenyi v. Creighton University, 2013 U.S. Dist. LEXIS 118121 (D. Neb., Aug. 19, 2013).

CASE EXAMPLE 3.2 • *Argenyi v. Creighton University (continued)*

supported his need for these accommodations, and he had used them both with success during his undergraduate education. Instead the university offered alternatives that the student stated did not provide him with the access he needed.

The student ultimately paid out of his own pocket for CART and interpreting services for the first 2 years of medical school, but when he got to the clinical portion of his education, the university refused to allow him to bring interpreters into the clinical setting, even if he paid for them himself.

The student sued the university for disability discrimination, and after several years of court battles, a jury ultimately held in favor of the student. The court ordered the school to provide the student with interpreters for the remainder of his medical education, and approved close to half a million dollars in attorneys' fees and costs to the student, although it declined to require the school to reimburse the student for the 2 years of CART and interpreter services he had already paid for himself.

Technical Standards

All academic accommodations must be considered in light of the program's fundamental requirements, or *technical standards*. Technical standards are a specific list of the abilities and characteristics established by faculty as requirements for admission, promotion, and graduation. Although the terms used may vary slightly among medical programs, the essence is fairly consistent and usually includes intellectual abilities, which encompass conceptual, integrative, and quantitative skills; physical abilities, including observation, communication, and motor functioning; and behavioral and social attributes. See Best Practices 3.1 and 3.2 for guidance regarding the creation of technical standards, and ensuring students are aware of the standards.

BEST PRACTICE 3.1
Disseminating Technical Standards

Schools should include their technical standards on each program's website as part of the admissions information, so that potential students are made aware of the technical standards prior to applying for a program. Once admission is offered, programs should again provide a copy of the technical standards, and ask all admitted students to sign a statement attesting that they can meet the standards, with reasonable accommodations if necessary. These practices help ensure that students are fully aware of the technical standards, so that those who cannot meet them due to a disability know this prior to enrolling.

Students unable to meet a program's technical standards, even with accommodations, should not be permitted to complete the program—regardless of disability. Health sciences programs are not required to modify academic or professional standards to accommodate a student with a disability (see Case Example 3.3). It is important, however, that technical standards are directly related to the educational needs of a program and do not serve as an arbitrary barrier to students with disabilities (see Best Practice 3.2). Furthermore, the school must create the technical standards it applies to students itself—the school cannot rely on the standards set by another institution, such as a clinic or practicum site.[6]

CASE EXAMPLE 3.3 • *McCulley v. The University of Kansas School of Medicine*[7]

A medical student with a physical disability who uses a wheelchair and has reduced arm strength requested the assistance of a staff person to do certain required tasks, including lifting and positioning patients and basic life-support measures (such as cardiopulmonary resuscitation [CPR]). The student argued that her planned specialty is not physically demanding, and therefore the more general requirements of the school's technical standards should be waived. The medical school, which offered an "undifferentiated degree" that prepares medical students to enter any medical specialty after graduation, denied the student's accommodation request, saying it would fundamentally alter the educational program.

The student sued, alleging disability discrimination. The court held that the school has the right to set its own curriculum, and the ADA does not require that a school make substantial changes to its curriculum as a disability accommodation. The court did note, however, that not all medical schools have such physically demanding technical standards, and suggested the student may succeed at another medical school.

BEST PRACTICE 3.2
Careful Creation of Technical Standards

The ADA regulations say that schools "shall not impose or apply eligibility criteria that screen out or tend to screen out an individual with a disability or any class of individuals with disabilities . . . unless such criteria can be shown to be necessary for the provision of the service, program, or activity being offered."[8]

(continued)

---

[6]Milligan College, Case No. 04-10-2235 (OCR Region VI, 2011).
[7] McCulley v. The University of Kansas School of Medicine, Case No. 13-3299 (10th Cir. 2014).
[8]28 C.F.R. 35.130(b)(8); 28 C.F.R. 36.301(a).

This means that a school's technical standards must focus on the *skill required*, but not a characteristic of a student.

For example, the technical standard "Ability to hear a heartbeat" would likely be impermissible because individuals who cannot hear may just as effectively rely on digital stethoscopes to "see" a heartbeat on a screen. The technical standard "Ability to *detect* a heartbeat" more clearly describes the desired skill, without screening out the entire class of individuals who cannot hear, in violation of the ADA.

The role of the DS office is to determine what disability accommodations are necessary and how they can be provided, while still ensuring that students with disabilities meet the program's technical standards. Whether a student meets a program's technical standards is determined on a case-by-case basis, by evaluating the individual's functioning in the particular clinical setting. DS providers should refer to a program's technical standards when discussing barriers and accommodation needs with students. For example, a common technical standard is the ability to communicate effectively with patients, coworkers, and other medical professionals. A student with a disability that affects speech may require an accommodation in order to facilitate spoken communication, such as use of a communication device (e.g., an iPad with speech production). If the accommodation allows the student to effectively communicate with the patient, then the technical standard is met, even if the student is not able to speak.

Didactic Versus Clinical Accommodations

Disability accommodations must be provided in clinical settings, just as in didactic settings. However, accommodations that may be appropriate in the classroom portion of a program could be considered unreasonable in a clinical setting, as the interactive patient care setting often requires physical and/or mental skills beyond those required in the classroom. For example, an adjustment to the attendance policy may be an appropriate accommodation in the classroom, where alternate modes of participation are available (e.g., listening to a recording of the lecture). However, a request for changes to attendance requirements would need to be carefully evaluated for the clinical environment, where substitutions for being present may not be appropriate (see also Chapter 4, Accommodations in Didactic, Lab, and Clinical Settings).

The program administrators and faculty have a more comprehensive understanding of the technical standards and essential elements or functions of their clinical programs; therefore, it is imperative to include these key stakeholders in the process of determining accommodations. The DS provider must contact the relevant program staff or faculty to discuss specific learning outcomes, technical standards, and clinical demands in order to determine if a requested accommodation is reasonable. For clinical accommodations, it is imperative that the DS provider, the student, and the program faculty and administrators engage in interactive discussions regarding the requested accommodations. Creating and finalizing the accommodations may require multiple meetings between the DS provider and relevant program officials. See Chapter 4, Accommodations in Didactic, Lab, and Clinical Settings, for examples of clinical accommodations tailored to specific needs.

KEY CONSIDERATIONS IN ACCOMMODATION DETERMINATIONS

Avoiding a Fundamental Alteration of the Educational Program

The ADA and its regulations require that a school make reasonable accommodations for students with disabilities unless the school can demonstrate that making the modifications "would fundamentally alter the nature" of the educational program.[9] A fundamental alteration occurs when an aspect of the program, including policies, practices or procedures, is amended in such a way that it changes the nature of the educational program being offered. When initially considering accommodations, DS providers can think of them in two broad categories: those that are clearly not a fundamental alteration of the program, and those that alter, or might alter, the program.

Accommodations in the former category, such as additional time on written exams, note takers, and sign language interpreters, can be thought of as "standard" accommodations. The DS provider can usually implement standard accommodations without needing to consult with faculty or other experts to determine whether providing these accommodations fundamentally alters the program. However, extended time on clinical exams is not so standard. For example, an accommodation of extended time for clinical exams that involve "standardized patients"—where a student is evaluated on a focused interaction and assessment of a mock patient—may not be appropriate, and might not allow faculty to accurately assess a student's ability in this area. Accommodations in clinical or mock-clinical settings can be thought of as "nonstandard" and may constitute a fundamental alteration.

When nonstandard accommodation requests are being considered, the DS provider has the responsibility to work with faculty and/or the professional administration to determine if the requested accommodations are reasonable or if they fundamentally alter the program. This determination will depend on the specific program's curriculum, requirements, and philosophy, and must be grounded in sound academic reasoning. Curricular requirements

---

[9] 42 U.S.C. § 12182(b)(2)(A)(ii); 28 C.F.R. § 36.302(a); 28 C.F.R. 35.130(b)(7).

that the OCR and courts have found to be fundamental in the past include a requirement that graduate school psychology students be required to work in groups on a particular project (denying an accommodation request that a student be permitted to work alone on the project),[10] attending a residency in person (denying an accommodation request to permit a student to complete the residency requirement of a master's degree program via telephone),[11] and a requirement that graduate students complete their PhD dissertation presentations orally (denying a disability accommodation request to defend the dissertation in writing).[12]

At times, a DS provider may be unsure about whether an accommodation would be considered standard, and therefore one that could be approved without consulting program faculty. Although a request may not seem like a nonstandard accommodation, if a DS provider is uncertain whether it would create a fundamental alteration, collaboration with the program faculty in the determination is imperative. For example, a nursing student may receive time and a half or double time when taking a didactic exam. Allowing the student to have that much extended time in a practical or clinical setting, when being evaluated on the student's skills to insert a catheter or IV, could very well jeopardize patient safety and comfort. If faculty and DS providers are unable to reach a consensus on whether a potential accommodation is a fundamental alteration to a program, it is advised that an outside expert be consulted. See the section "The Role of Faculty and Administrators" later in this chapter for further discussion of the role of health sciences faculty.

Patient Safety

When an accommodation request does not interfere with established technical standards, the next consideration involves patient safety. Health sciences programs have a responsibility to consider the health and safety of patients when determining reasonable accommodations. This is in line with the ADA, which states that an accommodation is not required where it poses a direct threat to the health or safety of others.[13] The ADA regulations caution, however, that the school "must ensure that its safety requirements are based on actual risks, not on mere speculation, stereotypes, or generalizations about individuals with disabilities."[14] The regulations provide very specific guidance for how to assess the potential risk posed by allowing accommodations where patient safety may be an issue: "In determining whether an individual poses a direct threat to the health or safety of others, a public accommodation must make an individualized assessment, based on reasonable judgment

---

[10]University of Massachusetts, Case No. 01-97-2095 (OCR Region I 1998).
[11]Maczaczyj v. New York, 956 F. Supp. 403 (W.D.N.Y. 1997).
[12]Oregon State University, Case No. 10-98-2071 (OCR Region X 1999).
[13]42 U.S.C. § 12182(b)(3).
[14]28 C.F.R. 35.130(h).

that relies on current medical knowledge or on the best available objective evidence, to ascertain: the nature, duration, and severity of the risk; the probability that the potential injury will actually occur; and whether reasonable modifications of policies, practices, or procedures or the provision of auxiliary aids or services will mitigate the risk."[15] See Case Example 3.4 for an OCR ruling regarding safety.

CASE EXAMPLE 3.4 • Office for Civil Rights (OCR) Letter to Baker College of Flint[16]

A student who had significant vision loss and profound hearing loss was enrolled in a veterinary technician program. Although she did well in the classroom setting, she encountered difficulties in the clinic, where her inability to detect an animal's body language made her unable to effectively control an animal for treatment, causing her to accidentally injure animals and contribute to an unsafe environment for others when an animal she was treating bit another student working with the animal. The program offered the student a number of accommodations, but ultimately determined that she was unable to satisfy the clinical requirements of the program without endangering animals and students.

The student filed a complaint with the OCR, alleging disability discrimination. The OCR determined that the student's disabilities prevented her from safely satisfying the program's technical standards and caused unacceptable safety risks, and therefore her dismissal from the program was not discriminatory.

Undue Burden on the School

The final consideration in determining the reasonableness of an accommodation request is whether approving a certain accommodation would constitute an undue burden—a significant difficulty or expense—for the school. However, cost alone is almost never a valid reason to deny an accommodation at an educational institution (see further explanation in the section "Cost" under "Factors That *Cannot* Influence Accommodation Decisions" later in this chapter). When considering a specific disability accommodation request, even a relatively expensive one, such as sign language interpreters—the institution should not allow consideration of the cost when making the determination. If a less expensive alternative *that effectively provides equal access* can be provided, an alternate accommodation may be appropriate.[17] Such a

---

[15] 28 C.F.R. § 36.208.
[16] Baker College of Flint, Case No. 05-06-2074 (OCR Region V 2006).
[17] Montgomery College, Case No. 03-99-2059 (OCR Region III 1999).

substitution should be explored with the student, to determine whether it would be as effective as the more expensive requested accommodation. See Best Practice 3.3 regarding documentation of decision making.

BEST PRACTICE 3.3
Documentation of Decision Making

An institution should always be sure to document in writing and keep on file the reasons for any accommodation determination made, as well as any alternate accommodation ideas that were considered, and why they were rejected.

There are limited circumstances in which cost-related limitations on disability requests are permissible. For example, an institution is not obligated to build an elevator in an older building or otherwise make substantial physical modification to a structure *if* the class or lab can be moved to another location that is equally as suitable as the original location. This is called a *program modification*, and is specifically permitted by the ADA, if an entity can prove that removing the physical barrier was not readily achievable.[18] However, any program modification must not cause students with disabilities to receive lesser access to their education than classmates receive.

Flowchart 3.1 is provided to assist the reader in thinking through the relevant considerations when determining the most appropriate, reasonable accommodations.

See Chapter 4, Accommodations in Didactic, Lab, and Clinical Settings, for more information about disability accommodations and auxiliary aids that are commonly provided in health sciences programs.

WHAT IF THERE IS NO REASONABLE ACCOMMODATION AVAILABLE?

At times, there may be circumstances where there are no accommodations that will allow the student equal access without fundamentally altering the program or endangering patients. The ADA requires that educational accommodations be provided to a "qualified individual with disability," which it defines as a student who "meets the essential eligibility requirements" of the institution—with or without accommodations. This means that students whose disabilities render them unable to complete the program—even with accommodations in place—should be dismissed, just as any nondisabled

---

[18]28 C.F.R. § 35.150(a); 45 C.F.R. § 84.22(a).

• FLOWCHART 3.1 Determining Appropriate Accommodations

Begin with Flowchart 2.1, then continue here:

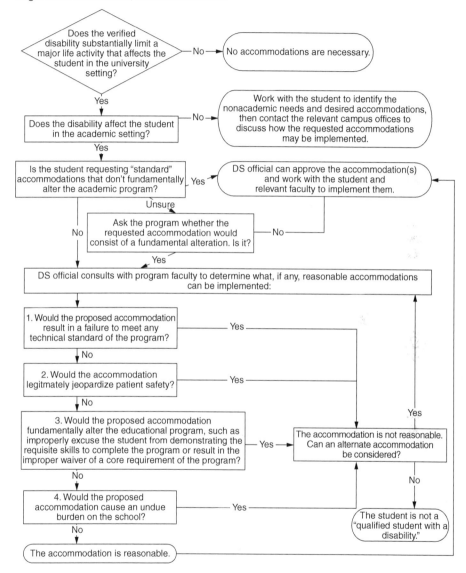

student who was unable to fulfill the program's requirements would be dismissed. This is also true for clinical placements.[19]

Prior to dismissing a student as "not otherwise qualified," however, it is important for the DS office, in conjunction with the student and

---

[19]Schwarz v. Loyola University Medical Center, 2012 LEXIS 82749 (N.D. Ill. 2012).

program faculty, to explore and consider potential alternative accommodations. If, however, it is determined that there is no reasonable alternate accommodation, a student may be not otherwise qualified for the program (see Case Example 3.5).

CASE EXAMPLE 3.5 • *Zukle v. Regents of the University of California*[20]

A medical student was provided multiple accommodations for her learning disability, including double time on exams, note-taking services, audio textbooks, and permission to retake courses and proceed on a decelerated schedule. Despite these, she did poorly in classes and clerkships and was ultimately dismissed from the school of medicine. She sued the school for disability discrimination. The court held that she was not a qualified individual with a disability under the ADA because she was not able to meet the school's requirements, even with disability accommodations; therefore, her disability discrimination suit failed.

It is important to note, however, that the court was only willing to defer to the institution's decision once it had determined that the school had taken seriously its obligation to enter the interactive process with the student and that relevant officials were involved in making a decision after carefully considering and weighing all options. Where the school has not done so, courts have ruled it has shirked its duty to the student requesting accommodations.[21]

In similar cases involving student dismissals for failing to meet academic standards, courts have held in favor of the school provided the interactive process was carefully undertaken.[22]

FACTORS THAT *CANNOT* INFLUENCE ACCOMMODATION DECISIONS

Cost

As discussed earlier (in the section "Undue Burden on the School"), the potential expense of an accommodation and the financial burden that may be incurred are usually not factors to be considered when determining

---

[20] Zukle v. Regents of the University of California, 166 F.3d 1041 (9th Cir. 1999).
[21] Wong v. Regents of the University of California, 192 F.3d 807 (9th Cir. 1999); Wynne v. Tufts University School of Medicine, 932 F.2d 19 (1st Cir. 1991).
[22] See, e.g., Brief v. Albert Einstein College of Medicine, 423 Fed. Appx. 88 (2nd Cir. 2011); McGuinness v. University of New Mexico School of Medicine, 170 F.3d 974 (10th Cir. 1998); Kaltenberger v. Ohio College of Pediatric Medicine, 162 F.3d 432 (6th Cir. 1998); Wynne v. Tufts University School of Medicine, 976 F.2d 791 (1st Cir. 1992).

accommodations. If a school's decision is challenged, the OCR or a court would consider the overall budget of the academic program and the institution—not just that of the DS office—when determining the ability to pay for an accommodation.

The "Real World"

A school cannot consider a student's possible postgraduation employment options when making the decision to admit or retain the student—the only legitimate concern is whether the student is able to meet the school's requirements to complete the degree program. An example of an impermissible consideration would be to claim that "a student who has only one hand should not be allowed to complete a nursing program because, 'in the real world,' no hospital would hire a nurse who could not use both hands to perform procedures." The student's ability to demonstrate mastery of the required skills, even in a nonstandard manner, is the only relevant consideration for the school. The only possible exception to this is where completion of the program itself is the only qualifying threshold to employment, such as whereupon completion of the program, a student is automatically licensed or certified.[23]

IMPLEMENTATION OF ACCOMMODATIONS

Accommodation Letters

After careful consideration and thoughtful deliberation of the requested accommodations, if deemed reasonable, they should be approved and implemented. At most institutions, implementation of accommodations begins with an accommodation or faculty notification (Appendix 3.2) letter created by the DS provider. Depending on the school's protocols, this letter may be delivered to the relevant faculty or staff electronically or in person by the student. Some institutions prepare these letters each new term or for each individual course, whereas others prepare one letter per academic year or for the duration of the program. Any method that conveys the relevant information so that the approved accommodations can be appropriately implemented and protects the students' privacy is acceptable, but the OCR has held that schools must have some established procedure for alerting faculty to approved accommodations.[24] A sample notification procedure is available in Appendix 3.3.

   Accommodation letters should contain information about the accommodations the student is receiving and the duration of the accommodations. They often also include standard language describing the process used to determine accommodations, references to applicable disability laws, and an invitation to contact the DS office with any questions. The letter should also briefly describe the process as an interactive one, inviting faculty to voice

---

[23] Northern Virginia Community College, No. 11-06-2036 (OCR Region XI 2006).
[24] Bates College, Case No. 01-96-2053 (OCR Region I 1997).

any concerns about the accommodations to the DS office. Letters should not include information about the student's specific disability, as such details are typically considered confidential and unnecessary for the faculty to know about in order to provide accommodations. An example of a typical accommodation letter is found in Appendix 3.2.

The Role of Faculty and Administrators

When faculty members receive an accommodation letter, they are required to implement the accommodations that have been determined by the DS office. In many cases, it may be beneficial for the student and the faculty member to engage in a conversation about the best way to implement the accommodations (see also Chapter 7, Professionalism and Communication About Disabilities and Accommodations). However, students do not have to disclose their type of disability, nor use the approved accommodations. Students often choose to use accommodations only in some classes. Student wishes regarding whether and to what extent they use their accommodations must be respected.

When faculty have questions or concerns regarding the recommended accommodations, they are responsible for contacting the DS provider for clarification. Faculty have a legal obligation to participate in the implementation of the approved accommodations.[25] As described earlier, faculty also play a significant role in the process of determining whether nonstandard accommodations are reasonable or if they would constitute a fundamental alteration of the program. As part of this process, faculty may be required to meet with one another or call in an outside expert to discuss whether a particular requested accommodation constitutes a fundamental alteration to a program. However, the OCR has held that the decision about whether an accommodation constitutes a fundamental alteration of the program cannot be left entirely with the faculty—disability experts must also be involved in the decision-making process.[26]

At some institutions, a designated administrator serves as a confidential liaison between the student and the faculty of a particular program within the school. This designee may be the dean of students, director of medical education, or some other person within the school or program. At institutions with a designated liaison, the DS provider or students may provide accommodation letters to this individual rather than directly to the faculty. A liaison can be a valuable partner in helping to inform and vet nonstandard accommodations, while maintaining an added level of confidentiality for the student by releasing a student's accommodation information only to those within the program who have a genuine need to know it. When concerns arise regarding the implementation of an approved accommodation,

[25]Kennesaw State University, Case No. 04-12-2275 (OCR Region IV 2013).
[26]University of California, Santa Cruz, Case No. 09-97-2169 (OCR Region IX 1999).

the designated liaison is often the initial point of contact for faculty and students, and will reach out to DS personnel as needed to resolve the concerns.

Confidentiality Regarding Accommodations

Unlike a student's diagnosis or disability status, a student's accommodation needs must be shared with those responsible for implementing the accommodations (e.g., relevant faculty, the clinical preceptor, testing center employees, the program's designated liaison). However, confidentiality regarding a student's accommodations still must be maintained as applied to all other individuals who do not have a need to know that a student gets accommodations and what those may include (see also Chapter 7, Professionalism and Communication About Disabilities and Accommodations).

A student's transcript must not reflect that accommodations were granted. Annotations or grades applied only to the transcripts of students receiving disability accommodations have been ruled by the OCR to be discriminatory (see Case Example 3.6). A transcript may contain unavoidable evidence that accommodations were granted, such as the completion of course work over a longer period of time than that of a typical student, but the transcript must not indicate in any way that the reason for the aberration was related to a disability.

CASE EXAMPLE 3.6 • New York Medical College[27]

A medical student with multiple sclerosis had difficulty completing her rounds in a clerkship due to her disability and, due to absences, ultimately completed the required clerkship hours over two semesters. The school added notations to her transcript indicating that additional course work was required of her and added, incorrectly, that her passing grade was a retake of the course. This differed from standard practices in which a grade of "Incomplete" was assigned, and then replaced with the earned grade once the clerkship was completed. The student filed an OCR complaint, asserting that these notations were discriminatory because they forced her to disclose and explain her disability to prospective employers reviewing her transcript for hiring purposes.

The school had no written policy reflecting this transcript notation practice. The OCR investigated and determined that nondisabled students who did not complete clerkships due to absences did not have such notations on their transcripts. The college acknowledged to the OCR that it had not used this notation system for any other student—the college had created it specifically to reflect this student's accommodations. The OCR found the school's actions to be noncompliant with disability laws, and changed the student's transcript to reflect her passing grade, without additional notations.

---

[27] New York Medical College, Case No. 02-13-2014 (OCR Region II 2013).

TIMING OF STUDENT ACCOMMODATION REQUESTS AND DS PROVIDER RESPONSES

Student Timing Responsibilities

It is the student's responsibility to disclose a disability to the institution (see Chapter 2, Disability Law and the Process for Determining Whether a Student Has a Disability). Students may wait until they are woefully behind or on the verge of dismissal before seeking disability accommodations. However, it is well settled that disability accommodations are not retroactive, and must only be applied after a request for accommodations is made.[28]

It is also critical for students to inform the DS office immediately if they are not receiving approved reasonable accommodations, if the accommodations are not working, or if the functional limitations of the disability change, such that new accommodations are necessary. The OCR has held that it is the student's responsibility to alert the DS provider to problems with accommodations and engage in an interactive process to adjust the accommodations as necessary.[29]

DS Office Timing Responsibilities

It is the institution's responsibility to provide accommodations within a reasonable time frame.[30] Some accommodations require additional time to implement (e.g., text conversion, class notes, adaptive technology, sign language interpreters). For this reason, campuses should publicize information about the importance of early disclosure of disabilities and making accommodation requests early on their websites, during new student orientations, on syllabi, and in any DS materials (see Chapter 2, Disability Law and the Process for Determining Whether a Student Has a Disability). Depending on the program's duration and structure, the accommodation of priority registration—permission to register at the beginning of the registration period, before classes are filled—may be appropriate in order to allow the DS office sufficient time to organize more time-consuming or time-sensitive accommodations, such as booking sign language interpreters or converting reading and other course materials into electronic format.

ADJUSTMENTS TO ACCOMMODATIONS

The process of requesting and receiving accommodations is fluid throughout the student's professional and clinical experience. The unique and

---

[28]Montgomery College, Case No. 03-99-2059 (OCR Region III 1999); University of New Mexico, Case No. 08-98-2070 (OCR Region VI 1998).
[29]Loyola University Chicago, Case No. 05-05-2139 (OCR Region V 2006).
[30]University of LaVerne, Case No. 09-96-2148 (OCR Region IX 1997).

novel environment of a health sciences program will oftentimes present barriers to equal access that were not originally anticipated. If this should occur, the interactive process described in this chapter should begin again to determine the reasonableness of the new request. For example, students with psychological or neurological disorders who were able to function well in the didactic portion of their programs may experience unanticipated difficulties in the clinical setting, with its often-frenetic schedule and long working days. To address new barriers, DS providers and students should review possible accommodations for clinical settings, such as being excused from overnight call duties or early release from clinic hours.

Adjustments to accommodations may also be necessary due to changes in a student's disability or treatment regimen. For example, a student with irritable bowel syndrome may find that increased stress has triggered a flare-up in symptoms resulting in the need for more frequent bathroom breaks during exams. The student is responsible for contacting the DS provider to request additional accommodations or an adjustment to existing accommodations.

Although many changes in disability require a reassessment of needs, a change may not require more accommodations; in fact, a change in disability can reduce or even eliminate the need for accommodations altogether. For example, a student with attention deficit hyperactivity disorder (ADHD) may begin a new medication that significantly improves her ability to focus and reduces her need for additional time on exams from time and a half to just an additional 15 minutes per exam hour.

Other changes to accommodations may be driven by changes in the learning environment. For example, a nursing student may discover that the ergonomic chair that had worked perfectly in the classroom does not fit in the nurses' station at the student's new clinical rotation, sparking the need for a new chair or alternate workstation. Or, a student with posttraumatic stress disorder (PTSD) may not have experienced triggers in a pediatric rotation, but during an emergency room rotation may encounter multiple triggers that require accommodation.

RIGHTS AND RESPONSIBILITIES

In order to ensure a fair, equitable, and lawful process is followed to determine accommodations for students with disabilities, all parties have a role to play. Table 3.1 outlines the rights and responsibilities for students, DS providers, faculty, and administrators. It is critical that all parties are aware of their responsibilities to create equal access for students with disabilities.

• TABLE 3.1 Summary of the Rights and Responsibilities of All Parties

	Rights	Responsibilities
Student	• An equal opportunity to access the courses, programs, services, and activities at the university • Request reasonable accommodations, academic adjustments, or auxiliary aids and services • Appropriate confidentiality of information regarding disabilities, except as disclosures are required or permitted by law	• Identify self to the DS office • Submit appropriate documentation to DS office • Request accommodations and participate in the interactive process • Meet the academic/technical standards of the program • Contact the DS office if accommodations are not being implemented • Follow DS procedures for requesting and maintaining accommodations
Disability services office	• Request and receive current documentation that identifies the existence of a disability and explains the functional limitations of the disability • Participate in the interactive process by suggesting appropriate and reasonable accommodations, academic adjustments, or auxiliary aids and services based upon documentation submitted to the office • Establish essential requirements and standards for courses, programs, services, or activities at the university, in conjunction with faculty and administrators • Select equally effective accommodations, adjustments, or auxiliary aids and services • Deny an accommodation, adjustment, or auxiliary aid that fundamentally alters a course, program, or activity	• Create clear, written policies and procedures for requesting and maintaining accommodations • Determine disability status • Maintain appropriate disability documentation for each student • Engage the appropriate individuals in the interactive process to determine reasonable accommodations • Assist students when accommodations are not properly implemented • Educate faculty, administration, and staff about the determination and implementation of reasonable accommodations and other relevant disability matters

(continued)

• TABLE 3.1 Summary of the Rights and Responsibilities of All Parties (*continued*)

	Rights	Responsibilities
Faculty	• Establish essential requirements and standards for courses, programs, services, or activities at the university in conjunction with administrators and the DS office	• Refer students to DS office when appropriate • Participate in the interactive process to determine reasonable accommodations • Assist with implementation of reasonable accommodations • Hold student accountable to academic/clinical standards of the program
School/program administration	• Establish essential requirements and standards for courses, programs, services, or activities at the university, in conjunction with faculty and the DS office	• Refer students to DS office when appropriate • Participate in the interactive process to determine reasonable accommodations • Assist with implementation of reasonable accommodations • Hold student accountable to academic/clinical standards of the program • Educate clinical faculty about the rights and responsibilities of students and the institution in creating and implementing disability accommodations

CONCLUSION

As described in this chapter, the process for determining appropriate accommodations for the health sciences educational environment is multifaceted, with the need for strong partnerships and effective communication between DS providers, faculty, administration, and students. In the following chapter, the process described here is applied to specific accommodations commonly provided in the health sciences environment.

Sample Questions to Help Determine Appropriate Accommodations

General questions for all students:

- What brought you to the DS office?
- How does your disability affect you in the educational environment?
- How have you dealt with your disability in the past (in or outside of an educational setting)?
- Have you had any recent medication changes? If so, how has this affected you and what accommodations might be needed as a result?
- Do you need to attend regular medical, therapy, or other treatment appointments?
- Do you have medication that needs to be specially stored and accessible at specific times?
- Have you ever had any experiences in clinical/lab environments?
  - Did you experience any disability-related difficulty in these environments?
  - If so, what strategies or accommodations did you use to address them?
- Do you anticipate any specific accommodation needs in clinical or lab environments in this program?
- What do you think would be helpful accommodations or adjustments for you in this program?

If student has used accommodations in the educational environment before:

- When did you first start using accommodations?
- What accommodations were effective or ineffective in the past?
- Are there other accommodations you did not have, but wish you had received?

If student is already enrolled in the program:

- What disability-related difficulties are you experiencing in your current classes?
- Do these difficulties vary depending on the class structure or requirements? If so, how?
- Explain any new challenges you are experiencing in this program that you didn't experience in your previous education.
  - To what do you attribute these new challenges?
  - What do you think would help to address them?

For students already in the clinical environment:

- How have your rotations gone so far?
- What rotations have you done so far and at what sites?
  - Which rotations are left to do?
  - Do you have any specific concerns about the remaining rotations?
- Are you experiencing any disability-related challenges in the clinic?
- Have you had any difficulties with writing case notes or "charting"?
- Have you had any interpersonal difficulties with peers, patients, or faculty?

Sample Accommodation Letter

Date

Dear Faculty Members,

I am writing with regard to [STUDENT'S NAME], who is a student in the [NAME OF SCHOOL OR PROGRAM] and is registered with Disability Services. Based on a thorough review of this student's disability and supporting documentation, Disability Services is recommending the following accommodations and academic adjustments for [SPECIFY DURATION]:

[LIST APPROVED ACCOMMODATIONS AS FOLLOWS:

- Accommodation 1
- Accommodation 2]

These accommodations are recommended after thoughtful analysis of the student's disability-related needs, the university's programs and curricula, and the university's legal obligations under the Americans with Disabilities Act (ADA) and Section 504 of the Rehabilitation Act.

The intent of all reasonable accommodations is to provide students with disabilities equal opportunity, not to lessen or undermine academic standards or course requirements. Please review the recommended accommodations and notify me if for any reason these accommodations are not appropriate in this context. I will consult with you through a deliberative process to determine the most appropriate reasonable accommodations for this student.

It is the responsibility of the student to request academic accommodations as needed in a reasonable and timely manner. The implementation of approved in-class accommodations is a shared responsibility between the instructor and the student. Disability Services suggests that all details (e.g., exam length, start times, format changes, locations) be decided as early as possible and recorded in writing.

After discussing with [STUDENT'S NAME], please do not hesitate to contact me at [NUMBER] to further discuss these recommendations or for assistance. I look forward to collaborating with you to ensure that students with disabilities have equal access to [INSTITUTION's] programs.

Sincerely,

[DS PROVIDER'S NAME AND CONTACT INFORMATION]

Sample Accommodation Notification Policy for Students

HOW TO REQUEST AND USE ACCOMMODATIONS: SCHOOL OF NURSING

Disability documentation will be stored confidentially in the Disability Services (DS) office. It is not necessary or recommended to give copies to the faculty. An Accommodation Letter prepared by DS notifies faculty of your eligibility for services and of the recommended accommodations.

1. **For accommodations in a <u>didactic/classroom setting</u>:**
   - **Before <u>*each*</u> semester in which you would like to use recommended accommodations**, contact the Nursing Dean of Students (DOS), who is the designated liaison with the DS office, to inform him which faculty you would like notified of your approved accommodations. The DOS will oversee the coordination of support for you, and work in collaboration with you and the faculty to discuss how the accommodation(s) can best be made in each of your courses.
   - Discuss the letter and recommended accommodations with each Faculty of Record (FOR) after the DOS has contacted them. It is recommended that you do so before the start of the semester, or, minimally, 2 weeks before an exam, if you have exam accommodations.
   - For note-taking and alternate-format media accommodations, follow procedures outlined by DS in advance of each semester.
     [PROVIDE LINK TO RELEVANT PROCEDURES]
   - **Meet with your advisor** to discuss the recommended accommodations. If your advisor changes in the future, you will need to provide the accommodation letter to your new advisor and discuss/request accommodations.
2. **For accommodations in the <u>clinical setting</u>:**

ACCOMMODATIONS IN THE CLINICAL SETTING ARE DETERMINED SEPARATELY FROM THOSE IN THE DIDACTIC/CLASSROOM SETTING

- If you believe you may need accommodations in the clinical setting, discuss your concerns with DS and make a request for clinical accommodations as early as possible.
- DS will work with the DOS, the FOR, and any other relevant administrators in the School of Nursing to determine if the requested accommodations are reasonable and do not alter an essential feature of the program requirements or technical standards.
- An updated Accommodation Letter will be provided to include those accommodations, specific to the clinical setting, if approved by Disability Services. You will then work with DS, the DOS, and the FOR to implement accommodations in the clinical settings.

F·O·U·R

Accommodations in Didactic, Lab, and Clinical Settings

Jan Serrantino, Lisa M. Meeks, Neera R. Jain,
Grace C. Clifford, and Jane Thierfeld Brown

INTRODUCTION

This chapter provides examples of accommodations that would be appropriate in the classroom (didactic) setting, as well as examples of the much more complicated issues that arise when determining accommodations in clinical settings (including a special section on obstetrics and gynecology, and surgery). Examples from multiple types of clinical settings (e.g., using live tissue, working with patients, accommodating overnight call, assisting students who are color-blind) and from multiple professions (e.g., dentistry, nursing, physical therapy, medicine) are offered, with an emphasis on maintaining patient safety while providing reasonable accommodations.

As discussed in Chapter 3, The Process for Determining Disability Accommodations, determining accommodations is an interactive process between the student and the disability services (DS) professional or responsible campus entity. Often, the academic accommodations requested in the health sciences setting are unlike those in any other campus department. Both standard and nonstandard accommodations are discussed in this chapter, with suggestions regarding how they might be collaboratively determined and most effectively implemented. Accommodations in three separate educational arenas are described: the didactic (classroom) setting, the lab setting, and the clinical (patient-focused) setting.

ACCOMMODATIONS IN THE DIDACTIC SETTING

Accommodation requests for the didactic setting are often the easiest to evaluate, as many students have a history of using accommodations in classroom environments. For example, extended time and a separate testing location are among the most widely afforded accommodations, and generally are considered typical or standard accommodations.

Written Exams: Additional Time and Breaks

Additional Time for Exams

Extended time to complete written exams is generally approved when a student's disability affects cognitive processing speed or the physical ability to respond (e.g., a hand injury that makes typing difficult). Students with learning disabilities, students with attention deficit hyperactivity disorder (ADHD), and students whose disability or medication causes cognitive "fogging" or slowing (e.g., fibromyalgia, chemotherapy, or depression) may require additional time to process information and accurately respond to exam questions. In these instances, the accommodation simply provides the student with adequate time to demonstrate mastery of the material. Notably, the literature suggests that in cases of disability, affording additional time does not give students with disabilities an unfair advantage over their peers. Instead, research demonstrates that whereas the performance of students with disabilities improves when provided extended time, students *without* disabilities who are afforded additional time on exams exhibit test performance that is consistent with their performance on exams taken with the standard amount of time (Runyan, 1991). Students with physical, cognitive, or learning disabilities often require additional time to properly demonstrate their mastery of the material to ensure their exam scores do not reflect the effects of their disabilities. The typical requests for additional time in health science programs are 25%, 50%, or 100% on exams and other assessments that do not involve working with patients.

Determining How Much Additional Time to Allow on Exams

The amount of extra time to provide will depend on the effect of the specific students' disabilities and level of interference it has on their speed of response in the testing environment. For students with disabilities that affect executive functioning (e.g., autism spectrum disorders, ADHD, anxiety), 25% or 50% additional time may provide sufficient time to refocus attention and organize their thoughts. In other cases, students may have a processing disorder that profoundly affects the speed at which they read, comprehend, and respond to questions, or they may have more than one disability that, when combined, exponentially reduce their ability to complete the exam in the allotted time. These students generally need 50% or 100% additional time for exams. Chronic health conditions can also affect cognitive processing, and as a result, affected students may also require additional time. In some cases, supervised breaks in lieu of extra time may better meet the needs of such students. For more complex cases, a combination of these two accommodations (extra time and supervised breaks) may be necessary.

Breaks During Exams

Some students with disabilities require additional time not for comprehension or processing, but to take medication, measure blood pressure or sugar levels, refocus, or rest, among other reasons. This need for additional time can be addressed via "stop-the-clock" breaks. In these cases the student is allowed breaks during the testing session, usually between sections to avoid exposure to test questions, and the "clock" measuring testing time is stopped until the end of the break. Therefore, students do not get extra exam time to work on the test with stop-the-clock breaks; they only receive extra time to address a specific, nonacademic need. In most cases, when rest breaks are offered, there is a set length and predetermined number of breaks based on the total length of the exam and an understanding of the student's needs (e.g., 10 minutes per hour of exam). However, in cases where the need for breaks cannot be scheduled (e.g., a student's blood sugar drops, multiple urgent extended bathroom breaks are needed), then the rest breaks may need to be provided on an as-needed basis rather than scheduling them in advance.

When evaluating requests for extra time, it is essential that DS providers review identified functional limitations and *how* these limitations affect the students on a daily basis and during intermittent flare-ups. Once understood, the DS provider can select the accommodation (e.g., extra time and/or additional breaks) to specifically address student needs (see Examples 4.1 and 4.2).

EXAMPLE 4.1 • Extra Time and Stop-the-Clock Exam Breaks

Students with diabetes may experience greater instances of blood sugar instability in times of stress (e.g., during exam periods). This may result in cognitive slowing, as well as the need for breaks to check blood sugar, administer medication, and/or eat a snack. Students with these more complex cases benefit from the extended time to address the cognitive fogging and from the extra breaks to address medication management.

EXAMPLE 4.2 • Breaks Versus Extra Time on Exams for a Chronic Health Condition

Another example of a multilayered disability need is a student with irritable bowel syndrome (IBS). This student may not have any disability-related needs on a daily basis; however, during an IBS flare-up, the student may experience increased need and urgency to use the restroom. The student in this example would benefit from breaks, rather than extended time, where time spent addressing the health issue (and not directly on the exam) is not taken away from the amount of exam time afforded, and thus does not penalize the student, nor award more time for the exam than is warranted.

Reduced-Distraction Environment or Private-Room Exams

Students with disabilities such as ADHD, processing impairments, autism spectrum disorders, or anxiety may become easily distracted by extraneous stimuli, resulting in their inability to take exams in the classroom. In these instances, DS providers should arrange for the student to test in a reduced-distraction environment. These environments should minimize interruptions and distractions that might affect the student's ability to concentrate or demonstrate mastery of the material. Examples of possible distractions include typical classroom noise (e.g., students coughing, erasing, tapping pencils), wall decorations, telephones, bright lighting, and interruptions when students get up, finish early, or ask questions of the professors.

If the student is exceptionally sensitive to stimuli, such as those students with significant anxiety or ADHD, or those with obsessive-compulsive disorder, it may be necessary to allow the student to take exams in a private testing room. This room is still considered a reduced-distraction environment and should eliminate the types of distractions just listed. One thing to consider is whether isolation is a distraction in itself. Some students experience exacerbated anxiety when placed in isolation; for these students, a reduced-distraction setting—but not a private room—is most appropriate for test taking.

Finally, students who use text-to-speech software, have scribes, or use other forms of assistive technology may need a private room to avoid disrupting other test takers. For the same reason, students who use self-talk or other active strategies to ameliorate the effects of their disabilities may also benefit from a private testing room.

Priority Seating

Another standard accommodation is priority or assigned seating accommodations for students with low vision, ADHD (or other disabilities affecting focus and concentration), and Deaf or hard-of-hearing (DHOH) students.

Students with ADHD are less distracted when given front-row seating; students with visual disabilities may need proximity to the whiteboard or projected slides to see them better, and DHOH students may need to be close to the front of the room to simultaneously view interpreters, captioning, or the faculty member (for lip reading) and the whiteboard or projected slides.

Other Considerations in the Didactic Setting

For certain teaching methods, small changes may need to be made to ensure the inclusion of students with disabilities in the classroom learning environment.

Group Work

Whereas some students with disabilities thrive when working in group settings, others with anxiety or processing disorders may find small-group discussions and other interactive activities a barrier to learning and demonstrating mastery of material. This is particularly challenging in those health sciences programs that employ a collaborative learning model with required small-group learning sessions. These sessions typically assign groups of students to teams that work through clinical scenarios together, guided by a teaching assistant or faculty member.

The following are some helpful ways to reduce the need for accommodations, lower anxiety regarding small-group discussions, and ensure that all students are fully engaged with the group:

- Set clear expectations about participation and workload.
- Identify roles for group discussions or activities.
- Provide supplementary discussion materials prior to lecture.
- Give clear verbal descriptions of visual materials and demonstrations.
- Paraphrase comments, questions, and answers.
- Summarize key points throughout the discussion.

Faculty should be encouraged to create options for electronic or written submissions as an alternative to oral presentation of materials (e.g., asynchronous online forums on course websites). Providing a notetaker, podcasts, or audio recording of sessions is an additional means of disseminating information to students in a meaningful, multimodal way that allows all students the opportunity to review and process the content of the small group after the session.

Clickers

Clickers are interactive technology response systems (similar to a television remote, or loaded on a smartphone via an app) that enable instructors to pose questions to students and immediately collect and analyze responses from the entire class (e.g., percentage correct). In large lectures with limited interaction, the use of clickers can improve or encourage participation. Unfortunately, clickers may pose a barrier to students with limited or no use of their hands, or those with disabilities that slow the processing of visual or auditory information. Clickers can also be inaccessible to students with sensory disabilities. DS providers should endorse the use of clickers that have the following accessibility features:

- Raised buttons that require less than 5 pounds of force to operate
- Ability to provide clear feedback when responses have been submitted (e.g., beep, light, and vibration feedback)
- Models that are accessible to both right- and left-hand-dominant users

Students who are not physically able to use clickers should be provided with the questions in advance and be permitted to provide responses in written form using preferred assistive technology such as speech-to-text software or other devices. *It is not recommended that clickers be used for graded quizzes or other assessments, as they make it difficult to appropriately accommodate students requiring extended time.* When used for "polling" the class, faculty should provide a reasonable amount of time for students to respond, taking into consideration the range of times needed by students with disabilities to formulate a response.

Other Standard Accommodations in the Didactic Setting

Although extended time and a reduced-distraction environment for exams are among the most frequently requested accommodations, several other accommodations are commonly utilized in the didactic setting. These accommodations include note-takers, readers, assistive technology, scribes, adjustments to classroom participation requirements, and podcasts, videos, or recording of the lecture (see Table 4.1).

ACCOMMODATIONS IN THE LABORATORY SETTING

Instruction in the lab setting is an essential part of all health sciences programs. As such, accessibility of lab materials and environments is critical (e.g., physical space, tools and equipment, safety and protective gear for all participants). Accommodations will need to be considered for each student with a disability who experiences barriers in the lab related to a disability. For the didactic portion of a program, most anatomy and skills labs (e.g., in physical therapy, pharmacy, dentistry, medicine) are focused on learning to identify physical structures, as opposed to manipulating them, but with advanced schooling comes more complex and delicate work in the lab. In addition to other accommodations, DS providers should consider adaptive or assistive devices for use in the lab that allow students with disabilities to independently perform the required tasks in the same, or similar, amount of time as their peers (see Chapter 6, Learning in the Digital Age: Assistive Technology and Electronic Access).

• TABLE 4.1 Other Standard Accommodations for the Didactic Setting

Accommodation	Potential Disabilities or Functional Limitations	Implementation of Accommodation
Note taking	Physical barrier to writing/typing Attentional issues Slowed processing speed Dyslexia Disorders of written expression Chronic health condition Deaf or hard of hearing	Peer note taker Smartpen Audio recording Video podcast Integrative note-taking app
Reader assistive technology and alternate-format text (electronic, large print, etc.)	Learning disability (e.g., reading disorder, dyslexia) Visual disability (blind, low vision) Slowed processing speed	Human reader[a] Screen-reading software Software or equipment to increase font, change visual contrast Provision of written materials in accessible formats
Participation	Chronic health condition Anxiety disorder Communication disorder (e.g., stuttering, expressive language disorder)	"Seat time"[b] attendance modification Read-and-respond method[c] Virtual attendance (limited)[d] Student-led responding[e]
Podcasts and video	All disabilities	Web-based posting of lecture material available for most programs
Interpreters, communication access real-time translation (CART)	Deaf Hard of hearing	American Sign Language (ASL), cued speech, or oral interpreters Live CART provider Captioned podcast Transcript

(continued)

• **TABLE 4.1 Other Standard Accommodations for the Didactic Setting** (*continued*)

Accommodation	Potential Disabilities or Functional Limitations	Implementation of Accommodation
Scribe	Limited or no use of hands Broken wrist, fingers Visual disability	A person who takes dictation from the student Voice-recognition software

[a] Reader should be able to correctly pronounce medical terminology, but should not have enough knowledge to inadvertently provide cues via changes in tone or enunciation of items.
[b] "Seat time" is an expression used in many medical schools to denote the amount of time a student must be physically in class.
[c] "Read and respond" refers to having the questions in advance and allowing all students to respond to them in writing on a shared space, as opposed to cold calling during class.
[d] Limited (short-term) virtual attendance via Skype or alternative format. Should not turn into distance learning and should be used only for flare-ups or short-term disabilities.
[e] "Student-led responding" refers to students volunteering to respond to questions instead of being called on. A set number of responses may be required to achieve expected participation levels.

Personal Assistants in the Lab

There are times when students with certain disabilities (e.g., blindness, low vision, chemical sensitivities, dexterity or mobility issues) require a personal assistant as an accommodation. A personal assistant operates much like a scribe in the exam setting—serving as the hands or eyes of the student with a disability. The personal assistant may be a nonpeer student employee or other individual hired to follow the explicit instructions of the student with a disability during certain lab activities. Student partners are an alternative to personal assistants, and may assist by occasionally manipulating sensitive instruments or chemicals. The student with the disability must maintain a directive role, by giving direction and recording results. When considering approval of a personal or lab assistant, DS providers must ensure that the program's technical standards are not compromised (see Example 4.3).

EXAMPLE 4.3 • Graduate Student Who Needs Lab Accommodations

> **Issue:** A graduate student with spina bifida, which reduces her ability to reach and grip very small items such as the tail of a research animal, is enrolled in a research lab involving mice.
> **How it impacts the lab work:** The lab requires that students use instruments and equipment to conduct research on the mice. This also requires that the student secure an individual mouse by holding the mouse's tail.
> **Goal:** The lab environment should be designed and organized to ensure that the student can participate to the greatest extent possible.

(*continued*)

EXAMPLE 4.3 • Graduate Student Who Needs Lab Accommodations (*continued*)

> **Resolution:** When necessary, the student's lab partner or personal assistant can hold the mouse by the tail or assist with instrumentation while the student conducts her research.

Chemical Sensitivities or Allergies

Chemical sensitivities and allergies to lab-related items (such as latex gloves) might warrant the need for accommodations in the laboratory setting. Additionally, some chronic medical conditions, such as multiple chemical sensitivities (MCS), render students unable to function when exposed to the low levels of chemicals typically tolerated by the average person. Chemicals used in anatomy courses and other labs can also act as barriers for a student with allergies or asthma. In each of these scenarios, students may need specialized equipment (e.g., masks with air canisters; protective gloves, eyewear, and clothing) to avoid exposure to chemicals or when working with chemically enhanced items (e.g., cadavers, tissue). Some individuals with MCS wear personal air purifiers at all times. These personal devices are not provided by the DS office, but are a form of self-protection.

Although protective gear can remove the disability-related barriers for most students with MCS in the lab setting, some students, as a result of a disability, are simply unable to tolerate the chemicals, and interaction with them may prove dangerous. In certain, limited situations, participation in a *virtual* lab can allow the student to demonstrate mastery of a lab skill, without having contact with preservative chemicals. Careful attention should be paid to the program's technical standards to ensure that a virtual lab results in the same learning outcomes as the standard lab environment.

Equipment and Ergonomics

In labs, students must demonstrate academic and practical knowledge, but students with disabilities may need to do so with accommodations such as adaptive lab equipment (e.g., talking thermometers and calculators, light probes, tactile timers, tactile or nonglass pipettes, large monitors attached to a microscope, a head lamp or loupe with light, and voltmeters). In addition to tools and equipment, students may also require adaptive or ergonomic furniture. Students with physical disabilities or injuries often require specialized seating or tables that allow them to participate in the lab or clinic, such as a height-adjustable table, an ergonomic chair, a chair with more cushion or back support, or a kneeling chair. In cases where a student requires specialized equipment due to a repetitive stress injury, a proper ergonomic evaluation by a qualified specialist is warranted to ensure the student's environment is adjusted appropriately. Finally, students who use mobility equipment such as motorized scooters should be provided a designated parking location in or very near the lab that is safe, secure, and easily accessible.

Safety

The safety of every participant in the lab is imperative, and the Americans with Disabilities Act (ADA) recognizes that there are times when accommodations requested by a student may conflict with standard safety protocols,[1] such as having a motorized wheelchair or service animal in the lab. When issues like these occur, lab protocols should be reviewed to ensure they are not inadvertently discriminatory. When considering whether to allow an accommodation, universities must carefully consider whether the concern constitutes a true safety issue. The Supreme Court has held that "the risk assessment must be based on medical or other objective evidence."[2] In order to proactively address potential safety concerns, DS providers should collaborate with lab faculty to determine the least restrictive environment for a student who requires specialized equipment or a service animal, and orient the student to the lab prior to the first day of class. DS providers should also conduct a walk-through of the lab, and consider organizing formal orientation and mobility training to ensure the student is able to locate workstations and equipment, and to determine the best paths of travel within the lab.

Practical Lab Exams

Practical exams in the lab environment require DS providers to consider two key components before determining accommodations: (1) the purpose and structure of the exam and, (2) the barriers experienced as a result of the student's functional limitations. For example, an anatomy instructor assigns students a two-part exam that contains a paper-and-pencil section and an oral identification portion. As previously discussed, extra time may be appropriate for the written portion of the exam, but accommodations for the oral or practical portion require further evaluation. During the oral portion of the exam, the class is given 3 minutes to orally identify each structure flagged on a dissected cadaver. A student with one hand may be assigned accommodations for the written portion of the exam only, while a Deaf student—who receives no additional time during the written portion—might receive extra time during the oral identification portion to allow for the additional time needed for an interpreter to receive and voice the student's responses. Another student with a processing disorder may be given extended time on both sections in order to provide sufficient time to process the information and formulate an answer. However, there are some practical exams for which giving extended time may not be appropriate, as with some patient simulations or some portions of clinical skills exams (see Example 4.4 and 4.5). Each case must be evaluated independently to determine the appropriate accommodations for that setting.

---

[1] 42 U.S.C. § 12182(b)(3).
[2] Bragdon v. Abbott, 524 U.S. 624 (1998).

EXAMPLE 4.4 • Extended Time for Practical Lab Exam

When practical exams include actual patients, the length of the exam is often a critical factor.

In most dental procedures, local anesthetic is used to block the nerves so that the patient does not feel any discomfort. Anesthetic is time-sensitive, fading over a specific period of time. Extending time to complete the procedure in these cases would not only pose a threat to the patient's comfort, but might require additional doses of anesthetic to finish the procedure, which can have a negative impact on the patient's health.

When determining whether a dental student should receive extended time on an exam that includes a live patient, the DS provider should collaborate with faculty to determine the nature and purpose of the exam elements.

For example, if the purpose of an exam is for students to demonstrate their ability to fill a cavity—a procedure that requires anesthetic—extra time is not appropriate. Where an exam is evaluating the student's ability to do a dental exam, additional time could be appropriate, if the technical standards are still being met.

EXAMPLE 4.5 • Deaf Student in a Practical Lab Exam

A Deaf student who uses an interpreter and is taking a practical exam with both a written and patient interaction portion will likely not require an accommodation of extra time for reading or typing clinical notes. However, it would be appropriate to allow the student some additional time to complete the patient interaction portion, to compensate for the additional time necessary for the interpreter to facilitate the student–patient dialogue.

Simulation Labs

Health sciences programs often utilize learning environments known as simulation labs (SIM labs). These settings provide students with applied learning opportunities through the use of human patient "dolls" that replicate basic to complex clinical scenarios in a simulated environment. SIM labs provide students with an opportunity to practice and hone their clinical skills in a formative manner. Disability accommodations can and should be provided in these settings, as these practical experiences are designed to better prepare all students for real clinical situations, without jeopardizing patient safety. Accommodations to consider include extended time or additional trials when conducting procedures, or use of assistive devices or strategies.

It is also necessary to ensure that simulation labs are designed for physical access, with height-adjustable patient tables and other access features. SIM labs can be the perfect setting to identify barriers a student may experience in the clinic, and test out possible accommodations (see Example 4.6).

EXAMPLE 4.6 • Student With Low-Vision and CVD Needing SIM Lab Accommodation

A nursing student has low vision and color vision deficit (CVD), or "color blindness," which creates a barrier when trying to manage multiple color-coded items. This issue becomes salient in the SIM lab when the student struggles to differentiate the various lines, tubes, catheters, monitors, and equipment in the mock intensive care unit (ICU) setting.

Possible accommodations include the labeling of the various items by name and color to accurately identify items until the student becomes familiar with the various shapes/sizes, which will ultimately inform the student's work in real clinical settings.

ACCOMMODATIONS IN THE CLINICAL SETTING

Accommodations in clinical settings require advanced planning and a team approach. It is beneficial for the DS provider to have a good sense of the required clinical rotations for each school's programs as well as the different types of clinical placement sites offered. This can be achieved through in-depth conversation and collaboration with the clinical placement coordinator and clinical program directors, by shadowing students or faculty in clinical placements, and by requesting feedback from students about their experiences. This knowledge, coupled with an understanding of the student's disability, will assist the DS provider to begin to identify potential roadblocks and stumbling points in the clinical environment, informing accommodation needs.

Accommodations for Clerkship Placements

Students with disabilities may need accommodations specific to their clerkship placement site. This occurs when a particular clerkship site acts as a barrier for a student with a disability, usually due to distance or lack of public transportation. A clinical site where the student had been a patient (particularly for psychiatric or other highly personal treatment) would also be cause for exclusion. The DS provider should have a good understanding of how clerkship placements are determined by the school (e.g., are clerkship placements randomly assigned with the aid of computer programs or by a human coordinator? Do students rank desired placements, and what is the timeline for making placements?) in order to make informed and timely recommendations for accommodations.

Clerkship Location

The distance from a student's home to the clinical site can act as a barrier for students with chronic health conditions or mobility issues, who may be unable to drive or travel long distances because their symptoms are exacerbated by the daily wear of a long commute or the lack of efficient public transportation to the site. Removing the barrier may involve excluding particular potential clerkship sites located outside a certain distance from the student's home or that are inaccessible via public transportation. In the event that sufficient clerkship sites, or those providing a unique learning experience preferred by the student, cannot be reached without a car, individual transportation paid for by the school may be a necessary accommodation to allow a student who cannot drive, but is otherwise capable, to complete the necessary clerkship.

Proximity of a clinical placement site to a student's established treatment team or health care facility may also be an important consideration for students with disabilities, such as chronic health, mobility, or mental health conditions, who require regular treatment to maintain their health and wellness. If a student placed in a distant clerkship is unable to arrange for temporary health care near the location of the placement or to receive care remotely (e.g., via phone or video conference), clerkships outside a reasonable commuting distance to their health care providers should be excluded from consideration. See "Time Off for Disability-Related Appointments" later in this chapter for further discussion about accommodations in the clinical setting for students with ongoing treatment needs.

Parking at the Clinical Site

Students who are able to drive but cannot walk long distances due to a disability should be provided with accessible parking privileges at the clinical site. Most students who qualify for this type of accommodation will have already established their eligibility for an accessible parking placard or license plate with the state, to enable them to use accessible parking spaces reserved for those with disabilities. Permission to park at the placement site, removal of parking fees, and the ability to park in designated accessible parking spots are among the many parking accommodations to be considered.

Scheduling Clerkship Order

Another accommodation to consider—especially for students with physical or chronic health conditions who may experience fatigue, a flare-up of symptoms, or reduced endurance—is the order in which required rotations are completed. For example, for medical students, changing the order of physically taxing clerkships such as surgery and obstetrics and gynecology

(OB/GYN), or intense cognitive clerkships such as medicine, to better balance the student's clinical year should be considered if medically necessary and appropriate. Other accommodations regarding clerkship order could include allowing a student to sit out for a block or rotation to address a medical need or providing extra breaks within the clerkship.

Seasonality may profoundly affect students with disabilities, causing a need for strategically arranging clerkship order. For students with chronic health conditions, flare-ups of their conditions often coincide with seasons of the year or weather. For students with psychological disabilities, time of year, lack of sunlight, or the anniversary of a triggering event might be known issues that significantly affect their functioning. In these cases, DS providers should work with the student to identify known difficulties in advance and try to schedule clerkships, breaks, or workload to allow for the anticipated reduction in functioning. Another consideration for accommodating the aforementioned concerns is to increase access to the student's health care team for additional care (e.g., therapy, medication management, physical therapy) through time off from clinic or a leave of absence.

Students Who Received Prior Medical Treatment at the Site

An appropriate placement accommodation may include exclusion of a clerkship at a hospital or clinic where a student has received treatment in the past. This is especially true for students with psychiatric disabilities. The DS provider, in consultation with the student, should determine whether or not this is a necessary accommodation. Providers should also consider, where possible, excluding clerkship sites (e.g., local emergency room, psychiatric hospitals or sites) where a student would be taken should he or she experience a psychiatric emergency in the future—especially if the probability of such treatment for the student is high.

Physically Inaccessible Clinical Site Locations

Section 504 of the Rehabilitation Act of 1973 requires that clinical facilities receiving federal funding should have been made completely physically accessible in the 1970s, and the ADA requires all other medical facilities to have become fully physically accessible by the early 1990s. Despite these federal laws, there may still be a few clinical sites that are not fully physically accessible to students with disabilities. If certain clerkship sites are physically inaccessible, removing those sites from the list of potential placements for a student with a mobility disability is necessary.

However, schools have an obligation to ensure that students with disabilities are offered the same opportunities as their peers. Institutions should be extremely cautious about maintaining partnerships with clerkship sites that are not compliant with disability laws; should a disability access lawsuit be filed by a student who is unable to participate in a desired clinical rotation due to physical inaccessibility or an institution's failure to provide reasonable accommodations, the school will almost certainly bear some of the liability for denying a student access, even if the program is not run by, nor the building owned by, the school.[3]

Attitudinal Barriers

It is possible that certain clerkship sites, or certain personnel within a site, may have a reputation for being less than inclusive of individuals with disabilities. Such *attitudinal barriers* are problematic and must be addressed through ongoing education and trainings. Whether to eliminate clinical sites with such a history from the sites available for placement of a student with a disability is a decision that should be made in conjunction with the student—some students may feel challenged to "prove them wrong" about people with disabilities, whereas others may prefer to avoid the potential conflict. As with physically inaccessible sites, the school should seriously consider eliminating partnerships with sites that have a known history of discrimination against, or unfavorable or unwelcome treatment of, students with disabilities.

Accommodations Within the Clinic

Although many students who receive accommodations in the didactic setting never need accommodations in the clinical setting, there are some students who will require accommodations in this setting. In order to prepare themselves for the clinical experience, it is beneficial for students to visit several clinical sites and rotate with faculty to get a better sense of the requirements and begin to determine, in advance, potential barriers. (See potential clinical accommodations in Table 4.2.) Armed with this information, students can more effectively work with DS providers and faculty before the rotation starts to formulate potential solutions or accommodations.

Time Off for Disability-Related Appointments

Some students with disabilities require ongoing treatment or regular therapy. Although treatment schedules can often be arranged around a student's schedule, this can be difficult in the intensive clinical training phase of education. Students who need to attend regular appointments for treatment, including counseling sessions, may need to be released from clinic duties to attend them. In addition, the recovery time following treatment may affect the student's ability to attend or meaningfully participate in the clinical environment immediately following the appointment, and this should also be factored into the arrangement. For those students

---

[3] Thomas M. Cooley Law School, Case No. 15-08-2067 (OCR Region IX, 2010).

• TABLE 4.2 Accommodations in Clinical Settings

Activity	Potential Disabilities or Functional Limitations	Implementation of Accommodation
Rounds, clerkships, preceptorships	Physical barrier to writing Attentional issues Processing speed Dyslexia/reading disorder Disorders of written expression Chronic health conditions	Voice-recognition software or dictation system Reading software Scribe Audio recording Previewing of patient files Adjusted schedule Use of calculator or handheld spelling device
Cold calling	Communication disability (e.g., stuttering, expressive language disorder) Processing disorder	Preview of questions or topic Written responses Oral responses at a later time Assistive device to facilitate speaking (e.g., iPad or smart-phone with speech software)
Patient care	Physical disability Deaf or hard of hearing Chronic health conditions Anxiety Communication disability Learning disability	Use of intermediary American Sign Language (ASL), cued speech, or oral interpreter Communication access real-time translation (CART) Assistive listening system Reduced patient load Note taker or smartpen during intakes Digital or amplified stethoscopes Automated blood pressure machine
Surgery schedule	Physical disabilities (e.g., limited range of motion, chronic pain, herniated disks) Chronic health conditions (e.g., fibromyalgia, chronic fatigue syndrome)	Modified schedule (e.g., no surgery over 4 hours in length, rest breaks during long surgeries) Chair or stool to sit periodically during procedures
Overnight on call	Chronic health conditions Sleep disorders Psychological disabilities	Modified schedule Reduction of overnight hours
Paging systems	Deaf or hard of hearing Blind or low vision	Visual, tactile, or vibrating paging devices Text pager

who do not need an in-person appointment, a reasonable accommodation may be to allow the student a private location within the clinic and sufficient time to have an appointment with a treatment provider via phone or videoconferencing.

Students with accommodations requiring a schedule change should not be required to work less time than their peers; in cases where students are released from clinic early, they should be required to make up the clinical time as determined by the clinic supervisor. Some faculty members have permitted a student to complete assignments, such as readings, charting, or a weekend shift, to make up time for early release.

Program Modifications

For students with chronic health conditions that do not necessitate a leave of absence, but may require more absences from clinical rotations than are permitted for other students, a modification of the policy regarding "normal time to degree" can be an appropriate accommodation, allowing for an extension to the standard length of a clerkship to account for increased absences. Other possible program modifications include a reduced patient load for a student who, for example, needs more time to write case notes or needs to avoid late hours at the clinic, which may trigger a flare-up of a disabling condition. It will be necessary to work with faculty to determine what is possible without fundamentally altering the clinical education requirements.

Overnight Call

Requiring students to complete overnight call, or long calls, is a standard practice in medicine and other health sciences programs. This practice exposes the student to a number of unique learning situations, for example, having an opportunity to work with a "skeleton crew." However, students with certain disabilities, such as psychological disabilities, chronic health conditions, or neurological disabilities (e.g., epilepsy), often require good sleep hygiene to maintain wellness, and may request an alteration or waiver of overnight call as an accommodation.

There is an inherent relationship between poor sleep and increased symptomatology in several disabilities, such as bipolar disorder (Soreca, 2014), autoimmune disorders (Luyster, Strollo, Zee, & Walsh, 2012), and epilepsy (Ahmed & Vijayan, 2014). In addition to increased symptomatology, there is a clear negative relationship between total sleeping hours and academic performance in medical students, even without any additional barriers experienced related to disability (Abdulghani et al., 2012). Therefore, it can be argued that achieving healthy sleep on a nightly basis is essential for health sciences students with specific disabilities.

In such cases, DS providers should consider excusing a student from overnight call as an accommodation. The most common accommodation for these situations is to require the student to take daytime weekend call in lieu of overnight call. Another possible accommodation is to ensure the student has a private "on-call" room at the clinical site to aid in maintaining good sleep hygiene, without excusing the student from overnight call altogether. When students have private rooms, they are better able to create an environment that is conducive to sleep (e.g., bedding, sound, temperature, medical devices). For example, being able to sleep may require certain sounds (or lack thereof), specialized medical equipment (e.g., continuous positive airway pressure [CPAP] machine), or feelings of safety (e.g., for a student with posttraumatic stress disorder [PTSD] or anxiety). When considering or suggesting this accommodation, DS providers should take special care to balance the accommodation needs of the student, the student's well-being, and the essential learning experiences of the clerkship.

Rounding and Cold Calling

In the clinical setting, students are often asked to respond to questions "on the spot" and in front of their peers and superiors. This is especially prevalent during rounds, where students have to "present" on their patients. During rounds, there is a predictable structure to the approach that students can expect. This allows students to prepare in advance for the presentations and answers required of them. For students who experience difficulty with presentations during rounds due to anxiety or disabilities that affect communication, practice and additional remediation often help to improve presentation skills. Students who stutter or experience extreme anxiety may request that their patients to be presented are preassigned (e.g., the night before instead of the day of) so they can practice presenting the patient in advance.

Cold calling occurs when a senior member of the team or faculty member asks unplanned questions, on any topic, in a group setting. This is usually practiced with one question per student, to multiple students, in a short period of time. Students with anxiety-related disabilities or communication disorders may experience difficulty responding to questions "on the spot." In these instances, an accommodation might include written responses to questions within a specific period of time (e.g., by 5 p.m. the same day as rounds) in lieu of responding to cold-call questions. For some students (e.g., students who are Deaf or hard of hearing, who are nonverbal, or who stutter), using an assistive device can be an effective accommodation to ensure their participation. Students can write their response to share with the group, use text-to-speech technology, or communicate via an interpreter.

A more aggressive and targeted form of cold calling, sometimes referred to as "pimping," is standard practice for some medical school faculty. *Pimping* is a slang term used in medical education to describe a method of questioning that incites shame or that is used to humiliate the learner and maintain a power differential between the learner and the senior members of a team. DS providers may wish to discuss limitations on aggressive questioning of all students, and particularly those with certain psychological disabilities, as it can often lead to an exacerbation of a student's symptoms.

Intermediaries

Intermediaries may be an appropriate accommodation for a student who can direct, but not physically perform, a necessary procedure. The DS provider must review technical standards and consult with faculty to determine exactly what skill is being assessed during an activity or exam, and the goal of the assessment or activity (i.e., is it important that the student understands the reasoning and process, or must the student demonstrate the ability to perform the activity?) An intermediary is only appropriate if the skill being measured can be performed through the use of the intermediary with complete cognitive direction from the student. For example, a medical student with a limited upper-body range of motion may have to examine a patient's ear with the assistance of an intermediary holding an otoscope in place while the student visually examines the ear. The discussion between DS and faculty should focus on the scope of the skill being assessed in the activity and whether or not the technical standards are met if an intermediary is used (see Chapter 3, The Process for Determining Disability Accommodations, for more information about technical standards).

Charting and Clinical Record-Keeping Accommodations

Charting and clinical record keeping are critical functions and essential tasks in any health sciences program. Essentially, all clinical sites use or are transitioning to electronic medical record (EMR) systems to maintain patient records. For students who need assistive technology to use computers, such as students with learning disabilities (e.g., dyslexia, written expression), visual disabilities (e.g., low vision, blind), and physical disabilities (e.g., limited use of hands), EMRs may not be accessible due to incompatibility between the system and the assistive technology. Widely varying software products and systems are available that allow individuals with disabilities to access EMRs (see Chapter 6, Learning in the Digital Age: Assistive Technology and Electronic Access, for a discussion about how to make EMRs more accessible).

Surgery and OB/GYN Clerkships

Surgery clerkships are known to be physically and emotionally demanding. The lack of sleep, the long days, and the urgency and intensity of the work all contribute to the demanding nature of this rotation. In an undifferentiated medical degree program that prepares medical students to enter any medical specialty after graduation, surgical clerkships are mandatory. Within the clerkship, students are called upon to either "learn" or "demonstrate" a skill. Although learning and communicating knowledge about the topic can be done without physical effort, demonstrating a skill often requires the ability to perform a taxing physical procedure on a patient (e.g., to demonstrate a thorough, diagnostic abdominal exam).

An essential portion of the surgical clerkship is spent in the operating room (OR). The OR is a dynamic setting where professionals from multiple disciplines work together on one patient. The setting also requires students to learn and follow an additional set of rules and regulations, both written and unwritten (Tahiri & Liberman, 2013). This makes navigating this nuanced environment difficult for all students, and particularly difficult for students with physical, psychological, or communication disabilities.

Preparation is of central importance for students with disabilities entering surgical clerkships. Students should be orientated to the techniques of scrubbing and gowning, and to the sterile field, which may require modified techniques or include the use of assistive devices. As well, practicing their skills (e.g., stapling, suturing, tissue handling) in a skills lab will likely reduce anxiety or trepidation concerning performance in the OR (Tahiri & Liberman, 2013). For students who require specialized equipment (e.g., infrared system, stand-up wheelchair, auto-retractor, specialized instrumentation, or other adaptive technology), time should be set aside in advance of the clerkship to test the equipment and orient them to its use in the OR (see also Chapter 7, Professionalism and Communication About Disabilities and Accommodations, for more guidance concerning communicating with treatment teams about clinical accommodations).

Finally, surgery is the clerkship that commands the longest days and overnight call, and may require additional accommodations related to sleep (see previous section "Overnight Call").

Obstetrics and gynecology (OB/GYN), like surgery, is a demanding clerkship that requires physical agility and typically commands longer hours, including overnight call. The physicality involved with labor and delivery is unlike that of other clerkships. In the course of the rotation, a student may be called upon to bear down on a mother's belly, hold a patient's legs, conduct pelvic exams, assist with a delivery, hold a retractor for a long period of time, tie a two-handed square knot, and deliver a baby. OB/GYN is also a surgical specialty and students are usually required to assist during a cesarean section, drawing on the same surgical skills and rules described previously. Like surgery, OB/GYN can be an exhausting clerkship, both physically and emotionally, and students should prepare for this using the same approaches that are listed in the previous discussion on surgery clerkships.

By addressing these items in a proactive manner, programs can support their students' learning and overall well-being throughout the surgery and OB/GYN clerkships.

ADDITIONAL ACCOMMODATION CONSIDERATIONS PARTICULAR TO THE HEALTH SCIENCES ENVIRONMENT

Clinical Skills Exams

Objective structured clinical examinations (OSCEs) are clinical skills exams used to assess clinical acumen with a *standardized patient* (an actor who portrays the same symptoms/responses for all students) instead of a real patient. OSCEs may also include interaction with clinical materials such as models, radiographs, and lab test results. Because the standardized patient's condition and presentation is the same for all students, faculty can more objectively assess each student's applied knowledge and performance on clinical skills (e.g., taking a history and physical, developing a differential diagnosis). These exams may be *summative* (i.e., graded) or *formative* (i.e., for review and clinical development). Regardless of the purpose of the exam, students with disabilities may encounter barriers in these settings, and require accommodations. Clinical skills exams usually consist of several multiple-step stations. Generally this includes:

- A reading portion, often referred to as "door notes," during which the student has a specified amount of time to read through initial information about the patient he or she is about to see (e.g., the patient's primary concern, lab results);
- A patient interaction in which the student examines and questions the patient; and
- Writing a case note summarizing the encounter, or an oral presentation wherein the student reports his or her findings to a faculty member.

Determining Accommodations for a Clinical Skills Exam

Because OSCEs constitute a hybrid of didactic and clinical settings, they may require both types of accommodations. In order to determine whether accommodations are necessary, DS providers must consider each section of the exam and identify if a barrier is present for the student. Then they must determine what, if any, accommodation is reasonable to provide for each section of the exam, depending on the purpose of the assessment and the barriers experienced (see Examples 4.7 and 4.8).

EXAMPLE 4.7 • OSCE Accommodations for a Student With Low Vision

A student with low vision and difficulty sustaining visual focus is scheduled to take a practice exam. The exam consists of 10 stations that include a combination of reading, writing, and standardized patient components. All students are allotted 3 hours to complete the exam.

(continued)

EXAMPLE 4.7 • OSCE Accommodations for a Student
With Low Vision (*continued*)

> The DS provider discusses the format of the exam with the faculty member and determines that the written portions of the exam will be administered on a computer with magnification software (Zoomtext) to enlarge the font. Use of this software can result in slowed reading speed due to the slightly cumbersome navigation of the magnified screen, so the DS provider and faculty together agree that 25% additional time will also be provided for these components.
>
> Because the student can experience eyestrain during periods of intense focus, an additional accommodation of "stop-the-clock" breaks of 5 minutes are provided after every other station to allow for eye rest.
>
> No additional time is required during patient interactions for this student.

EXAMPLE 4.8 • OSCE Accommodations for a Student
With Multiple Disabilities

> A student with one arm, who also has a learning disability that affects reading fluency, is taking her first OSCE exam. She has two disability-related needs: (1) the need for extra time to process written information and (2) the need to use specialized equipment or get assistance for the patient exam. The DS provider analyzes each section of the OSCE separately to determine if accommodations may be needed for that section.
>
> **Door Notes:** The student may require extra time and/or reading software to read and process the door notes.
>
> **Patient Interaction:** The student may require an assistant or may need specialized equipment to perform a patient exam (e.g., automatic blood pressure machine), if doing so will not interfere with the program's technical standards.
>
> **Written Report:** The student may require speech-to-text software to dictate the written report to accommodate for slowed typing speed.

In clinical skills exams, an electronic medical record (EMR) simulation is generally used to extract patient information and report clinical impressions (e.g., a SOAP note[4]). It is important to vet these systems for accessibility in advance. When these systems are not accessible, the DS provider may have to create work-around strategies for accessibility—for example, if the

---

[4]The SOAP note (an acronym for subjective, objective, assessment, and plan) is a method of documentation employed by health care providers to write out notes in a patient's chart.

EMR simulation software does not have a mechanism for enlarging text or is not compatible with assistive technology software (see Chapter 6, Learning in the Digital Age: Assistive Technology and Electronic Access, for more information regarding EMR accessibility).

Accommodations for Deaf and Hard-of-Hearing Students in Clerkships

Clinical settings include many competing auditory and visual stimuli, posing unique obstacles to Deaf or hard-of-hearing (DHOH) students. A DHOH student must attend to all of this information using visual channels. There are multiple ways to address the accommodation needs of DHOH students in health sciences settings.

For all settings—didactic and clinical—an interpreter, such as an American Sign Language interpreter, is appropriate when the student's preferred method of communication is manual. For the clinical portion of training, other accommodations may also be required (see Table 4.3). For example, DHOH

• TABLE 4.3 Accommodations for Deaf and Hard-of-Hearing Students[a]

Setting	Accommodation	Specifics
Lecture hall, classroom, or small group, surgical theaters	Amplification system (frequency modulation [FM] or infrared [IR])	Reduces background noise and maximizes listening by wirelessly broadcasting a speaker's voice, audio program, or simultaneous mix via FM or IR frequency delivered via a receiver or telecoil.
	Induction loop system	A "hearing loop" magnetically transfers a sound signal to hearing aids and cochlear implants that have a telecoil receiver.
Operating room, clinic, or isolation rooms	Transparent surgical masks	Allows student to read lips of colleagues. (*Prototypes in development— at press, not yet commercially available*)
	Communication access real-time translation (CART)	Allows student to see real-time captioning of spoken information, transcribed by a trained stenographer.
	Handwritten notes	Written instead of spoken communication between parties for clarification.

(continued)

• **TABLE 4.3 Accommodations for Deaf and Hard-of-Hearing Students** (*continued*)

Setting	Accommodation	Specifics
	Pocketalker® PRO System or other personal assistive listening system	Amplifies sounds closest to the listener while reducing background noise. Ideal for clinic setting.
	Sign language interpreters or cued speech transliterators	Students who prefer manual communication will require interpreters/transliterators in the clinical environment.
	Oral interpreters	Can mouth words to the student that may not have been visible to the student when uttered by the speaker and alert the student to auditory signals from operating room (OR) equipment.
	Infrared transmitter	Reduces background noise and maximizes listening by wirelessly broadcasting a speaker's voice, via infrared frequency, to a receiver. Ensures privacy, as broadcasted information does not travel beyond the room.
	Digital or amplified stethoscope	Visual display or amplification of patient vitals.
On-call room	Visual alarm/strobe	Alternative alarm notification.
	Bed shaker	When connected to phone or pager, will wake student when called.
Phone communication	Video phone, video relay service, or Internet Protocol (IP) Relay	Allows student to use sign language, lip-read, or type to communicate by phone.
	Caption phone	Visually displays spoken information from telephone communication.
	Vibrating text-based pager	Allows student to communicate with other treatment team members without using phone.

[a] See also Chapter 6, Learning in the Digital Age: Assistive Technology and Electronic Access.

students have successfully used communication access real-time translation (CART) in the OR environment (Meeks et al., 2015; UC Davis Health System, 2011). CART providers can work remotely, using audio feed from the OR via an Internet connection, and deliver captions to the student via an online host platform, such as GoToMeeting—a secure forum that meets federal patient privacy regulations. The attending surgeon can be fitted with a wireless high-quality lapel microphone to transmit sound to the CART provider. Captions can be viewed on existing OR screens, or on small portable devices such as an iPad, which provides flexibility to move around the room while allowing the student to easily view the text. A portable stand should be considered for the iPad, to ensure the student is able to position it for convenient viewing. The equipment and technology necessary for the accommodation of hearing disabilities in the operating room should undergo testing prior to use, because what works in an empty OR is not always effective when multiple speakers are present or when monitors and alarms are audible.

If interpreters are used in the OR, attention should be given to incorporating them into the OR team. They may have to be fingerprinted (per hospital requirements), and will need an orientation to the OR. Interpreters often scrub in for surgeries, and need instruction about the sterile field. They are often given a specific place to stand in the room. These processes take time and need to be organized as early as possible, often beginning in the first year of the student's program.

Color Vision Deficiency (CVD) or "Color Blindness"

Statistics suggest that one in eight individuals (mostly male) has a CVD.[5] Although this condition has historically not been regarded as a disability, in the context of the health sciences curriculum there are times when CVD places students at a significant disadvantage—for example, when identifying oral and throat lesions, icterus, and titration end points, as well as in tissue identification in surgical procedures (Pramanik, Khatiwada, & Pandit, 2012). A student with CVD could possibly endanger patient lives in cases where there is a pivotal observation,[6] such as seeing slight changes in color or patterns of rashes, or failure to identify stage 1 pressure ulcers (Mughal, Ali, Aziz, Mehmood, & Afzal, 2013). Therefore, DS providers may be called upon to identify accommodations for these students, or work with faculty to implement differentiated practices for learning.

In some cases, students with CVD may struggle with course work, most notably during histology, due to difficulty differentiating between colored

---

[5] http://ghr.nlm.nih.gov/condition/color-vision-deficiency
[6] A pivotal observation is a single sign that is essential to observe in order to take the correct action. If a health care provider misses this, the patient's medical condition will worsen but could easily have been prevented.

stains on slides. Although histology faculty often argue that size, shape, and contextual relationship cues are the key attributes for identification of any slides, and in fact are the primary cues needed to distinguish tissues and structures—not color—research has shown that using high-quality grayscale versions of histological images has allowed students with CVD to "discern structures that would otherwise be obscured by surrounding cells or other tissue components" (Rubin, Lackey, Kennedy, & Stephenson, 2009).

Although the switch to grayscale is easily accomplished within a controlled environment, it is not available in the clinical environment. Some clinical observations in particular are difficult for individuals with CVD: widespread body color changes (pallor, cyanosis, jaundice, and cherry red); rashes and erythema of skin; test strips for blood and urine; blood or bile in urine, feces, sputum, or vomit; ophthalmoscopy; otoscopy; and microscopy (Spalding, 1999).

Table 4.4 presents common concerns and challenges for health sciences students with CVD and potential accommodations. Students should

• TABLE 4.4 Common Issues and Potential Solutions for Color Vision Deficiencies (CVDs)

Challenge	Potential Solution/Accommodation
Histology slide reading, other microscopy	Use different color staining with colors student can see. Student works with faculty to develop nuanced ways to read slides (e.g., pattern recognition, pointing out configurations/indicators that are key). Provide high-quality, high-contrast grayscale photos of slides next to color slides to allow options for viewing in multiple ways (Rubin et al., 2009). Grayscale microscope (or attached monitor). Very high-resolution slide viewed in grayscale. Assistive technology (AT) that converts red, green, or blue parts of slides to an identifiable color, such as a Daltonizing algorithm. Specialized glasses, such as Enchroma. 15 minutes of extra time per hour for histology portion of exams. Color transparency overlays.
Difficulty distinguishing fresh blood/hemorrhage; blood or bile in urine, feces, sputum, vomit	Measure and monitor blood/fluid level.

(continued)

• TABLE 4.4 Common Issues and Potential Solutions for Color Vision Deficiencies (CVDs) (continued)

Challenge	Potential Solution/Accommodation
Drop in oxygen—color-related signs	Use appropriate monitors, especially pulse oximetry.
Identifying widespread body-color changes (e.g., pallor, cyanosis, jaundice, cherry-red) Missing "pink ear"	Close observation or cross checking (looking, touching, doing special investigations, and attention to lighting). Ask for help from others. Give more attention to the patient history and report.
Dermatology/rashes/erythema of skin	Diagnosis by color may be "superfluous" and can be done instead by pattern recognition (in some cases).
Reading charts, slides, prints, codes	Close observation or cross checking (looking, touching, doing special investigations, and attention to lighting).
Test strips for blood and urine	Reliance on shade or tone rather than on color; use a color meter.
Ophthalmology: disc pallor, diabetic changes, hemorrhage vs. pigment, glaucoma, hemorrhage in anterior chamber, Kayser-Fleischer rings	Close observation or cross checking (looking, touching, doing special investigations, and attention to lighting). Ask for help from others. Give more attention to the patient history and report.
Otoscopy: inflamed drum, wax vs. blood	Ask for help from others.
Mouth and throat conditions	Give more attention to the patient history and report.
Chemistry end points	Use color meters.
Color naming	Faculty should not ask for identification by color on exams; use other identifiers (arrows, numbers, or other descriptors).
Tissue identification (surgery)	Use other visual indicators.
Seeing arrows and pointers on lecture slides	Ensure all pointers and arrows are black.
Viewing laser pointers used by faculty during lectures	Use green instead of red laser pointers.

carefully consider the specialty they are studying, as some are highly reliant on differentiating color in everyday tasks (e.g., histology, hematology, bacteriology, surgery, pathology, dermatology, anesthetics, and retinal work in ophthalmology).

Autism Spectrum Disorders (ASDs)

The clinical portion of health sciences education is often the most challenging for students on the autism spectrum. For these students, interpersonal communication is the greatest disability-related struggle (Wolf, Brown, & Bork, 2009). A clinician must be able to listen to a patient's verbal descriptions of symptoms, and understand a patient's expression of pain or interpret body language. Patient communication often comes in the form of self-report and body language, and provides the clinician with clues about feelings like fear, anger, or hopelessness, even if the patient is unable to verbalize these emotions. Recognizing these unspoken cues, as well as explaining complicated diagnoses or procedures to patients in lay terms, requires sophisticated interpersonal communication skills.

Students with ASD often need additional communication guidance in the form of coaching via peers, faculty, or standardized patients. Virtual training has proven an effective method for teaching clinical skills such as those involved in surgery (Palter & Grantcharov, 2014). Most recently, simulated virtual reality exercises proved beneficial to individuals on the spectrum, for example, by improving job interview skills (Smith et al., 2014), social skill development (Stichter, Laffey, Galyen, & Herzog, 2014), and social cognition training (Kandalaft, Didehbani, Krawczyk, Allen, & Chapman, 2013). These simulated modules may be adapted to allow medical students on the spectrum independent opportunities to improve interpersonal skills specific to the clinical setting and history taking.

Critical to the success of any student, and specifically students with ASD, is specific and direct feedback on their performances. Video modeling can be used to teach a student with ASD about appropriate communication with a patient or superior (M. Rigler, personal communication, January 15, 2015). Videotaping faculty members in simulated clinical scenarios and then filming the student in the same setting is also recommended. The DS provider or faculty can play back the videos with the student, pointing out the differences between the videos and areas for remediation. Any remediation plan for a student with ASD should include both verbal and written feedback.

CONCLUSION

Developing accommodations for health sciences students requires creativity, detailed analysis, innovation, and collaboration. It calls upon DS providers to actively pursue a clear understanding of the unique culture, curriculum, and requirements of each health sciences program on the campus. In addition to this, DS providers must have an understanding of the standard policies and procedures for all students, so that appropriate and nonburdensome accommodations can be identified and implemented. So long as technical standards are met, the environment is ripe for creative and innovative solutions to ensure students with disabilities have equal access to the health sciences curriculum.

REFERENCES

Abdulghani, H. M., Alrowais, N. A., Bin-Saad, N. S., Al-Subaie, N. M., Haji, A. M., & Alhaqwi, A. I. (2012). Sleep disorder among medical students: Relationship to their academic performance. *Medical Teacher, 34*(Suppl. 1), S37–S41.

Ahmed, O. J., & Vijayan, S. (2014). The roles of sleep–wake states and brain rhythms in epileptic seizure onset. *The Journal of Neuroscience, 34*(22), 7395–7397.

Kandalaft, M. R., Didehbani, N., Krawczyk, D. C., Allen, T. T., & Chapman, S. B. (2013). Virtual reality social cognition training for young adults with high-functioning autism. *Journal of Autism and Developmental Disorders, 43*(1), 34–44.

Luyster, F. S., Strollo, P. J., Jr., Zee, P. C., & Walsh, J. K. (2012). Sleep: A health imperative. *Sleep, 35*(6), 727.

Meeks, L., Laird-Metke, E., Jain, N., Rollins, M., Gandhi, S., & Stechert, M. (2015). Accommodating deaf and hard of hearing students in operating room environments: A case study. *Journal of Postsecondary Education and Disability, 28*(4).

Mughal, I. A., Ali, L., Aziz, N., Mehmood, K., & Afzal, N. (2013). Colour vision deficiency (CVD) in medical students. *Pakistan Journal of Physiology, 9*(1), 14–16.

Palter, V. N., & Grantcharov, T. P. (2014). Individualized deliberate practice on a virtual reality simulator improves technical performance of surgical novices in the operating room: A randomized controlled trial. *Annals of Surgery, 259*(3), 443–448.

Pramanik, T., Khatiwada, B., & Pandit, R. (2012). Color vision deficiency among a group of students of health sciences. *Nepal Medical College Journal: NMCJ, 14*(4), 334–336.

Rubin, L. R., Lackey, W. L., Kennedy, F. A., & Stephenson, R. B. (2009). Using color and grayscale images to teach histology to color-deficient medical students. *Anatomical Sciences Education, 2*(2), 84–88.

Runyan, M. K. (1991). The effect of extra time on reading comprehension scores for university students with and without learning disabilities. *Journal of Learning Disabilities, 24,* 104–108.

Smith, M. J., Ginger, E. J., Wright, K., Wright, M. A., Taylor, J. L., Humm, L. B., . . . Fleming, M. F. (2014). Virtual reality job interview training in adults with autism spectrum disorder. *Journal of Autism and Developmental Disorders, 44*(10), 2450–2463.

Soreca, I. (2014). Circadian rhythms and sleep in bipolar disorder: Implications for pathophysiology and treatment. *Current Opinion in Psychiatry, 27*(6), 467–471.

Spalding, J. A. (1999). Colour vision deficiency in the medical profession. *British Journal of General Practice, 49*(443), 469–475.

Stichter, J. P., Laffey, J., Galyen, K., & Herzog, M. (2014). iSocial: Delivering the Social Competence Intervention for Adolescents (SCI-A) in a 3D virtual learning environment for youth with high functioning autism. *Journal of Autism and Developmental Disorders, 49*(2), 417–430.

Tahiri, M., & Liberman, M. (2013). What is an ideal surgical clerkship? *Canadian Journal of Surgery, 56*(3), 151–152.

UC Davis Health System. (2011, November 30). *Technology assures deaf student learns surgery at UC Davis School of Medicine* [Video file]. Retrieved from http://youtu.be/AwDvgFrbY5w

Wolf, L. E., Brown, J. T., & Bork, G. R. K. (2009). *Students with Asperger syndrome: A guide for college personnel.* Shawnee Mission, KS: Autism Asperger's Publishing Co.

F · I · V · E

The Process of Requesting Accommodations on Certification, Licensing, and Board Exams: Assisting Students Through the Application

Neera R. Jain, Colleen Lewis, Lisa M. Meeks, and Thomas H. Tucker, II

INTRODUCTION

Students in nearly every branch of the health sciences must complete a state or national standardized exam, such as the medical licensing board exam. Students must apply for disability accommodations directly to the testing agency. This chapter gives some insight into how the major testing agencies approach decision making, and provides guidance for the application process. It walks administrators through the process of writing letters in support of student requests for disability accommodations, including a guide for what to include. Finally, it provides administrators with information about how they can support students in making their applications.

LICENSING, CERTIFICATION, AND BOARD EXAMS
What Are These Exams?

Certification, licensing, and board exams can be a key part of the health sciences curriculum, and the gateway to practicing in the professions. These exams serve as licensing, advancement/promotion, or certification requirements in almost all of the health sciences professions. Some exams for professional health sciences include the National Council Licensure Examination

89

(NCLEX; nursing board exam), National Board Dental Examination (dental board licensing exam), National Physical Therapy Exam (national physical therapy licensing exam), North American Pharmacist Licensure Examination (national pharmacy licensing exam), Comprehensive Osteopathic Medical Licensing Examination (COMLEX; national osteopathic medicine exam), and the United States Medical Licensing Examination (USMLE) Step exams (medical licensing). These exams are a critical part of professional advancement, and require additional steps for students with disabilities requesting accommodations. Given this, it is important that disability services (DS) providers prepare students well in advance and help them understand the requirements for each individual exam.

Third-Party Exam Agencies and Boards

Students with disabilities must understand that requests for accommodations on these exams are made *directly* to the agency that administers the exam. In some cases, it is a separate licensing body that administers the exam, such as the National Board of Medical Examiners (NBME) or the state licensing board, which often oversees its own licensing exams and accommodation request process (such as for the nursing and physical therapy licensing exams). Such requests do not typically go through the DS provider or the school, although most schools offer to assist students with the process.

"Flagging" of Test Scores

When students take an exam with accommodations, some testing agencies and licensing boards annotate the score to indicate that the exam was taken under "nonstandard conditions." This practice is commonly known as *flagging*.

This is a contentious issue, as this practice effectively "outs" students with flagged scores as having a disability. The act of flagging scores may be a disincentive for students to request accommodations, as they fear it will negatively affect the future ability to gain admission to a program, match in residencies, or find employment. Further, the act of flagging a score subverts the initial intent of the accommodation—to level the playing field. As of September 10, 2014, the NBME discontinued the flagging of accommodated exam scores on transcripts and score reports for USMLE Step exams (USMLE, 2014a). The National Board of Osteopathic Medical Examiners (NBOME) followed suit, discontinuing the flagging of score reports and transcripts issued after February 1, 2015, for the COMLEX-USA examination series (NBOME, n.d.). Although this appears to be the direction in which testing agencies are moving, it is important for students to be aware that policies differ, and in the interest of informed decision making, DS providers should understand the score-reporting policy for each licensing exam their students may take.

THE PROCESS OF APPLYING FOR EXAM ACCOMMODATIONS

How Do Agencies Make Decisions About Accommodations?

Generally, an agency will start by considering the student's documentation and other information submitted with the student's application for evidence of a "physical or mental impairment" that "substantially limits a major life activity." In other words, the agency looks for evidence to establish that a student has a disability that rises to the level of needing accommodations.

The process includes examining how a disability affects a student across all areas of life—in academic settings (e.g., when taking exams), as well as in other domains such as daily living, work, and social relationships. The agency then makes a determination about how significantly it believes the person is impacted by the disability. In some cases, an agency may determine that a student's disability, although diagnosed and documented, has an overall impact that is "too mild" to warrant an accommodation by its criteria, or that the impact is limited to one area of life (e.g., test anxiety that is not generalized to all areas of a person's life), and may deny requests for this reason.

Varying Standards for Accommodations

Each agency sets its own requirements for requesting accommodations, including specifications for disability documentation, personal statements, and other required information for the application. The request process is usually outlined on the exam administrator's website. Unfortunately, in some cases, particularly where the exam accommodation approval is governed by a state licensing board, the information will vary and requires some research to fully understand the process. The variance among the agencies often requires a few phone calls, as well as close reading of a website to ensure that students have all the necessary information about making their requests. In addition, each agency sets a recommended deadline for accommodation requests, generally about 60 days prior to the exam date, and provides guidance regarding the expected turnaround time for a decision. The process of getting ready to submit a request for accommodations, however, can take 3 to 6 months. Students must factor in time to develop a personal statement, collect documentation, and file appeals, should the initial request be rejected. An appeal of a decision alone can often take several months. As such, students are highly encouraged to investigate the published timelines for decisions and start applying for accommodations *far* in advance of the exam date, in order to buffer for the possibility of an appeal process (see Appendix 5.1, and the section "How DS Providers Can Help Prepare Students" later in this chapter).

How Testing Agency and DS Office Accommodation Decisions Differ

The process for determining eligibility for accommodations used by testing agencies often differs from the process used by university DS offices. Many school-based disability providers take a more holistic approach to assessing students, and may rely more heavily on students' self-reports of their needs, on DS providers' own observations, and historical accommodation approval (see Chapter 3, The Process for Determining Disability Accommodations). Assessors for testing agencies, however, do not have the benefit of an in-person interview with an applicant. Therefore, it is essential that students provide a written firsthand, detailed account of their disabilities and prior accommodations, including a well-documented history, in their applications. DS providers can assist students by providing a letter of support that includes their professional observations and rationale for approving accommodations at the institution, in an effort to "fill in the gaps" for the testing agency. The burden of proving that a student needs accommodations rests with the student (see Tip 5.1, Three Burdens of Proof for Accommodations).

TIP 5.1 • Three Burdens of Proof for Accommodations

The key to receiving accommodations on certification and licensing exams is to build an "airtight" argument that:

1. The student has a disability.
2. There is a disability-related barrier to accessing the exam.
3. Accommodations will level the playing field, and best ensure that the student's performance is a reflection of his or her understanding and mastery of the material tested, without reflecting the disability.

Burden of Proof for Accommodations

Many test takers mistakenly assume that because they received accommodations on previous exams, they are assured accommodations for licensing and certification exams. Alternatively, students might assume that because they have never received accommodations before, they will not receive accommodations now, leading to a decision not to request them.

Although some students will receive the same accommodations for licensing and certification exams that they previously received in school, not all students who received accommodations before will also receive them on these exams, as the administering agency makes determinations about accommodation eligibility based on *specific criteria* (see Table 5.1). As a result, many students may also find that the accommodations approved are different from the ones they used previously in academic settings.

• TABLE 5.1 Differences in Requirements Among Three Major Testing Agencies

Process	United States Medical Licensing Examination (USMLE)	National Council Licensure Examination (NCLEX)	Comprehensive Osteopathic Medical Licensing Examination (COMLEX)
Test accommodation requests	Candidates who want test accommodations are referred to the overview and instructions, where there is also a link to the request form (USMLE, 2014b).	Requests are submitted by state or region where the candidate wishes to be licensed (National Council of State Boards of Nursing [NCSBN], 2014, p. 4). Some states, such as Missouri, refer to testing accommodations as "Exam Modifications" (Missouri State Board of Nursing, 2014). The NCLEX is administered by Pearson VUE, a private company, and candidates must have their accommodations approved before they can schedule an exam (NCSBN, 2014, pp. 4–5).	Candidates must provide "written, credible and objective documentation" establishing a "physical or mental impairment that substantially limits" the candidate's "major life activities, as compared to most people in the general population" (National Board of Osteopathic Medical Examiners [NBOME], 2014, p. 14).
Application for accommodation	Candidates are permitted to mail their requests to the address on the forms or to e-mail them with documentation submitted as PDF attachments (USMLE, 2014b, p. 7).	Make a written request for accommodations to your board of nursing and obtain approval before registering for the NCLEX (NCSBN, 2014, p. 4).	Candidates download the accommodation request from the NBOME website; complete it; and submit it, with supporting documentation, by mail (NBOME, 2014, p. 14).

(continued)

• TABLE 5.1 Differences in Requirements Among Three Major Testing Agencies (continued)

Process	United States Medical Licensing Examination (USMLE)	National Council Licensure Examination (NCLEX)	Comprehensive Osteopathic Medical Licensing Examination (COMLEX)
Required supporting documentation	Detailed evaluations from qualified professionals are required that provide a formal diagnosis of the impairment, a description of the diagnostic criteria and any tests used, identification of each major life activity limited by the impairment, and the recommended accommodation and why it is necessary (USMLE, 2014b).	Requirements vary between states. For example, some states, such as Illinois, require candidates to identify accommodations requested in writing and provide a justification of why they are necessary, detailed evaluations from qualified professionals identifying formal diagnoses, and descriptions of diagnostic criteria and any tests used (Continental Testing Services, 2011, p. 1).	Detailed evaluations from qualified professionals are required that provide a formal diagnosis of the impairment; a description of the diagnostic criteria and any tests used; and identification of each major life activity limited by the impairment, any treatment, how the impairment compares to the general population, the recommended accommodation and why it is necessary (NBOME, 2014, pp. 2–3).
Recentness of documentation	The USMLE requires that documentation be "current." In general, the USMLE expects documentation dated within the past 3 years (USMLE, 2014b). The USMLE also recognizes that recent documentation is in the "best interest" of the candidate and that some conditions change quickly (USMLE, 2014b).	Some states set no explicit limits on assessment dates, such as Missouri (Missouri State Board of Nursing, 2002, pp. 1–2) and California (California Board of Registered Nursing, 2004, p. 1).	The most recent evaluation must be dated within 3 years of the accommodation request date (NBOME, 1999, p. 2).

(continued)

Process	United States Medical Licensing Examination (USMLE)	National Council Licensure Examination (NCLEX)	Comprehensive Osteopathic Medical Licensing Examination (COMLEX)
Personal statement	Required documentation appears on page 1 of the application and the personal statement is listed first, "describing your disability and its impact on your daily life and educational functioning" (USMLE, 2014b).	Some states, such as Missouri, require "a letter from the applicant requesting the modifications and detailing the specific modifications" (Missouri State Board of Nursing, 2002, p. 2). Other states, such as California, do not, capturing similar information with their applications (California Board of Registered Nursing, 2004, p. 1).	The request for accommodation requires candidates to describe "each impairment," and to identify the limitations and circumstances under which "major life activity" is diminished (NBOME, 1999, p. 1). Otherwise, no separate personal statement is mentioned.
Scheduling the exam	Candidates will receive permission to schedule their exams, once applications are processed (USMLE, 2014b).	NCLEX candidates are prohibited from scheduling online and the NCSBN requires candidates to schedule their tests through the various state boards of nursing by telephoning the Pearson VUE NCLEX service representatives, identified on their authorizations to test, which are sent only by e-mail (NCSBN, 2014, pp. 2–4).	Candidates applying for accommodations may not schedule a date for testing "unless or until" they are notified of the NBOME decision (NBOME, 1999, p. 1). If a candidate schedules an exam date without accommodations, then the date may be adjusted, should accommodation be provided (NBOME, 2014, p. 15).

(continued)

TABLE 5.1 Differences in Requirements Among Three Major Testing Agencies (continued)

Process	United States Medical Licensing Examination (USMLE)	National Council Licensure Examination (NCLEX)	Comprehensive Osteopathic Medical Licensing Examination (COMLEX)
Time frames for submission of applications	Candidates must apply in advance for each Step or Step Component (USMLE, 2014b). Candidates must select an eligibility period, once approved for testing (USMLE, 2015, p. 15).	The California Board of Registered Nursing (2013) recommends candidates wait 6 to 8 weeks before checking the status of an application without accommodations. Additionally, once the state board of nursing reviews a candidate's application, it is then sent to the National Council of State Boards of Nursing, Inc. for final approval by Missouri (Missouri State Board of Nursing, 2002, p. 1) and California (California Board of Registered Nursing, 2004, p. 2).	Candidates are directed to apply at least 90 days before the desired testing date for Level 1, Level 2-CE, and Level 3 computer-based cognitive examinations and at least 180 days before the desired testing date for the clinical skills examination, Level 2-PE (NBOME, 2014, p. 15).
Subsequent examinations	The NBME permits an abbreviated form, "Subsequent Request for Test Accommodations," for candidates who were granted earlier Step exam accommodations, and requires no resubmission of documentation (USMLE, 2014b).	Some states, such as California, permit candidates to reapply for accommodations with an abbreviated form when repeating the exam (California Board of Registered Nursing, 2012, p. 1).	Candidates previously provided accommodation who are taking the next COMLEX exam must complete and submit a new "Request for Test Accommodation" (NBOME, 1999, p. 4).

(continued)

Process	United States Medical Licensing Examination (USMLE)	National Council Licensure Examination (NCLEX)	Comprehensive Osteopathic Medical Licensing Examination (COMLEX)
Notification	The NBME will e-mail candidates a confirmation of receipt of their requests within a few days of submission (USMLE, 2014b). Candidates should "allow at least 60 days for processing," and all notification will be made in writing (USMLE, 2014b).	The NCSBN confirms the provision of accommodations by e-mail when authorizing NCLEX candidates to take the test (NCSBN, 2014, p. 4).	Successful candidates are notified in writing and must contact the NBOME to register for their exams (NBOME, 2014, p. 16).
Reconsideration (appeal of adverse decision)	Candidates who consider their decision adverse (denied or provided alternative accommodation) may contact the NBME's disability services specialist by e-mail or telephone (USMLE, 2014b).	The NCSBN directs candidates to "request information" from their boards of nursing regarding accommodations (NCSBN, 2014, p. 4).	Candidates whose applications are denied or not approved as requested may submit "new and compelling data or information" that was "not previously available," and must also submit a "written and rational statement explaining the basis upon which the candidates contend the NBOME's decision should be reconsidered" (NBOME, 2014, p. 16).

(continued)

• TABLE 5.1 Differences in Requirements Among Three Major Testing Agencies (continued)

Process	United States Medical Licensing Examination (USMLE)	National Council Licensure Examination (NCLEX)	Comprehensive Osteopathic Medical Licensing Examination (COMLEX)
Personal item exemptions	Candidates with documented medical conditions who will need medicines or devices while testing can contact the "Personal Item Exception Coordinator" (USMLE, 2014b). Candidates requesting additional break time will apply to NBME's disability services (USMLE, 2014b).	There is no mention of personal item exemptions on the NCSBN website. They are alluded to by the California Board of Registered Nursing's "Candidates with Disabilities—Request for Accommodations," which states that any "examination accommodations, including aids brought into the testing center, must have pre-approval of the Board"—that is, requested as an accommodation (California Board of Registered Nursing, 2004, p.1).	The NBOME may provide limited special assistance if sufficient notification is provided to the NBOME, even though the candidate may not be a person with disabilities. Examples include the use of earplugs, dietary needs, or taking medication (NBOME, 2014, p. 17).

Accommodations Available on Standardized Exams

• TABLE 5.2 **Commonly Requested Accommodations and Points of Consideration for Each**

Accommodation	Points of Consideration
Extended time (standard time +25%, 50%, 75%, 100%)	• Base request on historically approved extended-time accommodations • If accommodation has not been received before, provide rationale for request • If extended time will necessitate exam being given over multiple days, consider if this will create further challenges
Additional or extended rest breaks	• Determine what the break structure is for all students • Consider if multiple short breaks or an extension to standard breaks will better meet disability-related needs • Specify the amount of time needed for each break, and the frequency of breaks needed
Multiple-day testing	• Can assist in combatting physical or cognitive fatigue from long testing days • Could be requested in addition to or in lieu of extended time, depending on need • Documentation should make a specific recommendation for the amount of time the test taker can work per day
Testing in a private environment	• May be requested related to anxiety, distractibility, inattention, panic attacks, or other similar concerns • May be used to allow the test taker to employ self-talk, or to walk around the room without disturbing others • Consider if breaks are helpful in addition to, or in lieu of, a private room • If approved, testing sites have a limited number of private rooms; secure a place at your preferred site early
Assistive technology	• Consider the exam format to determine what is necessary • Document a history of using specific technology requested (e.g., the student experiences a significant amount of eye fatigue, and thus needs large print and reverse-contrast screen colors; the student is very familiar with ZoomText software after 5 years of daily use, and should have access to the same software during the exam due to familiarity with keyboard shortcuts and settings) • Ensure that disability documentation makes a specific recommendation for the requested technology

(continued)

• **TABLE 5.2 Commonly Requested Accommodations and Points of Consideration for Each (*continued*)**

Accommodation	Points of Consideration
Oral directions: requesting a written copy or sign language interpreter	• This may be helpful for students with disabilities related to auditory processing, attention, or hearing deficits
Personal item exemptions	• Any disability-related item that will be needed in the exam room must be requested and approved in advance • Examples include food, water, medication, a special cushion, hearing aids or cochlear implants, and other medical devices • Students should check in advance with the testing agency/site to confirm if a formal exemption is needed • Once approved, students should confirm that this has been communicated to the testing site by the testing agency
Specific lighting requests	• Students with sensitivity to certain types of light might request this (e.g., those with migraines, seizure disorders, autism spectrum disorder [ASD], visual disabilities) • Disability documentation should explain the need • Provide history of receiving the accommodation

Ensuring Requested Accommodations Are Necessary

Eligible test takers can be approved for a variety of accommodations on high-stakes exams; however, in making an application, students should consider what accommodations are *required* to address their particular disability-related needs on that specific exam. Testing agencies and boards carefully review all submitted documentation to ensure that it provides evidence that students' disabilities significantly interfere with their ability to take the test under standard conditions. Disability documentation should clearly support the requested accommodation(s). (See Table 5.2.)

Know the Test Format

DS providers must ensure they understand both the *structure* and the *format* of the exam, in order to consider what accommodations students may require for equal access to the exam. Many professional school programs format their exams in line with certification and licensing exams; however, some do not. In order to prepare students for this high-pressure environment, DS providers also need to understand exactly how the exam is administered. Tip 5.2 provides some guiding questions to help in this process.

TIP 5.2 • Understanding the Exam Format

- Is it administered on a computer?
- If so, how does that computer system work?
- Can students go back and change an answer on a question?
- Can students skip a question, or get early questions wrong, or will they get "cut off"?
- What kinds of tools can students bring to the exam, or are any tools provided to all test takers (e.g., ear plugs, scratch paper, whiteboard)?
- What is the length of the exam, and how long and frequent are the breaks provided to everyone?
- Do any portions of the exam have a listening or practical component (e.g., listening to a recording of a heart sound, working with standardized patients)?

Disability providers and administrators should consider *what barriers* exist for students as a result of the format and structure of the exam, and how that interacts with the students' disabilities. For example, if the exam is very long (e.g., 8 hours) and a student's disability causes cognitive fatigue after 4 hours of intense focus, the *length* of the exam might be the barrier. However, if the exam is delivered on a computer, and a disability impacts a student's ability to read text on the screen, the *format and delivery* of the exam might be the barrier. Finally, if a student has difficulty reading, writing, or comprehending/ processing information within strict time limits, the *time limit* of the exam might be the barrier.

Once the barriers that are posed by the exam are understood, DS providers can best help students to determine what accommodations they require. This determination will also be informed by what accommodations the students have successfully utilized in the past. It is important to help students articulate *precisely* what accommodations they will need to have equal access to the exam, and why (see Tip 5.3).

TIP 5.3 • How Should Students Prepare?

1. Begin the process early; expect delays.
2. Submit recent, detailed documentation—obtain new documentation if necessary.
3. Locate multiple centers for accommodated testing.
4. Make requests for any personal item exemptions, including hearing aids and cochlear implants.

SUPPORTING STUDENTS IN THE REQUEST PROCESS

Early Discussions

Many students find the process of requesting accommodations for exams daunting on top of their already-busy academic schedules. As a result, students often put off completing the necessary paperwork until the last minute—a big mistake. The "last-minute scramble" results in unnecessary stress, and reduces the likelihood of a quality accommodation request. DS providers should remind students of the timeline for requesting accommodations early, and follow up with information about the process. Students should begin this process as early as possible, perhaps the summer before the exam. During the summer, students will have more flexible time in their schedules to gather evaluations, seek reassessment, and track down historical materials without having to balance course work and clinic requirements.

Gathering the Necessary Elements of Applications

Students need to provide some form of documentation of their disability status. DS providers should know the specific, nuanced requirements of the respective exams in order to help students identify the necessary documentation and other items to include in their applications (e.g., transcripts, previous standardized exam accommodation approvals, letters of support) well in advance of the identified submission date. The documentation on file with the school may not be sufficient to meet the requirements for the exam. Some of the requirements listed may be nonspecific. In these cases, DS providers and students should ask questions of the agency, and work with the agency to get specific guidance. The documentation required by an agency may be far and above that previously submitted to the school or DS provider. See Example 5.1 for the COMLEX requirements regarding submission of an extensive history of accommodations.

EXAMPLE 5.1 • COMLEX Requests for Student History

> 1. (d) Describe all examinations you have taken, if any, without an accommodation, including the date(s) or period(s) the examination(s) was administered, the testing agency, school or college administering such examination, and whether or not you passed or successfully completed the examination without an accommodation. (NBOME, 1999, p. 3)

Current Documentation

If a student requires new or updated documentation of his or her disability, this may require a referral to a specialist or the need to organize an appointment with the student's treatment team. The need for updated documentation adds to the timeline for requesting accommodations and highlights the need to begin the process early. The demands of academic programs, wait times for appointments with specialists, and cost of an evaluation all conspire to expand the time frame for obtaining a current assessment.

Even if a student has an evaluation or assessment that meets the documentation requirements for boards, the evaluation may be out of date. For example, the USMLE and the COMLEX require documentation current *within 3 years of the accommodations request.* The documentation used to obtain accommodations in a health sciences or medical school is often dated from the beginning of a student's undergraduate education, rendering it outdated for boards like the USMLE. Even if the content of the student's documentation meets the rigorous requirements of the licensing boards, it may well need updating.

Students' Limited Free Time

Students who require updated documentation or a review of their assessments need to plan ahead. Graduate health sciences students participate in rigorous programs, rarely permitting adequate time during the school year for an assessment worthy of the boards. Program timing may only leave a student with the summer or the holiday break to obtain an assessment.

Appointments

Many licensed professionals qualified to provide assessments are booked at least 3 months in advance. The assessment often takes a full day or more and the report can take up to 3 weeks to write. Together, this adds a potential 90 to 120 days to secure new documentation.

Cost

Some students, depending on their medical insurance and their geographic location, find they will spend $1,200 to $5,000+ for a typical assessment for a learning disability or attention deficit hyperactivity disorder (ADHD). Applicants may need to plan for the costs if they are paying out of pocket or seeking an adjustment to their financial aid package to cover the cost. We recommend that students obtain their evaluation 6 months to 1 year in advance of the date they plan to apply for accommodations.

Assisting the Evaluator

If students require a documentation update, it is helpful for students to approach the evaluator with a summary of the exam requirements, along with their reasoning for the requested accommodations (i.e., barriers posed by the exam, functional limitations associated with their disability). The evaluator may also wish to see all the historical evaluations that have been completed, if they are available. Providing the evaluator with this information in advance helps them best represent the student's needs and expedites the process.

Historical Evidence of Disability

Evidence of disability, historical accommodations, and the need for accommodation can bolster students' chances of receiving accommodations. The DS provider's observations about a student's experience with disability in the academic environment can also serve to help strengthen a student's application. Students with disabilities considered developmental in nature (occurring since birth or childhood, e.g., learning disability, ADHD) who have been diagnosed later in life *should* provide examples of how their undiagnosed disability affected their early years and education.

Leaving a Trail of Evidence

Students should provide a "bread-crumb trail" of evidence that they have experienced impairment throughout their lives (rather than simply because they have had difficulties with the rigor of the college or graduate school environment). Historical disability evaluations; letters from doctors; letters from previous institutions; letters or proof of approval for accommodations on previous graduate entrance exams (e.g., Medical College Admissions Test [MCAT], Graduate Record Examination [GRE], Dental Admission Test [DAT]); individualized education plans (IEPs); and report cards with comments referring to behavioral patterns, inattentiveness, or need for extra supports can help to substantiate a student's history of receiving formal or informal accommodations. For students who have acquired a disability recently that is not developmental in nature, the student should provide information about the onset of the condition and history of receiving accommodations since then, and explain any gaps or delays in using accommodations.

Transcripts

Some students wonder whether providing copies of their undergraduate transcripts or K–12 report cards would be helpful to substantiate early difficulties when accommodations were not provided. Students should consider the impression their transcripts might make if including them as part of the initial application for accommodations. If students were diagnosed later in their education (e.g., high school, college) and their transcripts show improved grades after they started using accommodations, then submitting them with a description of what happened might be helpful. In some cases, it may be better not to include transcripts unless the agency requests them, as agencies may consider evidence of prior success as a reason accommodations are not needed, overlooking that many students self-accommodated a disability for years.

Transcripts from elementary school, high school, and/or college should be provided if the records *clearly show* the impact of students' disability on their grades. For example, if a student has a history of dropping or withdrawing from course work to maintain a grade point average (GPA), this might serve as evidence that when given a reduced course load, the student excelled because he or she had the extra time necessary to devote to studying for each course. This can provide supporting evidence about the existence of a disability prior to formal diagnosis.

The Personal Statement

Most licensing boards require a personal statement or cover letter as part of the accommodation request application. This letter outlines the student's history of disability, its effect on functioning, history of receiving accommodations, and a summary of why the accommodations requested are necessary to ensure equal access to the exam. This is often the most time-consuming part of the process, but can be one of the most important and compelling parts of the student's application. *It is the student's only opportunity to share his or her personal experience of living with a disability.*

For many students, this process requires them to reflect on parts of their lives or educational experiences they might rather forget. Some students find the process of being reevaluated to prove their disability status frustrating and demoralizing. They may also worry about who sees this request, and how that might affect their future as a health care provider.

For students who have recently been diagnosed with a disability, do not have a long history of using accommodations, or are requesting accommodations for the first time, the personal statement serves to establish *why* the accommodations are necessary—and *why now*, when there is no history of accommodation. Some students will not have required extended time as an undergraduate because their previous institutions provided unlimited time, accommodated students "informally," or operated under a unique structure of the curriculum.

Students should discuss the circumstances around their diagnosis, and any effective self-accommodation strategies they may have used prior to an official diagnosis (e.g., reading texts over many times for comprehension, using extensive tutoring, utilizing a partner or study group to break down information for them, using reading or voice-recognition software or having a friend or family member read materials to them). If informal accommodations were provided, the student should describe what was provided, and how the provision came about (e.g., requested informally from professor, professor noticed that the student took longer to test and offered time), as well as documenting this via a third party (the professor, a proctor, a dean of students) wherever possible.

Points of Consideration for Personal Statements

1. Have students explain the *nature of their disability* and why they are requesting accommodations.

    Students should include a description of the day-to-day impact of the disability—not just the impact on academic tasks such as taking exams (e.g., the impact on interpersonal relationships, employment, course withdrawals, personal organization, driving record, financial management).

2. Focus on *areas of difficulty* rather than on strengths.

Highlighting weaknesses seems counterproductive because students with disabilities are taught to put their "best foot forward" and emphasize their strengths when speaking about themselves. However, the personal statement is not the time to talk about how well they have been doing. It is actually the place to emphasize and highlight what has been difficult. It is essential that students connect the requested accommodations to their successes.

3. Emphasize the *need* for the accommodation rather than a *preference.*

The burden to prove that the requested accommodations are *necessary* is on the student. Therefore, students should be very clear about the barriers posed by the test, and the anticipated outcome if the requested accommodation is not in place. The barrier must be grounded in the nature of the condition, and substantiated by the documentation they provide.

4. Students should pay close attention to the *language* they use to describe their needs.

Students should not say things like, "I would do better with" or, "to ensure my success," as accommodations are designed to ensure *access,* not success. Students should also avoid using phrases such as "learning differences," as agencies are only interested in disabilities that require accommodations, not "learning differences," which are applicable to everyone, and are not protected by the Americans with Disabilities Act. See Tip 5.4 for more on language use.

TIP 5.4 • Language Use

Language is powerful. Students should be intentional about the words they use and avoid these common word-use "pitfalls":

I would appreciate it if . . . (do not ask for a favor; ask for legally mandated access)
    It would be helpful to have . . . (some might say it would be helpful for everyone)

Instead say:

I require. . .
    As a result of [specify barrier], it is necessary that I am provided [specify accommodation].
    Throughout my education, [specify accommodation] has allowed me to demonstrate my understanding of materials on exams. I will require the same accommodation on this exam.

Letters of Support

Letters from professors, teachers, guidance counselors, or other people who can describe a student's previous academic performance may provide further evidence of how they are impacted by disability, or how the use of accommodations (formal or informal) and compensatory strategies improved their performance. These are not required portions of a student application, but can add weight to the application.

For students who were diagnosed later in life, a letter from the person who first suggested an evaluation for learning or other disabilities, or who first connected the student with disability-related supports, might be helpful to contextualize the student's circumstances.

Likewise, a letter from an employer providing further evidence of the effect of an as-yet undiagnosed disability on learning or performance while on the job (e.g., a letter from a former supervisor describing performance issues or additional support required on the job as a result of disability-related difficulties) can help to substantiate the effect of a disability, even if the student was diagnosed later in life. If formal accommodations or adjustments were needed in a workplace for a documented disability, providing evidence of this is also beneficial, as it shows that the student's disability affects the individual across areas of life, outside of a classroom or educational environment.

Disability Services or Academic Program Letter of Support

There is generally an additional form or requested letter of support that the DS office or academic program crafts, confirming the student's approved accommodations. If there are supplemental forms to fill out, it is important to determine who is qualified to complete the forms per the testing agency or licensing board guidance. Some require that a medical or mental health care provider (e.g., a psychiatrist, physician, psychologist), or the provider who conducted the evaluation, complete the form, whereas others accept forms completed by school officials (e.g., DS provider, dean of students office, office of student affairs).

The academic program or DS provider should offer to provide a more detailed letter in addition to the requisite form. Letters of this nature include additional information not captured in other forms, noting observations about the student's need for accommodations, how the school determined the approved accommodations and in what settings, as well as specific information about how the student's disability impacts him or her in the academic setting. It is critical that letters of support are specific to the student and do not resemble a form letter sent for all students. These letters are the opportunity for DS professionals to provide added value in the form of supportive justification for the student's need for accommodations. As such, letters of support should provide further explanation of the student's disability in a way that is distinctive to the student, and demonstrate the writer's expertise and understanding and observations of the student's needs. Example 5.2 provides a sample structure for a letter of support.

EXAMPLE 5.2 • Sample Structure for a Letter of Support

To Whom It May Concern:

I am writing at the request of [STUDENT NAME (REFERENCE NUMBER FOR APPLICATION)], to provide support for [HIS/HER] request for accommodations on the [NAME OF EXAM].

Section 1: Who you are and your expertise
- Describe your role, relationship to the student
- Provide information about your background and expertise in the work
- Explain when the student registered with your office and in what capacity the student was in attendance at your university

Section 2: Services and accommodations at your institution
- Describe the accommodations approved for the student at your institution
- Describe the duration for which the accommodations were approved
- Describe the documentation that was reviewed, and any other information that was used to make the determination
  - For example: in-depth intake interview with the student, conversations with therapist, record of historical accommodations, observed behavior, information from faculty
  - Where applicable, reference specific scores on evaluative measures or other quantitative data included in documentation
- Describe any particularities of the determination process
  - For example: initially approved 150% extended time but moved the student to 200% extended time after observing XYZ behaviors OR after XYZ changes in the student's status OR due to XYZ elements of the exam structure that created XYZ barriers due to XYZ features of the student's disability
- Provide any data regarding utilization of approved accommodations at your institution
- If the student has not been registered for the duration of the program at your institution, provide an explanation for this
  - For example: the student initially hesitated to register, hoping he would do well without accommodations, now that he had arrived at medical school; after failing his first two exams, he registered with DS and began consistently utilizing accommodations, and has achieved at a level commensurate with past performances that were accommodated
- Any additional information that will support the student's application, especially to fill in holes in documentation or to support the student's self-report of need
  - For example: if the student was first diagnosed while a student at your institution, provide background explanation of late diagnosis and your involvement with supporting the student and determining accommodations

(continued)

EXAMPLE 5.2 • Sample Structure for a Letter of Support (*continued*)

Section 3: The case for accommodations on this exam
- Explain your support for the student's requested accommodations on the licensing or board exam
  - Link the requested accommodations to the student's functional limitations and the impact of disability across multiple domains
- Provide rationales for any accommodations that the student is requesting that have not been previously provided at your institution, but that you believe are necessary to provide equal access to the exam
  - Explain the structure of your institution, and why the accommodation is not needed in that environment but is on this exam
  - Provide any support you can for why you believe the request is valid, given the structure of the exam and the impact of the disability as outlined previously

Section 4:
- Provide any final information that is additive to the student's request

Please do not hesitate to contact me at [PHONE NUMBER or E-MAIL] with any questions or concerns.

Sincerely,

[YOUR NAME]
[YOUR ROLE]

HOW DS PROVIDERS CAN HELP PREPARE STUDENTS

DS providers and administrators can be valuable resources for students in assisting them to prepare a request for accommodations. The following points outline the types of things that can be done to make the process less onerous for students (see also Tip 5.5).

TIP 5.5 • Testing Center Preparation

Multiple students report that visiting the testing center in advance of the test day, and practicing the check-in process, significantly reduces test anxiety. Similar to other establishments, testing centers vary in their size, staff, and level of activity. Some students seek out smaller testing centers in an effort to reduce stimulation and anxiety. Likewise, some students prefer to test at centers far away from the school to maintain a level of privacy about their accommodated situation.

1. **Work with students to identify the documentation they have** *early,* **and begin a file of historical documentation at the DS office.**
   - It is recommended that students begin this process as soon as possible, as it can take time to track down lost documentation or retrieve it from home.
2. **When reviewing the documentation students provide when they first request accommodations at the school, note whether the documentation is likely to meet standards for required licensing exams.** If it is not, have a conversation with the student at that time; explain why the documentation may need to be updated.
   - Alert students to the requirements for requesting accommodations to get them thinking about the process in advance of when they must begin working on it.
   - Assist students with early referrals for new or updated documentation. Students may need to find a new evaluator locally, or may prefer to seek an evaluation closer to home while on break. DS providers can assist here, too, by contacting a health sciences university in the student's hometown to request the institution's referral list for evaluators who are able to provide suitable documentation for the specific type of exam to share with the student.
3. **Set a recommended timeline for students to begin working on the application for accommodations, based on the timing of their required exams (see Appendix 5.1, Student Checklist and Timeline for Licensing Exam Accommodation Requests).**
   - We recommend starting the process at least 10 months before the exam.
   - Send reminders to students in advance of the recommended start time, then bi-monthly after that time, with tips and recommendations to motivate them throughout the process.
4. **Be available to review drafts of personal statements and coach students who are having difficulty with the process.**
   - Some students will be "old pros" at making these requests, especially if they successfully requested accommodations for an entrance exam. But other students may have more difficulty, especially if the process of requesting accommodations is triggering or new to them.
5. **When in doubt, reach out to colleagues for guidance.**
   - Testing agencies and licensing boards may change their processes or practices from time to time, and without warning. Discussing challenges with colleagues on other campuses may be helpful, as others may have found practical ways of addressing the issues, and multiple schools may wish to come together to make an inquiry about an issue to the testing agency.
   - See also Tip 5.6 on common mistakes to avoid in the process.

TIP 5.6 • Avoid Common Mistakes

Students should use special care to avoid these common pitfalls:
- Incomplete application for accommodations
- Weak historical evidence of a disability
- Documentation supplied does not provide clear evidence of a significant impairment in a major life activity
- Disability documentation is outdated

IF THE APPLICATION IS DENIED: THE APPEAL PROCESS

Supporting a Student Whose Request Is Denied

Testing agencies and boards will have an established appeals process, providing an opportunity for students to appeal a rejection. If the appeals process is not expressly stated in the denial letter, the student should contact the testing agency or licensing board to request information about the process. Most often, students are required to provide additional information or disability documentation with the appeals request. Appendix 5.2 provides a checklist to assist students in the appeal process. If the appeal attempt is not successful, students can decide to request further review of the request, or make a complaint to a higher authority, such as the Department of Justice. See also Tip 5.7 on the timeline for appeals.

TIP 5.7 • Watch the Clock

The clock resets with an appeal, usually for another 60 days! For this reason it is paramount that students begin the process early.

If students receive a denial letter, they should follow these steps to formulate an appeal:

1. **Read the denial letter carefully.**

   Ensure that the steps listed for appealing the decision are reviewed in detail. Each agency and board has a different appeals process and deadline.
2. **Ensure the appeal addresses the reasons for the denial.**

   In most cases, the letter will detail specific reasons for the denial. It may be helpful to go through the letter line by line to address each concern and directly tie these to the materials submitted, and to identify new information that will be required.

3. **Note the deadline for appeal.**

Most agencies or boards will not consider appeals received beyond the deadline. If students have a significant concern about meeting the deadline they should contact the testing agency or board immediately to discuss the concern and request an extension.

4. **Seek assistance as soon as possible.**

Students should be encouraged to contact the DS provider, and likely the health professional(s) who supplied documentation of the disability, to assist with the appeal. It is likely that students will only have a few weeks to appeal, and anyone assisting the student will need as much notice as possible. Students should not assume they can collect additional letters, test results, or evaluations on a moment's notice. They should allow ample time for practitioners to address their needs; 7–10 business days is a reasonable turnaround.

When requesting additional information from a provider, students should include a copy of the denial letter. The provider may be able to sort out the agency's main concerns and determine the type of additional documentation needed for the appeal. Additionally, the DS provider or health care provider may be able to write a second letter of support, provide guidance regarding the student's response, or provide a referral for a new evaluator, a private consultant, or an attorney who works on these types of cases.

What to Do if a Student Has a Poor Exam Experience

There are instances where students approved for accommodations by a testing agency or licensing board arrive at the exam site only to have something go awry. For example, the record of the student's approved accommodations was not sent to the exam site, or only a portion of the approved accommodations is recorded. As well, it may be that the site fails to properly execute approved accommodations (e.g., a private exam room is noisy due to location, rest breaks are not provided as approved, etc.). *It is advised that students raise any issues immediately, and refuse to sit for the exam until the issues are resolved.*

Students are often not permitted to take an exam again within a specified period of time. If they take the exam without approved accommodations in place, they may find themselves having to wait several months to take the exam again with the appropriate accommodations, even if it is due to exam center error. As well, it may not be possible (or may require a formal appeal) to "wipe" a grade from their records, and the poorly accommodated exam score may be reported to others (e.g., perspective residency sites)—even though it should not be considered a valid score.

If the student chooses to sit for the exam despite any issues, and notifies the DS office of these issues after the fact, the DS provider should advise the student to report the problems to the responsible testing agency immediately. Students may be able to appeal an exam administration and successfully argue for another exam administration with a fee waiver, as well as expunging the original score from their record. If students fail to report these incidents on the day of the exam, they lessen their grounds for appeal.

CONCLUSION

Requesting accommodations for certification, licensing, and board exams can be daunting for students. While engaged in a hectic and highly stressful program of education, they must once again build a case for requiring accommodations—this time on an exam that is critical to their future as a health professional. DS providers can provide valuable support to students in this process, beginning in their first interactions. Working alongside students, building structure to the process, and providing recommendations will assist them to navigate this phase of their education.

REFERENCES

California Board of Registered Nursing. (2004, January). *Candidates with disabilities—request for accommodations.* Retrieved from http://www.rn.ca.gov/pdfs/applicants/disable.pdf

California Board of Registered Nursing. (2012, January). *Request for reapply/repeat examination.* Retrieved from http://www.rn.ca.gov/pdfs/applicants/reapply.pdf

California Board of Registered Nursing. (2013). *Applicant frequently asked questions.* Retrieved from http://www.rn.ca.gov/applicants/lic-faqs.shtml#lic7

Continental Testing Services. (2011, April). *Reasonable accommodation request for examinees with disabilities.* Retrieved from http://www.continentaltesting.net/IL_ADA.PDF

Missouri State Board of Nursing. (2002, September). *Position paper: Requests for modifications from disabled candidates.* Retrieved from http://pr.mo.gov/boards/nursing/NursingADAPositionPaper.pdf

Missouri State Board of Nursing. (2014, January). *RN examination application instruction letter.* Retrieved from http://pr.mo.gov/boards/nursing/rnexam53003.pdf

National Board of Osteopathic Medical Examiners. (1999). *Instructions and forms, COMLEX-USA examinations.* Retrieved from http://www.nbome.org/docs/ADAApp.pdf

National Board of Osteopathic Medical Examiners. (2014, July 1). *COMLEX-USA bulletin of information.* Retrieved from http://www.nbome.org/docs/comlexBOI.pdf

National Board of Osteopathic Medical Examiners. (n.d.). *Information for candidates.* Retrieved from http://www.nbome.org/candidates.asp?m=can

National Council of State Boards of Nursing. (2014, January 1). *2014 NCLEX examination candidate bulletin.* Retrieved from https://www.ncsbn.org/2014_NCLEX_Candidate_Bulletin.pdf

United States Medical Licensing Examination. (2014a). *Announcements.* Retrieved from http://www.usmle.org/announcements/?ContentId=141

United States Medical Licensing Examination. (2014b). *Test accommodations.* Retrieved from http://www.usmle.org/test-accommodations/requesting-accommodations.html

United States Medical Licensing Examination. (2015). *Bulletin of information.* Retrieved from http://www.usmle.org/pdfs/bulletin/2015bulletin.pdf

Student Checklist and Timeline for Licensing Exam Accommodation Requests

> **Note:** This checklist is provided as a general recommendation. Students and DS providers should tailor the use of this checklist to the particular requirements of the exam, and the student's individual circumstances.

AT LEAST 10 MONTHS BEFORE YOU PLAN TO TAKE THE EXAM

☐ Find the information about the exam accommodation request process
☐ Find the deadline for making requests: _____
  - Identify the appeal procedure and any associated timelines
  - Aim to make your request 30 to 60 days **in advance** of the recommended deadline: _____
☐ Make a list of what historical documentation you need to gather:
  - All historical evaluations
  - Supplemental letters of support from previous instructors
  - Letters documenting historical accommodation approval
    - K–12
    - Advanced Placement (AP) exams
    - Scholastic Aptitude Test (SAT)/American College Test (ACT) exams
    - Undergraduate program
    - Post-baccalaureate program
    - Graduate school
    - Workplace
    - Professional school
☐ Locate the documentation requirements for making your request
  - Print a copy of the requirements
  - Compare your most recent documentation to the requirements
  - If your documentation doesn't match, identify the specific reasons why and make a list
  - If you'll need a new evaluation, begin contacting potential evaluators immediately to determine the cost and how soon you can be evaluated
    - Evaluators likely will want to see your historical evaluations
    - Evaluators will benefit from knowing what the requirements are for documentation

- Share the list of things you feel are missing from your historical documentation
- A good evaluator will summarize your historical evaluations and explain any inconsistencies between them, and between any new results
- Explain the deadline for submitting your application

☐ Schedule an appointment with your DS office to discuss your application
- The DS office might have copies of your historical evaluations or other materials you can include
- Make a request for a letter of support and/or for required forms to be completed
- Ask for tips and advice about your application, and inquire about other students' recent experiences
- Inquire about any financial support toward reevaluation, and recommended referrals

AT LEAST 8 MONTHS BEFORE THE EXAM

☐ Begin drafting your personal statement

AT LEAST 6 MONTHS BEFORE THE EXAM

☐ Ask someone from the DS office, or someone else you trust and who knows you and your disability experience well, to proofread your personal statement for completeness and clarity
- Note: It is not advisable for someone to heavily edit your grammar or language, particularly if your request is related to a learning disability or disorder of written expression

☐ Schedule a meeting with the DS office to review all the materials you've gathered and determine if there is anything else missing
- Collect any missing items and follow up with the responsible person if anything needs to be edited

☐ Finalize your package to send to the testing agency
- Give the DS office a copy of all the materials you've gathered to keep on file
- Make a copy of all materials to keep in a personal file

AT LEAST 4 MONTHS BEFORE THE EXAM

☐ Mail all materials to the testing agency; it is recommended that you send all materials tracked and with a return receipt or signature required to ensure that you know when the materials have arrived
- Track your package and confirm it was received

☐ Identify several preferred testing centers
- Determine your preference to take the exam close to school or close to home

ONCE YOUR APPROVAL IS RECEIVED

☐ Book your preferred testing location
  • Depending on the requirements of your exam this may be possible sooner; follow the instructions provided by the testing administrator
☐ Confirm that a record of your approved accommodations or personal item exemptions have been communicated to the testing site
☐ Consider a trial visit to the testing site to ensure you know the route and the check-in process

THE NIGHT BEFORE

☐ Lay out anything you'll need to take with you
☐ Get a good night's sleep
☐ Pat yourself on the back—you made it!

GOOD LUCK—YOU ARE AWESOME!

Student Checklist for Appeal of Denial of Licensing Exam Accommodation Requests

> **Note:** This checklist is provided as a general recommendation. Students and DS providers should tailor the use of this checklist to the particular requirements of the exam, and the student's individual circumstances.

IMMEDIATELY UPON RECEIPT OF DECISION

- ☐ Review the decision letter provided by the testing agency in detail
  - Schedule a meeting with your DS provider to get a second perspective to ensure you aren't missing anything
- ☐ Make a list of the issues identified in the letter
- ☐ Determine who can assist you with addressing the issues raised
  - Physician or other specialist health provider
  - Mental health provider
  - Evaluator
  - DS provider
  - Historical employer
  - Professor
  - Other: _____
- ☐ If you have materials to provide in answer to the agency's concerns, assemble these materials
- ☐ Contact each provider to make an appointment to request assistance and discuss how to address the concerns
  - Provide a copy of the decision letter
  - Highlight the issues you think they can assist with
  - Explain your deadline for submitting your appeal and provide a deadline for them to submit additional information to you
    - Generally 7 to 10 business days is reasonable, depending on what you are requesting and your timeline for submitting the appeal
- ☐ If you believe you will not be able to provide the necessary response in the timeline provided, contact the testing agency immediately to request an extension
- ☐ Craft a cover letter to respond to the agency's decision, and outline the additional information provided for consideration; address any issues raised that you are able to explain

2 DAYS BEFORE YOUR DEADLINE FOR PROVIDERS TO PROVIDE ADDITIONAL INFORMATION

☐ Follow up with the providers to provide reminders to ensure you receive necessary materials in time

ONCE ALL MATERIALS ARE RECEIVED

☐ Schedule a meeting and request that your DS provider look at your assembled materials
  • If possible, send a copy in advance of the meeting so the DS provider has sufficient time to review the materials and provide you with feedback
  • If you aren't able to provide materials in advance, advise the DS provider of what you're hoping he or she can do in advance so that the DS provider might be able to set aside time after your meeting to provide feedback quickly
☐ Make copies of all materials you will send and keep them for your records; if possible, also keep copies with the DS office for their records

BY THE DATE MATERIALS MUST BE POSTMARKED (APPEAL DEADLINE)

☐ Send all materials with tracking, return receipt, and/or signature required to ensure that they arrive on time and you have a record that they were received

S · I · X

Learning in the Digital Age: Assistive Technology and Electronic Access

Michael J. Kenney, Neera R. Jain, Lisa M. Meeks, Elisa Laird-Metke,
Joshua Hori, and Jonathan D. McGough

INTRODUCTION

This chapter provides a general overview of the relationship between educational technology and students with disabilities. The chapter focuses on two key aspects: first, ensuring that the technology provided to all students is inherently accessible to students with disabilities and, second, descriptions of some commonly used assistive technology to assist students in both the didactic and clinical settings. Although the chapter will touch on some of the most frequent issues involving accessibility, this chapter is only an overview of the vast array of assistive technologies available for the health sciences disability services (DS) provider.

ENSURING ALL CAMPUS TECHNOLOGY IS ACCESSIBLE

Now, more than ever, technology plays an important part in the recruitment, admission, classroom training, and clinical work of health sciences students. Although technology can be beneficial to students with disabilities, if a program implements a new technological system without first vetting its accessibility, it can create a new barrier for students. On June 29, 2010, the Office for Civil Rights (OCR) of the U.S. Department of Education and the Civil Rights Division of the U.S. Department of Justice issued a joint "Dear Colleague Letter" (DCL).[1]

---

[1] Joint Dear Colleague Letter from Assistant Secretary for the Office for Civil Rights Russlyn Ali and Assistant Attorney General for the Civil Rights Division Thomas E. Perez, U.S. Departments of Justice and Education, June 29, 2010.

The DCL stated that "requiring use of an emerging technology in a classroom environment when the technology is inaccessible to an entire population of students with disabilities" is discrimination prohibited by the American with Disabilities Act (ADA) and Section 504. For this reason, DS providers need to work with their institutions and educational technology staff to ensure that a robust assessment for accessibility is part of the review and procurement process for emerging technology and systems.

Despite the guidance of the Department of Education and the Department of Justice, institutions do not always ensure accessibility in their emerging technologies, websites, digital documents, and classroom management systems. Recent settlements show that schools must prioritize accessibility in the digital environment or the OCR will mandate the process for them (see Case Example 6.1).

CASE EXAMPLE 6.1 • University of Montana[2]

Students at the University of Montana filed a complaint with the Office for Civil Rights (OCR) in 2012 alleging that the university's documents, learning management system, library materials, classroom technologies (i.e., clickers), videos, and course registration system were not accessible. As part of the resolution, the university agreed to develop a comprehensive policy for accessibility in electronic and information technologies, put in place a coordinator to monitor and implement these standards, implement a mechanism to report any digital accessibility barriers, and develop a plan to assess products for accessibility before they are purchased. Additionally, the university now provides training to faculty and staff in creating an accessible digital environment.

Similar agreements have been reached with other schools whose campus websites and technology—even automated teller machines (ATMs)—were inaccessible, including the South Carolina Technical College System[3] and Penn State.[4]

OCR investigations are time consuming, but can also prove costly, and institutions can be held financially responsible for failure to comply (see Case Example 6.2, Louisiana Tech University).

---

[2] University of Montana, Case No. 10-12-2118 (OCR Region X 2012).
[3] Letter to South Carolina Technical College System, Compliance Review No. 11-11-6002 (DOJ 2013).
[4] The Pennsylvania State University, Case No. 03-11-2020 (OCR Region III 2011).

CASE EXAMPLE 6.2 • Louisiana Tech University (LTU)[5]

A blind student enrolled in a class that required all students to use an on-line learning system called MyOMLab™ to complete homework and take tests. The student was not able to access the system, even after contacting the system's vendor to request assistance. After a month of classes had passed without gaining access to the course materials contained on the site, he was forced to drop the online class. The student filed a disability discrimination complaint with the Department of Justice (DOJ). LTU agreed to pay the student over $23,000 in damages, implement a comprehensive policy regarding accessible technologies and materials, and provide ongoing training to faculty and staff regarding accessible electronic materials. In addition to developing a plan to incorporate accessibility into current and legacy webpages, the university was required to ". . . ensure that any new technology it makes available to students, prospective students or applicants, including web applications, hardware, software, telecommunications, and multimedia is accessible."

Developing a Team Approach to Accessibility

Learning from these cases, administrators are wise to devise plans that ensure existing and newly adopted technology and electronic resources are accessible to all students. Often, this is part of the role of a campus ADA or barrier removal committee; however, electronic barriers are quickly becoming the largest institutional issues with regard to accessibility. Each school should also identify an office (or individual) responsible for improving and enforcing electronic access campus-wide. This office should evaluate existing institutional technologies, including campus websites, then prioritize and respond to inaccessible electronic content and develop a mechanism for users to report electronic or digital barriers. The office would be charged with developing a plan to correct inaccessible technology, and implement assistive technology and universally designed technological solutions on campus. Finally, but perhaps most important, this office (or individual) should be engaged in building awareness and providing campus-wide training about electronic accessibility. When faculty and administration understand their role in maintaining an accessible environment, it reduces the number of barriers on campus, starting with individual courses.

CAMPUS-WIDE ACCESSIBILITY ISSUES

Online Exams

Increasingly, exams and quizzes are being administered on the computer, either through a campus learning management system (LMS; e.g., Moodle,

---

[5] Louisiana Tech University, Case No. 204-33-116 (DOJ 2013).

Blackboard, or Sakai) or with specific exam software, such as ExamSoft. However, before employing the aforementioned systems, it is essential that they undergo an accessibility evaluation, including compatibility with assistive technology such as screen-reading software. In addition, it is wise to ensure that "built-in" features to ensure accessibility are available, such as the ability to easily allow extended time on quizzes and exams for eligible students.

Exam software is designed to create a secure environment for exam administration by restricting access to the Internet and other computer functions while an exam is open. However, this otherwise useful feature may block the ability to access assistive technology programs needed by students with disabilities. Even if access features, such as a proprietary screen reader, are built in, their functionality may not be sufficient to ensure a student with disabilities equal access to the exam environment. If exam software used is not compatible with a student's assistive technology needs, the disability provider should assess alternate options, such as administering exams on a computer (without the inaccessible software) in a proctored environment to provide the desired security.

Lecture Capture/Podcasting/Vodcasting

In many universities, lectures are increasingly recorded using a lecture capture system installed in the classroom. These systems allow all students to access the course lecture later via playback of audio and/or video recordings. The playback is accessed as a streaming video to computers or portable devices through an LMS or some other web-based interface, such as YouTube. *Vodcasts* (video playback) and *podcasts* (audio playback) of classroom lectures that can be downloaded and retrieved later without an Internet connection may also be available to students. In these formats, students can review lecture material (e.g., PowerPoint slides or other projected material, audio and/or video of the speaker), at a time and location outside of the normal class hours.

This technology benefits all students, not just students with disabilities. For example, it enables students to review content at an individual pace and multiple times. This repetition can particularly benefit students with learning disabilities, sensory disabilities, and attention deficit hyperactivity disorder (ADHD). In addition, students who are unable to attend a class, whether for personal reasons or as the result of an illness, can keep pace with the course remotely, as long as it does not fundamentally alter the program (see section "Avoiding a Fundamental Alteration of the Educational Program" in Chapter 3). In order to make the recorded lectures accessible to students with various disabilities, captioning or audio descriptions may need to be added. These are explained next.

When selecting a lecture-capture system, it is important to determine if it has a built-in workflow to allow for ease of adding captions or audio description to videos. This will ensure that accessibility features can be added by simply selecting a "caption" or "audio describe" option for the course. Generally this triggers the file to be automatically sent to a designated captioning vendor upon upload, and allows for seamless reuploading once captioning and/or audio description is complete. Systems without a built-in workflow will require a manual work-around to be devised that is likely to be labor intensive and prone to errors. Some lecture-capture systems may also have a designated vendor to provide captioning or audio description. In these cases, it is also wise to review whether that vendor meets the university's needs in terms of technical expertise with terminology, and provides a competitive cost structure, in advance of selecting a system.

Captioning and Transcripts

Captioning is a transcript that is timed to the audio and printed at the bottom of the video image. In the case of audio-only recordings, a textual record of the audio material (transcript) should be provided alongside the audio recording. Note that a transcript alone is not considered sufficient to provide access to a video recording—captions should be provided in order for the student to have simultaneous access to the visual and audio material. If recordings of lectures are provided for all students, they will need to be captioned or transcribed for Deaf or hard-of-hearing (DHOH) students. If a DHOH student is enrolled in the course, any uploaded video of the lecture will need captioning.

Automated transcription or captioning is an emerging technology. Automated captioning systems, like those available on YouTube, are not yet accurate enough to provide captioning appropriate for some educational content, particularly in the health sciences environment. Automatic captioning tools could be considered for in-house captioning of short videos, but only when used in conjunction with careful manual editing. Lecture videos and podcasts would not be good candidates for these systems due to the length, volume, and technical language of the average health sciences class. As well, the time needed to manually edit these videos would be prohibitive.

Audio Description

For students with visual disabilities, audio description for lecture capture or vodcasting may also be required. Audio description provides a spoken description of key visual material. Most companies that provide captioning for videos can also provide audio description. Youdescribe.org provides the functionality for video owners to add audio description to their YouTube and Vimeo videos. In lieu of formalized audio description, however, DS providers should work with faculty of students with visual disabilities to ensure audio description of images used in the course. Universal design principals (see Chapter 10) suggest that every image presented include audio description to ensure that all current and future presentations are accessible to students with visual disabilities. Audio descriptions help ensure students with visual disabilities have context for, and benefit from, the images.

Websites and Digital Documents

The Web Content Accessibility Guidelines (WCAG) developed by the World Wide Web Consortium (W3C), require web-page authors to ensure that the content of their pages is accessible to users with visual disabilities by, for example, providing alternative descriptive text for images and content in their materials (Caldwell, Cooper, Reid, & Vanderheiden, 2008). When implemented properly, the WCAG enable screen-reader applications to "read" web pages, allowing the user to fully experience all information presented. Any institution with a web page must ensure that its content conforms to the current WCAG standards (see Case Example 6.2).

Similarly, Portable Document Format (PDF) documents also rely on the use of structuring and tags in order to be accessed with screen readers or other reading software. The American Foundation for the Blind has prepared a document outlining a process for ensuring the accessibility of PDF documents that clearly delineates the process of designing a structure and reading order as well as tags and navigational aids for enabling readability of the PDF by existing screen readers (American Foundation for the Blind & Adobe, n.d.).

Table 6.1 highlights other common technological barriers on campuses. It also provides suggestions for collaboration with IT professionals. DS providers must identify the office responsible for digital access and begin a collaborative relationship, working together to evaluate existing infrastructure and a protocol, if any, for addressing emerging concerns.

• TABLE 6.1 Opportunities for Collaboration: Technology

Technology	Collaborations
Websites	• Ensure all campus websites are accessible to applicable required standards, such as WCAG 2.0 level AA • Ensure accessibility is integrated into the university's website development "style guide" • If the university uses a web content management system with standard templates, ensure these are accessible • Implement a scanning and testing system for university websites to help in identifying those that are inaccessible and flagging them to be fixed
Digital documents	• Devise campus guidelines for creating accessible digital documents • Many institutions use a hosted service such as Sensus Access to assist faculty, staff, and students in creating accessible digital documents

(continued)

• TABLE 6.1 Opportunities for Collaboration: Technology (*continued*)

Technology	Collaborations
Procurement	• Ensure third-party technologies purchased are accessible to all students • University's request for proposal (RFP)/procurement guidelines must include a clause requiring accessibility of new software and hardware • Include key questions in RFP/procurement tool to assist in evaluating accessibility, or have software and hardware beta tested for accessibility *before* they are purchased

Technologies in the classroom	• Ensure emerging technologies are selected with accessibility in mind
	• "Clickers" and other audience response tools should be accessible to all students
	• Learning management systems should be fully accessible, including:
	  • Navigation possible with a screen reader
	  • Exam accommodations easily implemented
	  • Ability to implement captions for course videos and video conferencing features
	• Videos shown in the classroom should have captions and audio description where needed
	• Lecture-capture systems should have a built-in workflow to allow videos to be easily captioned

ELECTRONIC MEDICAL RECORDS (EMRs) AND ACCESSIBILITY

An electronic medical record (EMR) is a computer-based system that stores a patient's medical and clinical data from within that clinical facility or across a health care system (e.g., all affiliates of a managed care organization, or all affiliated facilities within a university medical center). EMRs are highly developed software packages, developed by third-party companies, which are then adapted and personalized for the purchaser.

Federal law requires that all providers implement EMR systems and that all patient records be stored electronically by 2015 (although this deadline was later extended).[6] As such, the entire medical community is striving to incorporate electronic records into all aspects of patient care and physician training. Issues related to the student use of EMR systems are a frequent topic of discussion in medical education programs; however, accessibility and other issues specific to the use of EMR by students with disabilities are often omitted from these discussions.

---

[6] Health Information Technology for Economic and Clinical Health (HITECH) Act of 2009, enacted under Title XIII of the American Recovery and Reinvestment Act of 2009 (Pub.L. 111–5).

If EMR systems used at clinical sites are inaccessible to students with disabilities, DS providers must work with staff at that site to determine a mechanism for ensuring access. Clinical sites and hospitals have IT staff members who are responsible, or other mechanisms in place, for trouble-shooting and maintenance of EMR systems. At times, the DS provider may know more about accessibility and/or the assistive technology (AT) software necessary to access the system (e.g., Kurzweil, Read and Write Gold, JAWS, ZoomText, Dragon Naturally Speaking), and will need to work with on-site staff to determine whether the two systems can work together. This process may require configuring the system to be compatible with a certain screen reader or other accessibility software on a designated assigned computer station as a workaround. In some cases, an iPad may be utilized instead of a desktop computer due to its built-in accessibility features providing an instant solution. However, in some instances, a technological solution may not be possible. Table 6.2 presents common barriers to accessing EMRs and possible solutions.

• **TABLE 6.2 Common Barriers to Accessing Electronic Medical Records (EMRs)**

Barrier	Issue	Considerations
• Difficulty reading and navigating material in EMR (students with print disabilities— visual, learning, etc.)	• Screen readers and other reading software often cannot be used with EMRs due to security features of the EMR **Possible Solution** • Some reading software has the ability to take a screenshot of a page and read it, allowing a workaround for EMRs that block reading software	• Screenshot conversions are not properly structured and thus can be laborious for someone who cannot see to easily "jump" to the relevant information • This solution does not solve the issue of navigating through the EMR • The time to make a conversion can be prohibitive **Bottom Line** • This solution may work best for a student with a learning disability who can see and identify what he or she wants to read more easily; however, it may be too cumbersome to manage • Consider employing a reader/writer to assist the student to navigate the EMR if other solutions are not feasible

(continued)

• **TABLE 6.2 Common Barriers to Accessing Electronic Medical Records (EMRs)** *(continued)*

Barrier	Issues	Considerations
• Difficulty seeing the EMR (low vision)	• Student's preferred enlargement software may not be compatible with the EMR • Computer stations provided do not have large enough screens to adjust resolution and navigate enlarged screen **Possible Solutions** • Try other enlargement software, including built-in enlargement software from the operating system • Have a computer station assigned to the student, and install a large monitor • Give the student an iPad to use with an EMR app (if available) that allows the student to enlarge text to the desired size	• Student may need training to increase facility with the new software or device • Designating one accessible computer station may not be sufficient if the clinic model is to write notes in the EMR while meeting with the patient; an iPad may prove to be a better option here, instead of or in addition to an accessible workstation • An iPad may be a viable option for mobile or quick uses, but may be more laborious to use for writing long notes and in-depth review of patient charts; it may be best to provide an accessible workstation for in-depth reviews and case note writing **Bottom Line** • Determine how all clinicians use EMRs, and determine the solution that will give students the greatest ease of use, commensurate to their peers
Barrier • Difficulty typing into the EMR (mobility disability, repetitive strain injury [RSI], etc.)	**Issue** • EMR may not allow voice-recognition software (VRS) to type directly into the system due to security features of EMR **Possible Solution** • Use VRS to type notes into a Word document, then cut and paste into EMR	**Considerations** • Will require clinic information technology (IT) support to install VRS onto clinic computer(s) • Student may require a designated accessible workstation due to cost of VRS licenses

When determining accommodations for EMRs, DS providers and clinical sites must take into consideration not only the student's needs, but also the required security and confidentiality necessary to protect patient information. For example, although the iPad may provide an instant solution for a student requiring access, it must be stored and password protected in line with the clinical site's privacy guidelines for mobile devices.

The issues just outlined highlight the difficulties that arise when systems are not built and selected with accessibility in mind. When an EMR is chosen, developed, and implemented, accessibility of the system must be a non-negotiable criterion for selection.

ASSISTIVE TECHNOLOGY AS AN ACCOMMODATION

Beyond ensuring that campus technology available to all students is fully accessible to students with disabilities, DS providers are also called upon to identify appropriate technology-based auxiliary aids to provide to students with disabilities as an accommodation.

What Is Assistive Technology?

Assistive technology (AT) refers to technological devices and software used to make course materials, instruction, and interactions with environments more accessible to students with disabilities. The goal of AT is to remove barriers to the educational environment. For a student with a visual disability, this might include the use of screen-reader technology to ensure the student can access written material. AT can also benefit students without disabilities, enhancing access to educational content. For example, a student with a strong auditory learning style may benefit from the ability to record lectures for playback at a later time.

AT Solutions for Students

Students with disabilities in health sciences programs often arrive armed with a number of compensatory skills and technological solutions that have contributed to their historical academic success. For these students, identifying AT solutions for the health sciences environment involves understanding what has worked in the past and securing, when appropriate, the same or similar technology. However, students with new or recent diagnoses, significant change to their disability status, or those who have not used AT before will require close attention and support to identify whether AT solutions may work for them.

Knowing which AT to recommend or purchase for students with disabilities and understanding how it works can be a daunting proposition for DS providers who do not have a technical background or access to an AT specialist. Although an AT specialist with specific technical skills and knowledge is a beneficial addition to DS departments, it is not always feasible to create such a specialized position. For those offices that cannot hire a specialist, DS providers can identify consultants from private industry or other colleges to assist on an as-needed basis. The information technology, educational technology, or engineering departments within your institution may also be able to assist DS providers with assistive technology needs, although recommendations from these sources must be paired with sufficient expertise in accessibility, as individuals from these offices may not be well versed in the needs of students with disabilities.

When assistive technology is installed onto a computer at a clinical site (e.g., screen readers or voice-recognition software) the DS provider should involve an IT specialist from the site. In most cases, clinic computers are "locked down" to comply with Health Insurance Portability and Accountability Act (HIPAA) regulations, and the information technology (IT) department will be needed to assist with installation of any software or applications.

DETERMINING THE STUDENT'S ASSISTIVE TECHNOLOGY NEEDS

Determining a student's AT needs involves more than an understanding of the available technology. An interactive discussion with the student, and some trial and error, may be necessary. The student's technical savvy and experience and the feasibility of a particular AT solution must also be considered, in concert with the requirements of the student's educational program. Flowchart 6.1 will assist the DS provider in determining how to approach identifying AT solutions for students.

Gauging Student Comfort With Technological Solutions

A student's level of comfort with using technology is critical to the process of identifying whether an AT solution will help to remove barriers and which solution best fits the student's needs. Understanding a student's general comfort with technology informs whether the student will benefit from a non-tech, low-tech, or high-tech solution (see Example 6.1). It also provides insight about what has and has not worked before.

EXAMPLE 6.1 • Key Questions for Evaluating a Student's Tech Savvy

- What tech devices do you use in your everyday life?
- Have you had any issues with using the required technology in school (e.g., issues with using the learning management system [LMS], accessing e-mail, using the clinic's electronic medical records [EMRs])? If so, what are they?
- What assistive technology (AT) have you tried before? What worked and what did not, and why?

• **FLOWCHART 6.1 Determining an AT Solution**

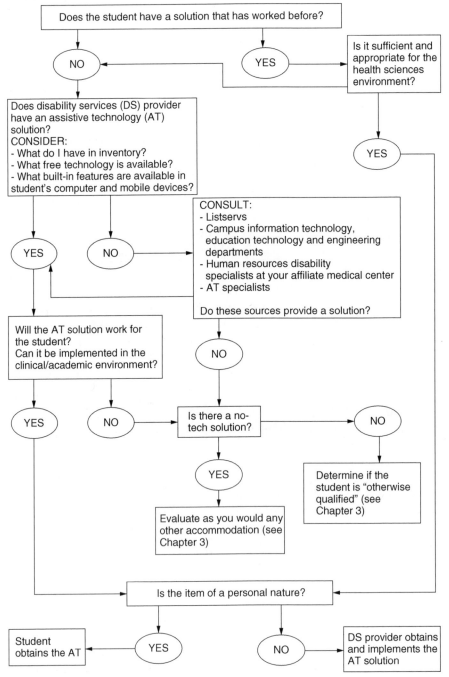

When demonstrating options to students, it is important to tune in to the student's response. If the student appears frustrated or suggests the technology is difficult to use, it is likely that he or she will not use the AT without a great deal of support and training. Often, health sciences students do not have the luxury of time to train and practice using AT. Therefore, the solution offered must be easy to use, reliable, and portable, and in line with a student's existing technological ability, or else it will likely be abandoned (Lang et al., 2014). For example, a student who has difficulty taking notes has a myriad of accommodation options requiring varying levels of technological comfort: a peer note taker—a no-tech solution; a digital recorder—a low-tech solution; a smartpen—a mid-tech solution; or integrated note-taking apps—a high-tech solution. Often, the most effective solution for a student is the simplest, and the one that most easily integrates with the student's existing technology.

Building Confidence, Knowledge, and an Inventory

In order to effectively serve students with disabilities in the digital age, DS providers must endeavor to build an understanding of the AT options available, and develop basic AT skills. They must also understand when to consult or refer to an AT specialist. All of these goals can be achieved by joining DS and AT-focused listservs, attending AT sessions at DS conferences or specialized AT conferences, attending AT fairs, and developing a trusted network of colleagues with AT knowledge. One reason that AT interventions are not successful is failure of the DS provider to choose an appropriate solution and provide product support (Lang et al., 2014). Until DS providers increase their knowledge base, students will not reap the full benefits of AT.

In addition to developing a knowledge base, DS providers should build an inventory of AT to loan to students for trial and extended use. This not only allows DS providers to begin experimenting with the items in order to familiarize themselves with the features and functions, it also empowers DS providers to talk about a technology and demonstrate its functionality in the moment. Having items available for immediate use is particularly beneficial for health sciences students, who are under time constraints and may lose interest (or need) if there is a significant delay between suggesting a device or software program and providing it.

Who Purchases the AT?

University and Student Purchases
DS providers (and their supervisors) often question the fiscal responsibility of an AT purchase. Generally speaking, if without the AT, the university environment—including the instructional environment and other university-provided and university-sponsored services—is not accessible, then the

university must bear the cost of AT. These items are typically purchased as loaner items for students, with the expectation that they will be returned in working order, allowing the purchase of expensive items to benefit multiple students over the life of the products. If the item is of a personal nature, and is something that will assist in accessing daily life, inside *and* outside of the university environment (e.g., wheelchair, hearing aid, eyeglasses), then the student bears the cost of the AT. In some cases, however, an item is necessary due to the specific requirements of the environment (e.g., student is in the clinic and requires a specific personal assisted listening system). In these cases, where failure to have a specific AT would provide a barrier to a student in the university environment, then the identification and purchase of the AT item is generally the university's responsibility.

Given this, DS offices should include funding for AT in their budgets. Slowly building an inventory of frequently used devices and technology can help to spread the cost over time. Careful consideration of existing resources should be made, as the DS provider will need access to funds to purchase specialized equipment, which can be costly. DS providers should also consider building a network with their peer institutions that allows for borrowing of devices not currently in use. This helps all institutions in the network reduce their costs and provides additional opportunities for interaction, relationship building, and collective group knowledge around emerging AT.

State Rehabilitation Agencies

Funding for AT assessment and/or devices may also be available to students through state vocational rehabilitation (VR) agencies, or through specialized VR agencies for people with visual or hearing disabilities (e.g., the Commission for the Blind in New York State). Linking students with state funding for services early in their educational careers is essential, as approval for services can take several months and is not guaranteed. Ultimately, the university is responsible for ensuring students with disabilities have equal access, and students cannot be required to register with VR agencies. Delays resulting from reliance on state rehabilitation agencies for funding may put universities at risk for being out of compliance, and this must be balanced in determining "who pays."

ASSISTIVE TECHNOLOGY ACCOMMODATIONS TO IMPROVE STUDENT ACCESS

Once DS providers have identified the disability-related barrier to the curriculum, and have a working idea of the type of AT needed by the student, they can choose from a number of options for accommodating student needs. Some of these options are described next (and in Chapter 4). Although this is not an exhaustive list, it represents a starting point that addresses many of the most commonly observed AT options available.

Audio Recording of Lectures

Digital Recorders

Students often experience difficulty retaining, recalling, or processing information due to their disabilities. These students may benefit from revisiting the information to solidify ideas and transfer information from short-term to long-term memory, or to improve the accuracy of the information received. In a health care setting that relies heavily on patient self-report of symptoms, having an accurate account of information is vital to providing good health care. For students who need to solidify information, listening to a recording of the information is sometimes the most efficient and effective way to review the material. Students can access audio recordings of lectures, small-group sessions, or patient interactions in several ways. Most phones now have a recording device, and mini digital recorders are also available, but for the most synergistic approach, students are using smartpens or note-taking applications.

Smartpens and Note-Taking Apps

Livescribe's smartpen, which records audio and syncs it with handwritten notes, is very helpful for removing barriers for students with disabilities. The recorded audio lecture and handwritten notes can be replayed and reviewed together, allowing students to jump to specific places in the lecture by touching the corresponding portion of the handwritten notes with the tip of the smartpen. It also creates a searchable PDF of the written notes and allows for syncing and sharing of the notes on several social media sites.

There are also note-taking apps available, such as AudioNote, Sonocent, SoundNote, or Notability, which offer similar functionality to the smartpen but are used on a laptop or tablet computer.

Caution: Recording Patient Information

The use of smartpens and note-taking app technology has revolutionized access to information for students with disabilities; however, not all information can or should be recorded. When patient information is being shared—whether in the classroom or in the clinical setting, disability accommodations must comply with HIPAA, which protects the confidentiality and security of health care information, including requiring that patient health information must be securely contained in a password-protected/encrypted environment. If students need to use recording devices, including smartpens and note-taking apps, as disability accommodations in a health care setting, specific protocol and security measures must be enacted to maintain HIPAA compliance (see Example 6.2).

EXAMPLE 6.2 • Using the Smartpen in the Clinical Setting

Request: A student with a disability that affects processing speed requests to use a smartpen while taking patient histories, to aid in accuracy of charting later in the day.

Concerns: Administrators want to provide a suitable disability accommodation to the student while also adhering to HIPAA regulations.

Solution: The smartpen can be stored in a locked area in the clinical setting and the patient history recordings can be deleted with the notes shredded at the end of each day. This allows the student to use a needed disability accommodation, while still protecting the patients' confidential medical information.

Speech-to-Text and Text-to-Speech Technology

Another AT solution that assists students who have disorders of written and oral expression, or physical disabilities, is the use of speech-to-text and text-to-speech technology.

Speech-to-Text Technology

Dragon Naturally Speaking

Dragon Naturally Speaking, from Nuance Communications, Inc., is the most commonly used speech-to-text software and is frequently used by physicians and other clinicians to dictate patient notes. For everyday note taking on a small scale, students can download the free Dragon mobile application to a smartphone. Voice-recognition software requires the investment of time to "train" the software to accurately transcribe the nuanced speech patterns of each individual student before the full benefits are achieved.

Communication Access Real-Time Translation (CART)

CART providers work, on-site or remotely, to capture audio feed from the intended source (e.g., faculty member, small groups, labs, clinical procedures) and provide a real-time written transcript via computer for DHOH students. Captions can be viewed on many existing devices, including an iPad, computer, or a large lecture screen. Thus, CART can be utilized in both clinical and didactic environments. CART can be a good option for students with newly acquired hearing loss and those whose preferred communication is not manual. It is also ideal for use in locations where the presence of additional people may pose a risk, such as the operating room (increased individuals in the operating room increase the risk of infection; Meeks et al., 2015).

Text-to-Speech, Screen-Reader, and Screen-Enlarging Software

These tools read aloud printed and encoded text from websites and electronic documents in order to provide access to students who cannot otherwise read the material due to visual, physical, or learning disabilities. Screen readers and text-to-speech software vary in their range of features (e.g., multiple voices, the ability to navigate a screen using keyboard commands, the ability to enlarge text or manipulate screen contrast, the ability to highlight words with multiple colors for coding different ideas, a built-in dictionary and other options for improving access to text), and some are specifically tailored for individuals with visual or learning disabilities. They are available as "built-in" accessibility features of a computer's operating system (e.g., VoiceOver on iOS devices), and as separate software packages available for free online (e.g., NVDA), or for purchase (e.g., JAWS, Read & Write Gold, Kurzweil, and ZoomText).

In order to access printed course materials, such as the text of a book or article, via reading or enlargement software, the materials must be converted to an accessible electronic version. An overview of the available products and how they provide accessibility for various disabilities is discussed next.

E-Texts

Many textbooks, articles, and other references can be found in digital format, either as an e-book or PDF. DS offices can access these items through a number of resources such as Accesstext, BookShare, Alternate Media Exchange (AMX), Google Scholar, Learning Ally, or by request directly to the publisher. Some books may be available for purchase as an e-book; however, these versions may not be sufficient to meet a student's needs if they are not compatible with the student's reading software. In some cases, DS offices may need to create their own electronic-format materials for students (by cutting, scanning, and editing a book with publisher permission), or by having them created by a vendor.

Having these items in a digital format may meet a student's need for a lightweight and compact alternative to textbooks, particularly for those whose disability makes it difficult to manipulate and carry heavy texts to and from class. However, if a student requires the use of reading or enlargement software as well, specific formats of digital files will be required, depending on the software the student is using. At a minimum, an accessible PDF or Word document will be needed (see previous section in this chapter, "Websites and Digital Documents"). Universal design principles (Chapter 10) recommend that faculty post all course materials in accessible formats, thus eliminating the additional time required for document conversion (see "digital documents" in Table 6.1).

For Students With Visual Disabilities

As introduced earlier, there are specific screen-reading software packages that are used by individuals with low and no vision. JAWS (Job Access with Speech), which provides voice and braille output (when used with a specific braille display) for text content, is among the best known of these applications. Others include Window-Eyes, MAGic, ZoomText, and NVDA.

Other tools to enlarge screen areas and/or improve readability for individuals with low vision include Closed Circuit TV (CCTV) devices, loupes and magnifiers, handheld or screen-mounted video magnifiers, and portable video magnifiers used with a computer display to enlarge anything in a room (e.g., Enhanced Vision's Transformer device). An advantage of all these devices is that they allow functionality for enlarging physical printed materials, including prescription labels, notes written on the board at a distance, and live tissue.

One of the biggest challenges for individuals with visual disabilities is the use of images on web pages and PDF files for printed materials. Although magnifiers can make these appear larger for those with low vision, neither PDF files nor web pages can be read by screen readers *unless* specific attributes are included in the development of documents for the web or PDF documents, as described earlier in this chapter (see previous section, "Websites and Digital Documents").

For Use With Students With Reading or Other Learning Disabilities

Often, students with learning disabilities, ADHD, or other disabilities affecting cognitive processing require the previously described reading software to increase the comprehension or fluency of reading, rather than due to a visual disability. The ability to "hear" the words benefits students for other reasons as well. For some students, such as those with ADHD, anxiety, or depression, the ability to listen to material while simultaneously exercising helps students to maintain a workout regimen during their otherwise limited time, as well as tapping into the benefit for some to move while learning, improving their retention of material.

Many types of screen readers exist on the market, although several products are the most widely used, including Kurzweil, Read and Write Gold, and VoiceOver. Each product has unique features, strengths, and weaknesses, and they can also vary in price. DS providers (or an AT specialist) should assess which will match student needs best. As stated earlier, students will require reading materials to be in an accessible format in order to access them with their software.

Assistive Listening Systems

DHOH students with some residual hearing may benefit from assistive listening systems (ALSs), which amplify sounds in the environment. Although hearing aids and other personal devices to assist in hearing are the legal obligation of the student to purchase, an assistive listening device must be provided by the institution in spaces designed for listening, such as lecture halls and classrooms.[7]

In the clinical setting, where background noise may vary, DS providers should work with students interested in using an ALS to test out a variety of systems, microphones, and headphones or other delivery methods to see which system works best. Providers need to consider the nuances of various clinic environments to ensure the most effective solution is identified and to consider whether a different or supplemental accommodation may be necessary (see Chapter 4). As well, the need for confidentiality of patient information will influence the type of ALS selected. Generally, systems that use infrared waves, or that gather and transmit sound in a closed system (i.e., by wire), are more confidential, as there is not the risk of sound "leaking" to an unintended audience. If confidentiality of information is a concern, DS providers should consider an infrared device, such as the Sound Choice SC-186K. The benefit of infrared is that information is limited to "line-of-sight" receivers and will not leave the closed room. This is essential in clinical environments where sensitive patient information is discussed.

Students often use ALS in conjunction with other accommodations, such as sign language interpreters, note takers, or CART, depending on the environment (see Chapter 4 for discussion of accommodations for DHOH students in clerkships). What works in one environment, such as a clinic with small rooms and one-on-one conversations with patients, may not work in a more stimulating environment like the emergency room.

Organizations such as Pepnet 2, or a student's audiologist, can provide additional guidance on selecting the appropriate ALS to meet a student's needs (see Appendix 9.1 in Chapter 9 for information about additional organizations). Table 6.3 describes ALSs for DHOH students.

Amplified and Visual Stethoscopes

Health sciences students depend on stethoscopes to properly examine a patient's circulatory, respiratory, and/or gastrointestinal systems. Amplified stethoscopes can amplify sounds 30 times louder than an acoustic stethoscope. In addition to amplification, these stethoscopes are available with visual displays of the phonocardiogram or phonopneumogram to help the clinician in identifying sounds. These products can be used with different headphones and hearing aids by wearing them in the ear (ITE) or behind the ear (BTE). Students should work with their health care providers to determine which stethoscope is best for use given their individual needs. Organizations such as the Association for Medical Professionals with Hearing Loss (AMPHL) offer mentorship and advocacy for health care professionals with hearing loss. The AMPHL offers a rich discussion of the subject in its online

---

[7] 28 C.F.R. 36.303.

• **TABLE 6.3 Assistive Listening Systems (ALSs) for Deaf and Hard-of-Hearing (DHOH) Students**

Device	How It Works	Considerations
Frequency modulation (FM) system	Sound is transmitted via FM (radio) waves to a receiver integrated with existing hearing device, or headphones if no hearing device is used	FM waves can travel approximately 50 feet and thus can be accessed outside the intended hearing area; may not be appropriate for clinical settings
Infrared (IR) system	Sound is transmitted via infrared waves to a receiver integrated with an existing hearing device, or headphones if no hearing device is used	May not work well in tiered auditoriums or spaces that are not enclosed
Induction loop	Uses magnetic fields to transmit sound directly to hearing devices equipped with a "telecoil" switch; can also transmit to a portable receiver that can be used with headphones when a telecoil is not available	May be built into an environment (installed in the floor or ceiling), and thus can only be used for fixed areas such as auditoriums or meeting rooms, or a mobile version can be utilized
Personal ALS (e.g., Pocket Talker, MINI IR system, Sound AMP-R app)	A small portable device or integrated app that transmits sound gathered via a short-range microphone, amplifying sounds closest to it, to a receiver integrated with a hearing device; microphone may be directly connected, or may use FM or IR waves to transmit sound	Best suited for a small-group or clinical environment. Consider the mode of transmitting sound to ensure it is appropriate for the environment of use (i.e., FM systems are likely not appropriate for confidential discussions for reasons discussed earlier). Note concerns described earlier in chapter if app includes a recording feature

forums, as do other organizations for Deaf health professionals (see Appendix 9.1 in Chapter 9 for a list of professional organizations).

Paging and Telephone Systems

There are two general types of paging devices that clinical environments may provide clinicians—text pagers, which offer the ability to send a message, and basic pagers, which display only a phone number. Generally, for DHOH students, it is helpful to list as an accommodation that the student should be provided a text pager with vibrating mode. This allows the student to connect and communicate with team members using text messages as much as possible, as opposed to using the phone, which poses additional concerns.

The type of accommodation for a DHOH student who needs to use a phone system in the clinical environment will depend on the student's level of residual hearing, needs, and communication preferences. Hard-of-hearing students may find that a phone system with built-in amplification features is sufficient, whereas video or audio relay systems may be necessary for students with more profound hearing loss. Certain telephone captioning systems, such as Captel, may not be reliable enough for transmitting medical information that needs to be exact, so caution should be exercised when selecting a telephone accommodation.

The DS provider should have a good understanding about the standard ways that phones are used in the clinical environment to assist a student in determining the best accommodation. Where possible, efforts should be made to select a telephone accommodation that will work across multiple settings—each clinical site may have a different type of telephone system, and creating one solution that works in all the sites will save all of the parties much time and frustration.

Patient privacy is less of a concern for telephone accommodations than for ALS selection. Telecommunication relay services such as relayed captioning, Internet protocol (IP) relay, and video relay services are HIPAA compliant, and can be used to communicate with patients and with fellow health care professionals regarding protected health information (Federal Communications Commission, 2004).

Accessible On-Call Rooms for DHOH Students

DHOH students who are required to do overnight call rotations may need to implement specific assistive technology in the clinical setting to ensure that they are able to wake up when called, similar to those provided in the dorm setting. Possible accommodations include a light or "bed shaker," which vibrates in order to wake the person, connected to the student's phone, pager, or other alert system used to contact clinicians during "on-call" shifts.

CONCLUSION

Assistive technology can prove highly beneficial to students with disabilities. The key for DS personnel is to work closely with the student to ascertain the student's individual needs and comfort levels, and current use of technology. In addition, DS personnel should foster collaborative relationships with IT staff to ensure that the technology in place is both useable by the student and maintains the security of the privileged information prevalent in a health care environment. In many cases, DS personnel can work closely with faculty and other administrators to design materials and instruction that reduce the need for accommodation. The principles of universal design (see Chapter 10) should be used in conjunction with AT to ensure maximum accessibility for students with disabilities. As well, technology utilized in instruction and available to all on campus must be selected with accessibility in mind, in order to ensure that minimal "work-around" solutions are required for all students to access it, with or without the use of additional AT.

REFERENCES

American Foundation for the Blind & Adobe. (n.d.). *Accessing PDF documents with assistive technology, a screen reader user's guide*. Retrieved from http://www.adobe.com/content/dam/Adobe/en/accessibility/pdfs/accessing-pdf-sr.pdf

Caldwell, B., Cooper, M., Reid, L. G., & Vanderheiden, G. (Eds.). (2008). *Web content accessibility guidelines 2.0, W3C World Wide Web Consortium recommendation, 11 December 2008*. Retrieved from http://www.w3.org/TR/WCAG/

Federal Communications Commission. (2004). *Clarification of the use of Telecommunications Relay Services (TRS) and the Health Insurance Portability and Accountability Act (HIPAA)* [Press release]. Retrieved from http://hraunfoss.fcc.gov/edocs_public/attachmatch/DA-04-1716A1.doc

Lang, R., Ramdoss, S., Sigafoos, J., Green, V. A., van der Meer, L., Tostanoski, A., . . . O'Reilly, M. F. (2014). Assistive technology for postsecondary students with disabilities. In G. E. Lancioni & N. N. Singh (Eds.), *Assistive technologies for people with diverse abilities* (pp. 53–76). New York, NY: Springer Science+Business Media.

Meeks, L., Laird-Metke, E., Jain, N., Rollins, M., Gandhi, S., & Stechert, M. (2015). Accommodating deaf and hard of hearing students in operating room environments: A case study. *Journal of Postsecondary Education and Disability, 28*(4).

Professionalism and Communication About Disabilities and Accommodations

Lisa M. Meeks, Neera R. Jain, Erin K. Phair, and Shelby Acteson

INTRODUCTION

This chapter addresses the importance of professional communication concerning disabilities and accommodations between university personnel and students. Administrators and faculty may be tempted to slip into their roles as health care providers when working with students with disabilities, so guidance will be offered to help avoid accidentally blurring the boundaries of the academic setting. Students may struggle with how to discuss their disabilities with faculty and supervisors. Sample e-mails and conversations to aid disability services (DS) providers working with students to understand the principles of professional communication are included in Appendix 7.1. This chapter also includes information about why students might hesitate to disclose their disability status at school and work, and how to help students navigate the benefits and pitfalls of sharing information about their disability with others.

For all students, the transition to graduate or professional school requires the use of many skills to adapt to the new environment. One's professionalism, especially regarding communication skills, is crucial to making an effective transition. Students with disabilities have added responsibilities in the educational environment: They must disclose their disability, request accommodations, engage with DS providers to discuss possible accommodations, and then work with faculty and staff to access approved accommodations. It is essential that all parties communicate well with one another to ensure that access to approved accommodations is timely and occurs smoothly.

This chapter helps administrators and DS personnel effectively communicate with graduate and professional students in the health sciences regarding their disability needs, as well as their classroom and clinical placement accommodations. It also outlines several key issues for working with students with disabilities, including: (1) the appropriate boundaries for how faculty/staff and students share information, (2) guidelines for professional communication, and (3) the student's role and responsibilities in this process.

PROFESSIONALISM

Professionalism encompasses several aspects of behavior, including professional relationships, work habits, ethical principles, external standards, and communication. In 2012, as an initiative of the American Board of Medical Specialties (ABMS),[1] a new working definition of "professionalism" was developed. Wynia, Papadakis, Sullivan, and Hafferty (2014, p.712) developed the definition for the ABMS, which states, "Medical professionalism is a normative belief system about how best to organize and deliver health care. Believing in professionalism means accepting the premise that health professionals must come together to continually define, debate, declare, distribute, and enforce the shared competency standards and ethical values that govern their work."

In the health sciences, these skills are viewed as critical in forming relationships with patients and other health care team members that are based on respect, integrity, and responsiveness to the needs of others. They are also viewed as integral to students becoming professionals who can apply ethical standards to their practice. Research demonstrates that lapses in the professionalism of health sciences students are predictive of similar difficulties in future professional behavior (Papadakis, Hodgson, Teherani, & Kohatsu, 2004; Papadakis et al., 2005). For these reasons, in every school, professionalism is included among the technical standards that must be met in order to complete the program. This means that ongoing or egregious breaches of professionalism can be the sole reason a student is dismissed or denied a degree (see Case Example 7.1, and Chapter 8, Case Example 8.1).

CASE EXAMPLE 7.1 • *Al Dabagh v. Case Western Reserve University*[2]

A medical student who excelled academically throughout his medical education completed the requirements to earn his medical degree but was not certified for graduation by the school. Instead, he was dismissed at the

(continued)

---

[1] The ABMS is the umbrella group for 24 U.S. specialty and subspecialty boards that certify individual medical and surgical specialists.
[2] Al-Dabagh v. Case Western Reserve University, 777 F.3d 355 (2015).

CASE EXAMPLE 7.1 • *Al Dabagh v. Case Western Reserve University (continued)*

> very end of his program due to breaches of professionalism that began in his first year and continued throughout his education. The professionalism concerns included excessive tardiness; complaints about his working demeanor from patients, nurses, and others during internships; allegations of sexual harassment from fellow students; and a conviction for driving while intoxicated. The student sued the school for failing to honor its contract with him as a student (disability was not a factor in this case).
>
> The lower court ruled in favor of the student, but the court of appeals reversed and upheld his dismissal, noting that professionalism is repeatedly identified in school documents describing expectations for students, as well as being an important part of the medical profession, and schools may exercise academic judgment regarding whether a student has fulfilled the necessary requirements to receive a degree.

COMMUNICATION

Clear and appropriate communication between faculty, administrators, and students is essential for creating a solid foundation for the accommodation process throughout the student's tenure at an institution. Open lines of communication ensure that all parties are on the same page in terms of policies, procedures, and expectations, and make it easier to discuss difficulties that arise along the way. More important, open communication with students regarding disability services conveys a welcoming atmosphere for students in which they feel comfortable disclosing a disability, or issues that arise regarding accommodations.

How Is Communication Different in Health Sciences Professional School Settings?

In graduate and professional schools, there is an expectation that students demonstrate a higher level of self-direction and self-advocacy in their behavior and learning, compared with their earlier education. Particularly in professional health sciences schools, language and communication are essential aspects of safe patient care, and are integrated into the competency of "professionalism" that is embedded in the curriculum to support the professional development of students as they become health care providers. This is evidenced by the 1999 decision by the Accreditation Council for Graduate Medical Education (ACGME) to include professionalism and interpersonal and communication skills as two of six "core competencies" as graduation requirements for medical residency programs (ACGME, 1999). Similarly, the Commission on Collegiate Nursing Education (CCNE) requires that nursing students demonstrate competencies in leadership communication, conflict management, ethical decision making, and cultural competence, among others (CCNE, 2008).

Research also demonstrates the need to make professional behavior a requirement in health sciences education. A study by Papadakis and colleagues (2004) found that shortcomings in professionalism in medical school—evidenced by "poor reliability and responsibility," "lack of self-improvement and adaptability," and "poor initiative and motivation"—were linked to subsequent discipline by licensing boards. Building on this research, Papadakis and colleagues (2005) later reported that students who had been deemed "irresponsible" in medical school were eight times more likely than others to be disciplined as doctors.

Although research will continue to define and measure behaviors that are indicative of inadequate development of professionalism, the challenge still exists to develop behavioral remediation in health sciences education that will show positive results in future professional behavior (Kirk & Blank, 2005).

How Is Communication Measured in the Professional School Setting?

Professional communication skills are measured in the didactic and clinical portions of health science studies through course objectives, exam questions, and skills demonstrations. However, when students enter the clinical practice of their fields, expectations for professionalism (communication, behavior, and interpersonal interactions) are often not clearly articulated and remain vague and subjective.

Many students struggle with the unspoken rules and hierarchies of the clinical environment, especially when it is assumed that they have the skills to interpret subtle cues and situational nuances absent of clearly identified action/reaction parameters. For example, on one rotation, students might be encouraged to address attending physicians by first name, whereas on another, this could very well get them written up for unprofessional behavior. If there is an expectation that students demonstrate professionalism as an essential competency of the clinical experience, the institution should clearly define the competency and provide the instruction and feedback necessary for students to develop these skills.

There is also a challenge when clinical faculty members exude the "all-knowing, paternalistic" culture of the past. Despite the increased emphasis on professionalism, as noted earlier, students still may encounter bullying in their educational experiences. In a study published in 2012 and conducted over the course of 13 years at the David Geffen School of Medicine at the University of California, Los Angeles, more than 50% of medical students across the United States said they experienced some form of mistreatment (Cohen, 2006).

If there is an expectation that students demonstrate professionalism as an essential competency of the clinical experience, then it is important that the culture of the institution also reflects this evolution, and provides the instruction and feedback necessary for students to learn that competency. The old adage "Do as I say, not as I do" is becoming less applicable to the emerging team-based nature of health care.

By establishing clear objectives and standard policies regarding professionalism that govern all clinical experiences, students, faculty, and clinical staff are able to more successfully and consistently communicate expectations in the clinical environment. Moving away from subjective evaluation of student behavior is beneficial to all students, but especially for students with disabilities, who may require specific feedback in order to develop and improve their communication skills with each new environment.

Communication Skills and Students With Disabilities

Students with disabilities are, of course, students first. They are held to the same standards of behavior as all other students. Standards of professionalism are consistent expectations for a student's interactions and behaviors across all facets of the academic environment, including accessing disability-related accommodations and supports.

Communicating one's disability-related needs is an important step in a student's path to accessing accommodations. Like any other communication with faculty, communication about a disability is a reflection of a student's professional communication skills and conduct. For many students, this communication is anxiety provoking. Students may be reluctant to share information about their disabilities out of shame or fear of stigma from school administration, peers, or faculty. Some students may have had negative experiences in the past and, as a result, may display behaviors that reflect their reluctance to access accommodations. Other students are new to discussing their needs with faculty, either due to the structure of their undergraduate environment or a new diagnosis or exacerbation of an existing condition. In these instances, a student may be unsure about what to say and how to say it. This can lead to poorly executed communication from the student, including: (1) late notification of a need for accommodations; (2) sending brief or excessively lengthy and detailed communication; (3) taking an overly defensive, emotional, or aggressive stance in communication; or (4) simply not reaching out to ask for assistance.

Poor communication in the health sciences environment leads to potentially strained relationships, or misinterpretation around expectations. Additionally, failure to clearly communicate accommodation needs contributes to unnecessary stress and burden for both faculty and students. Both parties should strive to maintain a professional relationship, as they will soon become part of one professional network, and faculty may be called upon for references for jobs or other future pursuits.

Faculty may feel that it is an unfair burden, on top of their already layered responsibilities, to think about or manage students' accommodations. Practicing and developing professional communication skills regarding accommodations for the faculty, DS provider, and the student will help every member of the process improve communication regarding disability-related needs.

Benefits of Disclosure

The most significant benefit of disclosing a disability is to receive accommodations in the academic environment, thereby giving students equal access to the educational experience. Despite the DS providers' best efforts, many students still choose not to disclose until *after* they experience difficulties in the academic program. Of the students who disclose, some may not fully disclose the extent of their disability-related needs, resulting in underaccommodation.

Effective Disclosure

Students with disabilities may arrive at graduate or professional schools lacking a good understanding of their disabilities and having difficulty communicating their needs. They often share feelings of uncertainty about how much they should reveal, and with whom to share this information (see Tip 7.1).

TIP 7.1 • A Student's Disclosure of Personal Health Information

Students are not obligated to disclose personal health information, nor the nature of their disability, to faculty, administrators, or other program personnel in order to access accommodations approved by the disability services office.

Students studying the health sciences might feel compelled to share details about their diagnoses as a way of justifying their need for accommodations. They may also believe that disclosing the nature of a disability will result in a more empathetic response and enhanced understanding of their needs, given that faculty are health professionals.

The DS office should carefully protect a student's confidential disability-related information and maintain written policies that ensure a student's privacy. Accommodations should be "vetted" in advance with the respective schools to ensure that technical standards are not compromised. Faculty should *never* inquire about the nature of a student's disability or request additional documentation (e.g., doctor's notes, documentation of illness, medical evaluations). No additional "justification" of disability or need for accommodation is necessary or warranted once the identified office on campus determines accommodations (see Tip 7.2).

TIP 7.2 • Engaging With Students About Disability Specifics

Faculty and administrators should exercise caution against engaging in a dialogue about medical or disability specifics (e.g., diagnosis) with students. Any questions concerning disability should be directed to the disability services office.

Faculty and students, particularly in the health sciences, can easily slip into an in-depth medical dialogue about diagnosis, prognosis, and course of treatment when discussing a student's disability. Conversations of this nature place both the student and faculty in a vulnerable position, and can invite unwanted medical advice and future questions about status and well-being. Students may leave a conversation of this nature feeling vulnerable, or sense that they have shared too much. Even though faculty may have good intentions, future interactions can end up focusing on the student's medical status instead of his or her learning and education as a result. Similarly, faculty should avoid giving advice concerning the topic of disability accommodations and supports and allow the appropriate office (usually, disability services) to confidentially determine the most appropriate course of action. *At all times, faculty members and administrators should remember that their role is "educator," not "health provider," in this relationship.*

PROCESS FOR DISCLOSING A DISABILITY

Students are responsible for following the procedures for accessing accommodations outlined for their school or program each quarter or semester (see Chapter 3, Table 3.1 and Chapter 4). DS providers should communicate this process to students in person and in writing, and have these processes accessible online for both students and faculty, ensuring a transparent and easily referenced policy (see Appendix 3.3 in Chapter 3).

Counseling Students Regarding Disclosure

When DS providers counsel students about whether they should share their medical information directly with faculty, it is helpful to first ask them to consider *why* they are sharing. Sharing information of a sensitive or personal nature can be perceived as an attempt to elicit sympathy or seek favoritism, or as a mechanism for explaining subpar performance. Formal accommodations should *eliminate* the need to discuss specifics about a disability and support performance-based assessment of the student. Faculty and students should be made aware that the DS office is available to assess eligibility for additional accommodations, including modifications to policy and procedure, when necessary, and to consult with faculty about appropriate disclosures.

There are a number of reasons that students do not disclose or do not fully disclose. Trammel and Hathaway (2007) conducted a review of the literature regarding help-seeking behaviors of college students with disabilities and concluded that a student's decision to seek help is "complex, multilayered, and highly correlated to the climate and disability environment on campus, as well as to personal factors related to motivation, which vary from student to student" (p. 6). This issue is magnified in the health sciences, where the "culture of excellence" is less tolerant of students who demonstrate their knowledge in nontraditional ways. For example, a clinician may feel that a student receiving extra time on a clerkship shelf exam is not as competent as a student who completes the exam without this accommodation.

In their interactions with students, faculty should in no way imply that those who receive accommodations exhibit less intellectual rigor compared to their peers. Faculty who suggest that students will be viewed negatively for seeking disability accommodations run the risk of discouraging them from doing so and, furthermore, could be engaging in disability discrimination (see Case Example 7.2). It is important that faculty and clinical teams are educated about the applicable disability laws (e.g., Americans with Disabilities Act [ADA] amendments and Section 504) and how and why students with disabilities are provided with accommodations.

CASE EXAMPLE 7.2 • *North v. Widener University*[3]

A graduate student disclosed to a trusted faculty member that he has attention deficit hyperactivity disorder (ADHD). The faculty member advised him not to disclose this fact to other faculty, because it could indicate to them that the student was not suited for the program (a doctorate of psychology). The student followed this advice, but was ultimately dismissed from the school, having failed to pass his qualifying exam by one point. The student sued the school for disability discrimination, alleging that the school knew he had a disability and that was why he was dismissed. He never applied for or received accommodations.

The court held that although a student must formally disclose a disability through proper channels to request accommodations, where the school was on notice about the student's disability through his informal disclosure to one professor, which the professor also shared with other faculty, the student's disability discrimination lawsuit against the school regarding his dismissal could go forward.

---

[3] North v. Widener University, 869 F. Supp. 2d 630 (E.D. Penn. 2012).

In an effort to identify trends in students' reluctance to disclose, a study by Marshak, Van Wieren, Raeke Ferrell, Swiss, and Dugan (2010) categorized barriers to seeking and utilizing disability support services into five major categories:

1. Identity issues
2. Desire to avoid negative social reaction
3. Insufficient knowledge
4. Perceived quality and usefulness of services
5. Negative experiences with professors

Expanding on this model, Table 7.1 provides additional examples of barriers—some specific to the health sciences—and makes suggestions for ways that students and DS staff can minimize these barriers.

• TABLE 7.1 Barriers to Seeking and Utilizing Disability Support Services (Marshak et al., 2010)

Barrier: Identity Issues	
Examples	If a new diagnosis, reluctance to integrate it into identity or accept it as part of identity If disability status is not new, it may be that the student wants to reframe his or her identity in a new environment (e.g., transition from undergraduate program to medical school) Desire for self-sufficiency; belief that they can overcome disability limitations without accommodations
Student actions	Work with health care providers and/or counselors to better understand disability Connect with other students with disabilities, interest groups, etc.
Disability services (DS) office actions	Work with students to identify needs, define barriers and accommodations Connect students with other disability resources on campus and in the community
Barrier: Desire to avoid negative social reaction	
Examples	Fear of resentment from other students for "special treatment" Fear of resentment, perception they are not as competent as other students from faculty/clinical staff Not wanting to be singled out, especially in a competitive program

(continued)

• **TABLE 7.1 Barriers to Seeking and Utilizing Disability Support Services (Marshak et al., 2010) (*continued*)**

Student actions	Learn how to effectively communicate to others about disability needs and rights under the law
DS office actions	Provide general presentations to faculty and students to increase disability awareness Work with clinical faculty to increase awareness of microaggression, stigma, and unintentional bias Provide success stories, examples from similar programs
Barrier: Insufficient knowledge	
Examples	Question fairness of receiving accommodations; don't feel deserving of services Confusion about accessibility and disability services—especially at the graduate level and in the clinical environment Lack of training in how to explain disability needs to others Lack of understanding about privacy and confidentiality Unsure if needs are due to new environment or disability or combination; this impacts scope of requests
Student actions	Learn more about disability services process Seek out additional resources to better understand needs
DS office actions	Provide information about disability services in a variety of formats Ensure that equal access is promoted as part of diversity and inclusion efforts of institution
Barrier: Perceived quality and usefulness of services	
Examples	Lack of understanding of disability services process (i.e., collaborative process between student, DS office, and program) Not sure if disability services are applicable—especially in a clinical environment Expediency of service delivery—it may take time to put accommodations in place May not feel that accommodations are worth the extra process to get them implemented
Student actions	Be proactive in seeking disability services early, not after academic difficulties arise
DS office actions	Provide various opportunities for students to learn about disability services and interact with disability services staff at the beginning of each term (e.g., orientations, syllabus statement, etc.)

(*continued*)

• TABLE 7.1 Barriers to Seeking and Utilizing Disability Support Services (Marshak et al., 2010) (*continued*)

Barrier: Negative experiences with faculty	
Examples	Faculty question need for accommodations, especially with an "invisible" disability
	Faculty assume that a disability equates to lack of competence and/or threat to patient safety
	Faculty confuse academic standards and essential job functions
Student actions	Learn how to effectively communicate about disability needs
	Utilize support from the DS office where needed to address difficulties with communicating with faculty
DS office actions	Educate faculty on disability law, specific disabilities, accommodations
	Collaborate with other institutions to educate faculty

COMMUNICATION ABOUT DISABILITY PRIOR TO ENROLLMENT

Although the majority of accommodation needs are determined after a student arrives at the institution, it is important to start communicating about potential accommodation needs from the initial application to the time of enrollment. Including a short statement about disability services on the application, interview materials, and letters of acceptance will help alert potential or accepted students that accommodations are available. Suggestions for sample language are as follows:

Application

[Name of university or program] welcomes students with disabilities who meet the technical standards of the program, with or without accommodations. If you are an applicant with a disability who needs accommodations to complete this application, please contact [Insert DS office name and contact information for office].

Interviews

[Name of university or program] welcomes students with disabilities who meet the technical standards of the program, with or without accommodations. If you are a student with a disability who needs accommodations during your interview, please contact [Insert appropriate office and contact information for office].

Acceptance Letters

[Name of university or program] welcomes students with disabilities who meet the technical standards of the program, with or without accommodations. If you are a student with a disability who needs accommodations to fully access the [Insert program or school], please contact [Insert DS office and contact information for office]. Accommodations are never provided retroactively. Students are therefore encouraged to register with [DS office name] far in advance of the start of the program.

COMMUNICATION ABOUT DISABILITY AFTER ENROLLMENT

Orientation

Even after students are accepted to a school, they may still be hesitant to disclose a disability. Having a representative from the DS office speak at orientation may help ease student apprehension about self-identifying. By presenting at orientation, disability providers can help demystify the process of applying for services and put a face on the DS office, rather than simply being known as the "disability office." Students report feeling more comfortable approaching a familiar face and having some knowledge of how things work at the institution. In addition, having a representative at orientation speaks to the program's commitment to diversity and inclusion, and the expectation that students with disabilities will indeed be a part of the community.

Syllabus Statements

Having faculty include a disability statement on course syllabi is another effective way of indicating that the institution welcomes and encourages students with disabilities to participate in programs. Many schools offer a standard syllabus statement for faculty to use. Faculty can also contact the DS office to inquire about crafting a statement for a syllabus. Examples 7.1 and 7.2 provide well-written and poorly written sample statements.

EXAMPLE 7.1 • Well-Written Syllabus Statement

"[Name of School] is committed to providing equal access to learning opportunities to students with documented disabilities.[a] To ensure access to this class, and your program, please contact [designated contact person for disability services] to engage in a confidential conversation about the process for requesting accommodations in the classroom and clinical settings.[b]

(continued)

EXAMPLE 7.1 • Well-Written Syllabus Statement (*continued*)

> Accommodations are not provided retroactively.[c] Students are encouraged to register with [name of office responsible for DS] as soon as they begin their program. [Name of school] encourages students to access all resources available through [name of office responsible for DS] for consistent support and access to their programs. More information can be found online at [DS website], or by contacting the office at [DS phone number].[d]"
>
> [a]Indicates a welcoming educational environment.
> [b]Makes the student aware there is a process to follow before accommodations can be made.
> [c]This is important for students to know prior to starting a class.
> [d]Make information about contacting the office readily available.

EXAMPLE 7.2 • Poorly Written Syllabus Statement

> "Please contact the Disability Services office for help with accommodations."[a]
>
> [a]This statement, although valid, does not encourage the student who is struggling with or unsure of the correct process to seek help. It also suggests, with its lack of detail, that the university may not be welcoming of students with disabilities.

When a Student Discloses a Disability Directly to Faculty

Although the DS office strives to make its services known to potential and incoming students, a faculty member is often the first person to whom a student discloses his or her disability. In these situations, it is important for faculty to be knowledgeable about the DS office and the types of services offered. Faculty should direct students to the DS office and explain that the students must register with DS to be eligible for accommodations. Determining accommodations is the responsibility of the DS office, and faculty should not determine or implement accommodations without official notice. Any medical documentation a student attempts to present to faculty should be refused, and students should be encouraged to visit the appropriate office for disclosing such documentation. It is important for faculty to follow up with students via e-mail, reiterating the referral. This is critical, as the students have disclosed to faculty, who are *agents of the institution* and therefore have a duty to direct them to the appropriate office. By following up via e-mail, faculty members document the date and time they referred the student, and can summarize the discussion with the student (see Examples 7.3 and 7.4).

EXAMPLE 7.3 • Well-Written Follow-Up E-Mail After a Student Self-Identifies

Dear Student,

Thank you for meeting with me today. Because you self-identified as having used disability-related accommodations in the past, I wanted to follow up with information about the Office of Disability Services here at _____ University. Information about applying for services can be found on the school website at www.xxxx.edu/ds. I have also copied the Director of Disability Services on this e-mail, as you expressed interest in speaking with a DS staff member.[a] I encourage you to make an appointment to explore the possibility of using accommodations. I hope you find this resource helpful.

Best,
Prof. Smith

[a]Following up with specific contact information provides the student with a clear and easy way to get information about accommodations and follow up with the appropriate contact.

EXAMPLE 7.4 • Poorly Written Faculty Follow-Up E-Mail After a Student Self-Identifies

Dear Student,
Thank you for coming in today. After our discussion, it sounds like you will be fine in the course without any accommodations. If you need help the office is always there, but hopefully you keep working hard and will not need the office![a]

Best,
Prof Smith

[a]This e-mail minimizes the student's request for accommodations by implying that if a student works hard enough, he or she should not need accommodations. The statement also vaguely refers to the DS office, but it is not clear, and does not give the student any specific information about next steps or contact information. The tone is too casual and almost dismissive of the needs of the student.

E-MAIL COMMUNICATION BETWEEN FACULTY AND STUDENTS

E-mail is possibly the most common form of communication on college campuses today. It is fast and convenient, and provides documentation of virtual conversations. However, there are times when it is necessary to meet in person, for example, to discuss parameters concerning flexibility with deadlines for a student with a chronic health condition. In order to ensure that all parties agree on changes or the terms of a specific accommodation, faculty should send a follow-up e-mail summarizing the main points of the conversation, along with any expectations and goals established during the face-to-face meeting (see Examples 7.5 and 7.6).

EXAMPLE 7.5 • Well-Written Faculty Follow-Up E-Mail Regarding Accommodations

Dear Student,

Thank you for meeting with me today. I would like to summarize the goals and expectations that we established for the semester, so that we are both on the same page going forward.[a]

When you have a flare-up of your condition, you should contact me as soon as possible in order to negotiate a new deadline for any missed assignments.[b]

New deadlines [spell out the deadlines in detail] must be met or you will be penalized for a late assignment [explain what the penalty is].[c]

If you need to miss class because of a flare-up, contact me as soon as possible, but no later than 1 hour before class, to let me know you will be absent. In order to meet the standards of the course, it may not be feasible for you to miss more than four classes.[d]

We will meet again mid-semester (or prior to that, if necessary) to gauge how things are going and review these expectations. Do not hesitate to contact me should you need any assistance moving forward.[e]

Best,
Prof Smith[f]

[a]Confirms meeting and provides a written summary of the discussion.
[b]Provides clear instructions on the process, what to do in the event of a flare-up.
[c]Provides clarity concerning any accommodation that involves deadlines and clearly spells out consequences.
[d]Emphasizes the need for communication in a timely manner, also sets larger standards regarding total number of possible absences.
[e]Invites student to reach out if there is a change in the condition and to reassess.
[f]Focused solely on the accommodations (not disability) and maintains clear boundaries with student.

EXAMPLE 7.6 • Poorly Written Faculty E-Mail Regarding Accommodations

Dear Student,

Even though you are approved for absences from class and extended time for assignments, I do not believe you can be successful if you are not in class. I hope you will be able to meet deadlines; otherwise your grade could suffer.[a]

Prof. Smith

[a]Clearly states that the faculty has no intention of following the accommodation. Also places pressure on the student to attend class regardless of health condition.

Avoiding Unintended Discriminatory Behavior

It is very important for faculty members to understand that they may be the first individuals of the school community to whom students disclose their disabilities. Students may already be hesitant to reveal disability information; therefore, it is important that faculty members confronted with this information convey that the institution is welcoming of students with disabilities. Discouraging students from disclosing a disability for fear that it will affect standing in an academic program or indicate that they are somehow less qualified than other students is discriminatory (see Case Example 7.2).

MAINTAINING CONFIDENTIALITY OF STUDENT DISABILITY INFORMATION

All disability-related information, including accommodation letters, correspondence, and consultations, is considered confidential and must be managed in line with the Family Educational Rights and Privacy Act (FERPA) regulations (see discussion in Chapter 2 on confidentiality of students' documentation). This includes electronic, paper, oral, and any other types of communication.

Faculty "Need to Know"

In addition to fulfilling legal obligations, maintaining a high standard of confidentiality also serves to maintain an environment in which students with disabilities feel respected, safe, supported, and protected. Breaches of confidentiality can lead to complaints of discrimination if students feel that they have been treated unfairly because information about their diagnosis or disability status was shared inappropriately. Even if the perceived treatment has nothing to do with a student's disability status, when information is shared inappropriately, it leaves the institution open to potential complaints. Furthermore, students may perceive unauthorized breaches of confidentiality as signs of a hostile environment.

Unauthorized disclosures of student information must be documented, and can result in the institution being in noncompliance with federal regulations. The Office for Civil Rights (OCR) may audit FERPA compliance and require corrective actions. Additionally, such disclosures may violate state privacy laws and may subject the institution and the individual to liability. Disclosures of information are generally inadvertent. For this reason, a high level of vigilance to avoid unintentional, but inappropriate, disclosure of disability information must be maintained. Faculty members should contact the DS provider if they have any questions, issues, or concerns regarding maintaining confidentiality of information.

Once a student discloses his or her registration, or unofficially discloses additional information about his or her diagnosis to faculty or administration, there remains an obligation to keep that information confidential. This information should be used only to coordinate approved accommodations or provide educational support to a student. For example, if a student discloses that she has a learning disability and suggests that she would benefit from having information presented visually, her instructors can use this information to shape their teaching, but it would not be appropriate to discuss the learning disability at length with the student, nor share the information off-hand with other faculty or support staff in the department.

Sharing Information

Faculty and administrators are often not sure whether it is appropriate to share information that has been disclosed to them in order to support the work of their colleagues in the department who are also training or educating the student. It seems logical that other faculty or administrators should be advised to ensure the timely provision of accommodations. However, faculty and administrators should use *great caution* in communicating a student's disability-related needs. Although information can be shared on a "need-to-know" basis under FERPA, it is important to question the need before sharing information. If there is a co-faculty member, teaching assistant, or administrator from the same course who is responsible for coordinating testing accommodations, he or she may need to know the nature of the accommodations approved, but would not need to know the nature of the student's disability. In other cases, such as a perioperative (surgical) environment, it may be necessary for key staff beyond the student's direct clinical supervisor to know about a student's approved accommodations, in order to ensure that they are appropriately implemented, although not all staff members need to be informed. However, sharing information about specific students and their accommodation needs with faculty who may teach them in future courses or rotations would generally be inappropriate.

If there are administrative concerns about time frames for organizing accommodations, these should be discussed with the DS provider. Together, the DS provider and the department can work out a balance between the need for confidentiality, student-led disclosure of accommodations, and the logistical realities of administrating accommodations. For example, instead of naming registered students and their accommodation needs for all faculty in the department, it may be possible to disclose the number of students anticipated and their respective accommodation needs so that each faculty member can make appropriate arrangements in advance. It is good practice to discuss nonroutine disclosures with DS providers, and to work through any complicated scenarios in advance (e.g., surgical environment, scheduling changes). Another alternative is to identify a single administrator who organizes exam accommodations, space, proctors, and logistics, so that faculty members are informed only when necessary for purposes of education and learning.

As a rule of thumb, the highest level of confidentiality should be applied at all times to the nature of a student's disability and diagnosis. This information should not be shared unless there is explicit agreement with the DS office and the student that it is appropriate and necessary to do so. It is rare for DS to release information about a student's diagnosis or nature of disability, and this information will be provided only for a specific purpose. Confidentiality should also be applied to students' status as persons registered with disability services. This information should be shared only with individuals who need to administer an accommodation, or who facilitate the accommodation and require guidance. See Tip 7.3 on confidentiality.

TIP 7.3 • Ensuring Confidentiality of Student Information

- All information that students share with faculty related to their disabilities is to be used specifically for arranging reasonable accommodations for the course of study.
- Do not leave student disability information visible on your computer or in any format that others can see.
- Letters of accommodation should be filed in a safe place and disposed of securely at the end of the quarter.
- Refrain from discussing a student's disability status and necessary accommodations within hearing range of fellow students or others who do not have an "educational need to know."
- Do not assume that students registered with the DS office are aware of other students' disability status. If, for some reason, you feel it might be beneficial for students with disabilities to know each other, discuss this with the DS office.
- When sending e-mails to a group of students, even if they are all registered with the DS office, blind copy (BCC) students so they are not privy to other students' information, or send a separate e-mail to each student.
- At no time should the class be informed that a student has a disability, except at the student's request.
- Discuss accommodation letters and logistics of implementing accommodations with students in private. Make yourself available by e-mail, during office hours, or by appointment to discuss.
- Casual conversations with colleagues about a student's disability status are not advised. Confidential disability information, to which you have access, should be released to other faculty or staff members based only on their *need to know* (e.g., they are course co-instructors, proctoring an exam, arranging for exam space, assisting you to identify a note taker in the course). In such cases, disclose only the necessary information. For example:
  - A course coordinator proctoring an exam would only need to know the student's approved exam accommodation (e.g., 1.5 extended time and private room).

(continued)

TIP 7.3 • Ensuring Confidentiality of Student Information (*continued*)

- A teaching assistant (TA) who is providing the DS office with a list of the required books for the course only needs to know that the book list is needed, not which student the request is related to.
- A clinical supervisor only needs to know the approved on-site accommodations, not why the student requires them.
- Requesting specific information about students' disabilities is inappropriate. Instead, faculty should contact the DS office with any inquiry on how students' learning is affected by their disabilities.
- Requesting a letter from the student's physician is inappropriate. The accommodation letter is all that is needed to justify the accommodation, and supersedes any letter from the student's care provider.
- If students voluntarily disclose the nature of a disability to you, even if it is obvious, do not disclose it to others.

Ensuring the proper office is involved in the process

- If students try to provide you with their primary disability documentation, *refuse to read or accept* it, and refer the student to the DS office. Your university likely designated one office as the repository of all disability documentation for students with disabilities.

Appropriate Disclosure

As noted previously, it is rare that the DS office, in partnership with the student, will formally disclose the nature of a student's disability while organizing accommodations. This is purposeful, as it is unnecessary for others to need to know a student's diagnosis or disability category to ensure equal access in education. However, there are some cases in which disclosure may be appropriate, such as when the disability is not visible but some visible side effects of the condition may be of concern, or if there is a possible risk to safety that needs to be discussed. Yet, even in these cases, it may not be necessary to disclose the actual diagnosis, and it may be sufficient to simply describe the important feature of the disability, or any risk, in order to discuss possible accommodations (see Examples 7.7 and 7.8).

EXAMPLE 7.7 • Disclosing an Aspect of a Disability

A student who has narcolepsy may be prone to falling asleep during class. It may be necessary for faculty to be made aware that this is a feature of the student's disability, and is not simply laziness or a result of having been up all night, which might invite a concern about the student's professionalism.

EXAMPLE 7.8 • Safety-Related Need to Disclose Disability

For a student with a seizure disorder entering the clinical environment, it may be necessary to disclose the disability to supervisors and discuss in more detail the general pattern of seizures (e.g., Does the student experience an aura to warn of an impending seizure? How much time usually elapses between the aura and the onset of a seizure? Are there preventative measures that can be taken, and what do they require in terms of time and urgency of action?), as well as preferred methods for responding to a seizure should it happen suddenly, which may need to be checked against a medical center's general policies for responding in situations where an individual is suddenly incapacitated.

Navigating Disclosure in Clinical Placements

Placement or clerkship coordinators might be concerned about what information to disclose to a prospective site, as well as how to disclose such information. Relationships with clinical sites may be fragile, and in many disciplines the sites are voluntary and have no obligation to take on students. In these cases, coordinators find themselves at the mercy of the individual sites with regard to student placement. Despite the difficulty in working with these sites, confidentiality must still be held at a premium.

Information about a student's disability should not be shared with a clinical site unless expressly approved by the student and the DS office. It is illegal and discriminatory for a clinical site to refuse to accept a student simply because he or she has a disability, as long as the student is able to perform the essential requirements of the clinical work, with or without accommodation. If a clinical site refuses to accept a student with a disability, or pulls out of hosting a student after learning the student has a disability, the institution should seriously consider whether to continue working with that clinical site, as the site is practicing disability discrimination, placing the institution at risk.

Once a student has been placed at a site, the timing of disclosure will depend on the student's needs. In some cases, students wish to wait to develop a relationship with the clinical supervisors before identifying as students with disability. Of course, these students run the risk of having performance-related difficulties without the accommodation, and the university may not be able to "turn back the clock" to remedy the poor performance, as accommodations are not made retroactively. They also run the serious risk of damaging the relationship with the clinical supervisor. Therefore, students should consider disclosing disability-related needs to the clinical supervisor and site far in advance of starting the placement, giving the site time to prepare for any adjustments to current practices.

Discriminatory Actions

If students feel that they have been discriminated against due to their status as persons with disability, there are formal channels to address this. Each university is required to have a published procedure available to make a claim of discrimination on the basis of disability. Generally, the university's Americans with Disabilities Act (ADA) compliance officer manages these claims (see Chapter 1's discussion of grievances and formal complaints). Although we recommend that students first seek to resolve a situation within the institution, students also have the option to make a formal complaint through the Department of Education's Office for Civil Rights, or through private legal means.

MAINTAINING APPROPRIATE BOUNDARIES

Faculty and Student Boundaries in Communication

We have discussed what happens when students willingly share too much information, but what happens when faculty do not recognize boundaries, and ask questions of a personal nature? When this occurs, it is usually done without malicious intent and comes from a place of a general concern for the student's well-being. Good intentions, however, do not trump the need to keep conversations professional and to stress to your faculty that it serves everyone well to respect a student's privacy.

Although it is a difficult conversation to initiate, *it is important to set a professional tone between faculty and students concerning communication about disabilities and to keep personal information confidential.* The perfect time to set boundaries is during the initial disclosure of a student's status as a student with a formally registered disability. Students should be encouraged to follow the guidance offered in the section "First Contact" in Appendix 7.1.

Faculty, DS providers, and students can set a professional tone through their e-mails by focusing on accommodations and not a student's disability or diagnosis. Also, by maintaining a formal and professional tone in the initial e-mails, faculty and students set a standard for future communication.

Emotionally Loaded Communication

At times, students make emotionally loaded statements in their communications with faculty; this is not professional, and should be addressed directly. Although it is understandable that students might have genuine concerns about how they are perceived, it is not productive to attribute feelings or intention to others. Instead, DS professionals should encourage students to remain focused on their own circumstances and work toward a positive resolution of any concerns.

In Appendix 7.1, you will find examples of straightforward, appropriately assertive, and objective communication. Faculty should respond very directly to any emotionally loaded statements in communication about accommodations, and advise students not to use such statements. DS providers and faculty can assist students with avoiding the following types of language when communicating about approved accommodations:

- "I know you must be upset. . ."
- "Please don't think I'm lazy. . ."
- "You've been ignoring me!"
- "You seemed angry when. . ."
- "I know it's a real pain for you to make these arrangements for my accommodations. . ."
- "Could I ask you for a favor?"
- "I feel horrible asking this, but. . ."
- "Please forgive me for asking, but. . ."
- "I assure you that my condition is real. . ."

It is important to keep in mind that students with disabilities are entitled to the accommodations approved by the DS office. They should not apologize for a disability or need for accommodations. Formal accommodations approved by the DS office have been determined reasonable, and are tools to facilitate equal access to learning. They should not be considered a burden, unfair advantage, or benefit to students with disabilities, and communication with the student should focus solely on the implementation of the accommodation.

School Procedures and Faculty Responsibilities

Professional communication and responsible behavior in accessing accommodations is a two-way street. In addition to the students' responsibility to follow procedures and communicate effectively in a timely manner, it is also expected that faculty will respond in kind. If a faculty member is not responding in a timely or respectful manner, the DS office should facilitate communication. Faculty should respond to a student's disclosure within 24 business hours, when possible. A simple return e-mail that acknowledges receipt of the e-mail (and, often, the letter of accommodation) is appropriate.

Suspected Disability

Faculty members who suspect that a student has a disability, but are unsure, should tread carefully. This is particularly important in the health professions, where faculty and administrators often have clinical expertise and may be tempted to form an armchair diagnostic opinion based on observations.

In an article about medical faculty with disabilities, Steinberg, Iezzoni, Conill, and Stineman (2002, p. 3149) state that "physicians are the putative arbiters of true impairment." They assert that "colleagues or supervisors often think their medical training gives them special insight into the faculty member's abilities and needs. But [they] may have inaccurate perceptions or limited knowledge about specific diseases or disorders; they may thus harbor overt or hidden biases or misconceptions" (p. 3149). It is dangerous territory, and bad medicine, to form a presumptive opinion or provide medical advice without full information. In addition, faculty, DS providers, and administrators are well advised to remember that their role here is that of an educator or administrator, not a clinician, when working with students.

If a student alludes to a long-term learning difficulty, or mentions having health problems or seeing a counselor as an explanation for difficulties with performance, faculty should refer the student to the DS office.

If a student displays behavior that leads a faculty member to believe that the student may have an undiagnosed condition, including a learning disability, the faculty member should discuss this with the DS provider. Some DS offices conduct prescreenings with students to determine if a referral for a disability-related diagnostic evaluation is warranted. Understanding the available resources on campus helps faculty make an informed referral for these types of cases (see Example 7.9).

EXAMPLE 7.9 • Response to a Student Alluding to a Disability

Faculty response:
I am sorry to hear you are having difficulty. You may want to seek assistance with the student support offices available, including the learning center, the counseling center, and the disability services (DS) office. These offices may be able to provide some support for you academically, and many students find them helpful.

Outcome:
This statement normalizes help-seeking behavior and lets the student know that you encourage disclosure and work well with the DS office. By referring a student to multiple supports at once, along with the referral to the DS office, you offer guidance that is nonthreatening, particularly if a student does not explicitly mention a diagnosis or use of health or mental health support to explain the difficulty.

This approach also has the benefit of normalizing the students' difficulties, by indicating that the faculty member has worked with these offices before. The referral is supportive and remains focused on improving the students' ability to learn, which falls within the purview of an educator, and does not suggest a specific diagnosis, which would fall under the purview of a clinician. At times, students may push back on the idea of going to the DS office and not think of themselves as someone with a "disability," particularly those with chronic health conditions, including mental health diagnoses. It is helpful to explain to the student that disability is a broad "catch-all" term that includes a spectrum of situations, and that the DS office can often be a good source of support and referral to other offices if deemed necessary. It goes without saying that referrals should be done in a confidential space, out of earshot of other students, faculty, and staff. If a student raises a concern with a faculty member at the end of class, the faculty member should schedule a meeting to discuss the issues in a private space.

CONCLUSION

The manner in which students, faculty, and administrators communicate about accommodations is a critical part of maintaining a professional atmosphere in the health sciences. Communication must be clear and respectful, with due attention to confidentiality. Attention to boundaries in these relationships is also an important part of maintaining professionalism, ensuring that the discussion does not move into the realm of clinician–patient types of interactions. By ensuring that communication is transparent and respectful, students will be well served in the educational environment, and the university will protect itself from risk associated with miscommunication.

REFERENCES

Accreditation Council for Graduate Medical Education. (1999). *General competencies.* Retrieved from http://www.acgme.org/acgmeweb/Portals/0/PFAssets/ProgramRequirements/CPRs2013.pdf

Cohen, J. (2006). Professionalism in medical education, an American perspective: From evidence to accountability. *Medical Education, 40*(7), 607–617.

Commission on Collegiate Nursing Education. (2009). *Standards for accreditation of post-baccalaureate nurse residency programs.* Retrieved from http://www.aacn.nche.edu/ccne-accreditation/standards-procedures-resources/nurse-residency

Kirk, L., & Blank, L. (2005). Professional behavior: A learner's permit for licensure. *New England Journal of Medicine, 353*(25), 2709–2711.

Marshak, L., Van Wieren, T., Raeke Ferrell, D., Swiss, L., & Dugan, C. (2010). Exploring barriers to college student use of disability services and accommodations. *Journal of Postsecondary Education and Disability, 22*(3), 151–165.

Papadakis, M., Hodgson, C., Teherani, A., & Kohatsu, N. (2004). Unprofessional behavior in medical school is associated with subsequent disciplinary action by a state medical board. *Academic Medicine, 79*(3), 244–249.

Papadakis, M., Teherani, A., Banach, M., Knettler, T., Rattner, S., Stern, D., . . . Hodgson, C. (2005). Disciplinary action by medical boards and prior behavior in medical school. *New England Journal of Medicine, 353,* 2673–2682.

Steinberg, A., Iezzoni, L., Conill, A., & Stineman, M. (2002). Reasonable accommodations for medical faculty with disabilities. *Journal of the American Medical Association, 288*(24), 3147–3154.

Trammel, J., & Hathaway, M. (2007). Help-seeking patterns in college students with disabilities. *Journal of Postsecondary Education and Disability, 20*(1), 5–15.

Wynia, M., Papadakis, M., Sullivan, W., & Hafferty, F. (2014). More than a list of values and desired behaviors: A foundational understanding of medical professionalism. *Academic Medicine, 89*(5), 712–714.

Professionalism in Communication: A Guide for Graduate and Professional Health Sciences Students With Disabilities

Neera R. Jain and Lisa M. Meeks

For all students, the transition to graduate or professional school requires the use of many skills to adapt to the new environment. One's professionalism, especially regarding communication skills, is key to making an effective transition. It is essential that students with disabilities effectively communicate with faculty, colleagues, and other administration and staff in order to ensure access to approved disability accommodations.

This guide was developed to assist graduate and professional students in the health sciences to effectively communicate information about their disabilities and their classroom and clinical placement accommodations with faculty and administrators. The goal is to outline several key issues for students with disabilities, including: (1) the appropriate amount of information to share, (2) tips for professional communication, and (3) the students' roles and responsibilities in this process.

WHAT IS UNIQUE ABOUT GRADUATE AND PROFESSIONAL SCHOOL STUDY?

In graduate and professional schools, there is an expectation that students will demonstrate a higher level of self-direction and self-advocacy in their behavior and learning than they did during earlier education. Particularly in professional health sciences schools, the competency of professionalism is embedded in the curriculum to support the professional development of students as they become health care providers.

WHAT IS PROFESSIONALISM?

Professionalism encompasses a number of aspects of professional behavior, including professional relationships, work habits, ethical principles, and external standards. In the health sciences, these skills are seen as critical in developing the ability to form relationships with patients and other health care team members that are based on respect, integrity, and responsiveness to others' needs. It is also seen as integral to students becoming professionals who can apply ethical standards to their practice.[1] Research demonstrates that lapses in the professionalism of health sciences students are predictive of similar difficulties in future professional behavior.[2]

HOW DOES PROFESSIONALISM APPLY
TO STUDENTS WITH DISABILITIES?

Students with disabilities are, of course, students first. They are held to the same standards of behavior as all other students. Standards of professionalism are maintained for all aspects of a student's interactions and behaviors in the academic environment, which includes accessing disability-related accommodations and supports.

Communicating with faculty regarding your status as a student with a disability is an important step in accessing accommodations. Like any other communication with faculty, it is a reflection of professional conduct. For many students, this can be an anxiety-provoking task. Students may be reluctant to share information about their disabilities out of shame or fear of stigma from school administration, peers, or faculty. Some students may have had negative experiences in the past and, as a result, may display behaviors that reflect their reluctance to access accommodations. Other students are new to discussing their needs with faculty, either due to the structure of their undergraduate environment or due to a new diagnosis or exacerbation of an existing condition, and may be unsure of what to say and how to say it. This can lead to poorly executed communication from the student, including: (1) late notification of a need for accommodations; (2) sending brief or excessively lengthy and detailed communication; (3) taking an overly defensive, emotional, or aggressive stance in communication; or (4) simply not reaching out to ask for assistance.

In a health sciences school, poor communication leads to potentially strained relationships with faculty. Additionally, failure to clearly communicate accommodation needs can contribute to unnecessary stress and burden for both faculty and students. All students should strive to maintain a professional relationship with faculty members, as they will soon become part of

---

[1] http://meded.ucsf.edu/ume/md-competencies
[2] Papadakis, M. A., Teherani, A., Banach, M. A., Knettler, T. R., Rattner, S., Stern, D. T., Veloski, J. J., & Hodgson, C. S. (2005). Unprofessional behavior in medical school and subsequent disciplinary action by state medical boards. *New England Journal of Medicine, 353,* 2673–2682.

their professional network and may be called upon for references for jobs or other future pursuits.

It may seem unfair that students without disabilities do not have to think about or manage this extra layer of responsibility. However, it is a reality of having a disability and being in a graduate program. It also mirrors the process that people with disabilities follow in the workplace to access accommodations for a job. Practicing and developing professional communication skills regarding accommodations as a student will help you to refine your ability to communicate concerning your disability-related needs as you enter the workplace.

WHAT ABOUT DISCLOSING A DISABILITY TO FACULTY?

Students with disabilities may arrive at graduate or professional schools lacking a good understanding of their disability and having difficulty communicating their needs. They often share feelings of uncertainty about how much information to share, and with whom to share this information.

Students are not obligated to disclose personal health information, nor the origin of their disability, to faculty, administrators, or other program personnel in order to access accommodations approved by the disability services (DS) office.

Students studying the health sciences may feel compelled to share details about their diagnosis as a way of justifying their need for accommodations. Students might also believe that disclosing the nature of the disability will result in a more empathetic understanding of their needs, given that many of their faculty members are health professionals.

The DS office carefully protects a student's confidential medical information and has protocols in place to ensure a student's privacy. Accommodations are "vetted" in advance with the respective schools to ensure that technical standards are not compromised. As such, faculty members are strictly prohibited from inquiring about the nature of a student's disability or requesting additional documentation (e.g., doctor's notes, documentation of illness, medical evaluations). No additional "justification" of a student's disability or need for accommodation is necessary or warranted.

We caution students against engaging in a dialogue about medical or disability status with faculty and administration, aside from the DS office. Faculty and students, particularly in the health sciences, can easily slip into an in-depth medical dialogue about diagnosis, prognosis, and course of treatment when discussing a student's disability. Conversations of this nature place both the student and faculty in a vulnerable position and can invite unwanted medical advice and future questions about status and well-being. Students may leave a conversation of this nature feeling that they have shared too much. Although faculty members often have good intentions, future interactions may become focused on the student's medical status instead of the student's learning and education.

When a student is determining whether or not to share medical information, the student should consider *why* he or she is sharing. Sharing information of this nature can be perceived as an attempt to elicit sympathy or seek favoritism, or as a mechanism for explaining subpar performance. Formal accommodations should eliminate the need to discuss specifics about a disability and allow faculty to keep assessments strictly performance-based. The DS office is available to assess eligibility for additional accommodations, including modifications to policy and procedure, when necessary, and consult about appropriate disclosures.

WHEN FACULTY ASK PERSONAL QUESTIONS

We have discussed what happens when students willingly share too much information, but what happens when faculty do not recognize boundaries and ask questions of a personal nature? When this occurs, it is usually done without malicious intent and out of a general concern for the student's well-being. Good intentions, however, do not trump the need to keep conversations professional and for the student to vocalize his or her desired privacy.

Although a difficult conversation to initiate, *it is important for students to set a professional tone with faculty regarding their status as a student with a disability and their desire to keep personal information confidential.* The perfect time for students to set boundaries with faculty is during the initial disclosure of status as a student with a formally registered disability. For guidance on the first contact with faculty, see Section I, "First Contact." Students can set the tone in their e-mails by focusing on their accommodations and not their disability diagnoses. Also, by maintaining a formal and professional tone in their initial e-mails, they set up expectations for future communication.

EMOTIONALLY LOADED COMMUNICATION

Emotionally loaded statements made by students in communication with faculty, including attributing feelings about accommodations, disability, and associated malicious intent to others, is less than professional. Although it is understandable that students may have concerns about how they are perceived, it is not productive to attribute feelings to others. Instead, students should remain focused on their own circumstances and moving toward a positive resolution.

The subsequent sections present examples of straightforward, appropriately assertive, and objective communication. We recommend that students avoid emotionally loaded statements in communication about accommodations, such as the following.

- "I know you must be upset. . ."
- "Please don't think I'm lazy. . ."
- "You've been ignoring me!"
- "You seemed angry when. . ."
- "I know it's a real pain for you to make these arrangements for my accommodations. . ."
- "Could I ask you for a favor?"

- "I feel horrible asking this, but. . ."
- "Please forgive me for asking, but. . ."
- "I assure you that my condition is real. . ."

It is important to keep in mind that students are entitled to accommodations that have been approved by the DS office. Students should not apologize for a disability, or for the need for accommodations. These adjustments have been determined reasonable, and are tools to facilitate equal access to learning. They should not be considered a burden, unfair advantage, or benefit to students with disabilities.

SCHOOL PROCEDURES AND FACULTY RESPONSIBILITIES

Students are responsible for following the procedures for accessing accommodations outlined for their school or program each quarter or semester. Students should note the process for their school or program in the student handbook and make sure to follow these procedures carefully.

Professional communication and responsible behavior in accessing accommodations is a two-way street. In addition to the student's responsibility to follow procedures and communicate effectively in a timely manner, it is also expected that faculty will respond in kind. Students who find themselves in a situation where a faculty member is not responding in a timely or respectful manner should contact the DS office or the DS liaison to obtain assistance.

DISCRIMINATORY ACTIONS

If students feel that they have been discriminated against due to their status as a person with a disability, there are formal channels to address this. Each university is required to have a published procedure available to make a claim of discrimination on the basis of disability. Generally, the university's Americans with Disabilities Act (ADA) compliance officer or equal opportunity office manages these claims.

Although we recommend that students first seek to resolve a situation within their university, students also have the option to make a formal complaint through the Department of Education's Office for Civil Rights,[3] or through private legal means.

GENERAL RECOMMENDATIONS AND REMINDERS FOR COMMUNICATION

1. It is important that communication **be clear and concise.**
2. It is essential that students **communicate and follow up in a timely manner.**

---

[3] https://wdcrobcolp01.ed.gov/CFAPPS/OCR/contactus.cfm

3. **Most faculty members are very aware of the expected processes for accessing and providing accommodations,** and have experience working with students with disabilities.
4. **If students encounter any difficulties with faculty, they should contact campus resources** (disability services, or identified liaisons in your school) **immediately to avoid any delay or disruption to services.**
5. **Students must take responsibility for following up.** Many students find it helpful to set reminders on their calendars in advance, outlining when to send communication to faculty or when to follow up if they haven't heard a response, and to schedule periodic check-ins regarding upcoming exams.
6. **Students are not obligated to disclose personal information unrelated to accommodations.** Legally, students are not required to disclose the nature of a disability or to submit additional documentation (e.g., psycho-educational or other evaluations, medical records, letters from health care providers) to other university departments, faculty, or personnel once they have become registered students with the DS office.

I. FIRST CONTACT

The first contact with your faculty about your need for accommodations lays the groundwork for your relationship. It should be short and to the point. Most important, no in-depth disclosure about your disability is necessary.

This first communication should address your needs, including a request for information about when, where, and how your accommodations will be provided. Your university likely has specific guidelines for notifying faculty of your registration with the disability services office, and your need for accommodations. Most schools encourage students to notify faculty in advance of the semester or quarter, or at least 2 weeks in advance of an exam. Depending on the structure of your course (e.g., those with exams or quizzes within the first 2 weeks), it may be advisable to contact faculty in advance of the start of the class.

Some accommodations, such as a change in clinical site or the need for specialized equipment, alternate-format course materials, or sign language interpreters, require additional time to arrange. In these cases, the DS office and faculty should be notified well in advance. Part of professional communication is allowing for the time necessary to coordinate your accommodations. Your student handbook or DS procedures guide should outline expected timelines for arranging such accommodations.

Timely communication with faculty is the first step in establishing a good working relationship. Most faculty convey that the only issue they have regarding students with disabilities is the failure of students to communicate their needs in a clear and timely manner.

Example of a Well-Written First E-Mail

Dear Professor Smith,

My name is XXXX and I am a student in your Adult Med/Surg course.[a] I am writing because you have received an e-mail from the nursing school liaison confirming my registration with Student Disability Services and outlining my approved accommodations for your course. I am hoping to speak to you to discuss how I will access my exam accommodations. Per my accommodations, I require 150% time for my exams, as well as a private room.[b]

Could you please advise me on when and where I should report for my exams?[c] If you would prefer, I would be happy to meet with you in person to discuss this. Generally, once we have finalized the plan, I send a reminder to my faculty of my needs 2 weeks in advance of my exams to confirm the arrangements.[d]

If you have a course coordinator or proctor whom you prefer I contact, or whom you would like copied on these e-mails, please let me know. I look forward to working together to facilitate these accommodations.

Thank you in advance for your assistance.
Best regards,

[a] This introduction informs the professor who you are, and introduces you as a current student first.
[b] Reminding professors that they have already received communication about your circumstances will prompt them to look back in their e-mails to refresh their memory about your case.
[c] You ask for the specific information needed to access your accommodations.
[d] Taking responsibility to remind your professors that you require accommodations 2 weeks before an exam will help to avoid any confusion or miscommunication on the day of the exam, when you are hoping to stay focused on the exam material.

Example of a Poorly Written First E-Mail

Dear Professor Smith,

I am a disabled student[a] in your Adult Med/Surg course this quarter. I have a lot of needs[b] because I have a significant learning disability,[c] and I hope that I will do okay in your course.[d] I was only diagnosed 3 years ago.[e]

I need extended time for my exams.[f]

TY,[g]

[a] There are different philosophies regarding the language used to refer to people with disabilities. Some people choose to refer to themselves as a disabled person first, such as "I am autistic" or "I am a disabled student," denoting that the disability is an inherent part of their cultural identity. Others choose to use person-first language, such as "I am a person with autism" or "I am a person with a disability," denoting that they are a person first and having a disability is one of a number of qualities that describes them, not the only descriptor. You may find it helpful to think about how you would like to refer to yourself, what it means to you, and what message it conveys to others. This can be a valuable exploration into your personal disability identity and philosophy. There is no "wrong answer" to the question, "how will I refer to myself?"

[b] Reporting to faculty members that you have "a lot of needs" can leave the impression that working with you will take up a good deal of their time and energy. Instead, specifying your approved accommodations better conceptualizes your needs for faculty. Some students feel guilty for taking up faculty time and will communicate this in e-mails. Using an apologetic tone is not necessary. Accommodations are available to allow students equal access to a program, and should not be considered a burden or excess work. It is best to proceed in a matter-of-fact manner.

[c] Disclosing your disability is not necessary in this context.

[d] Saying that you "hope you do okay" or similar language reads as if you are trying to elicit sympathy. This type of communication can be perceived as less than professional. Moreover, you, like any other student, have met the admissions requirements for the program, and are as qualified as any other student to be in the class.

[e] This may seem basic, but we'd like to remind students that using emoticons and emojis in your e-mails is less than professional. We recommend that you refrain from using them in your communication with faculty.

[f] This statement is not specific—how much time does the student need? It does not refer back to the official approval notification that the faculty member should have already received from your school liaison.

[g] Closing an e-mail with an informal salutation does not convey a professional tone. Even though you are a student, you are expected to communicate as a professional adult in all situations, including e-mail. We recommend that you refrain from using abbreviations common to "Internet speak" such as LOL, SYS, TY, and ROFL, as they are not sufficiently formal for this type of writing.

II. FOLLOW-UP E-MAIL

A. Follow up to no response

There are two types of follow up e-mails to the first contact that students generally send to faculty. The first is intended to follow up should you not hear back within a reasonable period of time.

If there is no response to your initial e-mail, it is generally recommended that you follow up within 3 to 5 business days. This follow-up e-mail should include the previous e-mail and be approached as a gentle reminder that you are waiting for a response.

Example of a Well-Written Follow-Up E-Mail

Dear Professor Smith,

I hope this e-mail finds you doing well.[a]
    I am following up on the communication below in order to finalize arrangements for my approved accommodations in your course.[b] For clarity and ease of reading I've put my questions in bullet format.[c] If it would be helpful for us to meet in person instead, I would be happy to do so. Please let me know which works best for you.[d]

- QUESTION 1
- QUESTION 2
- QUESTION 3

Thank you!
Best,

[a] Begin with a friendly tone.
[b] Inform the professor about your needs, and reference your initial e-mail, which is copied below.
[c] Make e-mail communication easy by bulleting or numbering items.
[d] Make yourself available in case the professor has more questions or wishes to see you in person.

Example of a Poorly Constructed Follow-Up E-Mail

Dear Professor Smith,

I am very worried about the upcoming exam[a] because I haven't heard back from you about the e-mail I sent last night![b] I really, really need the accommodations[c] and I think I will fail your exam without them.[d]

As you should know, I'm entitled to these accommodations under federal law. I hope I don't need to make a complaint about not getting my accommodations.[e]

Sincerely,

[a] Does not communicate confidence.
[b] You are anticipating an unreasonably short turnaround ("e-mail I sent you last night").
[c] This sentence makes it appear that you are desperate for the accommodation. The writing style is also informal.
[d] Accommodations are intended to level the playing field—not to ensure that students pass. This argument also appears unprofessional and emotionally charged.
[e] It is generally not helpful to remind faculty of legal obligations at this juncture. This statement as written appears threatening. It is more helpful to use a collaborative tone, and reach out to the DS office or your school liaison for support if collaborative efforts are not successful.

B. Follow up to confirm arrangements

The second type of follow-up e-mail is more general in nature and is used to confirm details for accessing accommodations. It should be simple and concise, confirming any agreed-upon details from your previous conversations.

Example of a Well-Written Follow-Up E-Mail

Dear Professor Smith,

I am writing to confirm the arrangements for accessing my accommodations in the upcoming Adult Med/Surg exam scheduled for December 5.[a] As we discussed previously, I will take the exam in CL 214 at 8:30 a.m. Because the standard time for the exam is 60 minutes, and I am allotted 1.5 times the normal administration time, I should have 90 minutes, completing the exam by 10 a.m.[b]

Please let me know if there have been any changes to these arrangements.[c]

Thank you, again, for your assistance.
Best regards,

[a] Gives very specific information about the test day, time, and location. The professor can extract the information if needed and forward to any proctors.
[b] Reminds the professor of the approved accommodations and states the end time, helping the professor plan for proctors.
[c] Invites the professor to respond if there are any changes.

Example of a Poorly Constructed Follow-Up E-Mail

Dear Professor Smith,

I'll be at the test tomorrow. Let me know if anything has changed.[a]

Best,

[a]Very casual; does not elicit cooperation in the tone, or communicate your understanding of any arrangements previously made.

III. COMMUNICATING CONCERNS AND COMPLAINTS

Sometimes, despite everyone's best efforts, something goes wrong in the process of accessing your accommodations. It is important to raise concerns as soon as possible so they can be addressed expeditiously. Ideally, if there is a concern during an exam (e.g., a student who is approved for a private room is placed in a shared room, or there is a noise complaint), you should notify your proctor in the moment so it can be addressed immediately. However, if there is a concern that is not or could not be addressed in the moment, you may want to inform the professor in writing. It is recommended that you copy the DS office on this e-mail so that the DS office can provide technical assistance to your faculty or school regarding the incident.

When communicating a complaint, it is helpful to inform your faculty about the facts of the incident as you understand them, note your concerns about what happened, and propose or inquire about a desired solution. Although a situation may have been upsetting, it is helpful to try to use a neutral tone, and be as clear and objective as possible. Using a neutral tone does not take away from what you have experienced. In fact, you may feel quite upset and troubled by what happened. However, your communication is a means for reporting and documenting your concerns. Taking a neutral and collaborative tone helps to create a "paper trail" around your concern, and demonstrates and documents your professional approach in the process. Using a neutral tone also tends to be the most successful in eliciting cooperation, and can go a long way in resolving your concern.

Note that although we recommend that students attempt to address concerns informally first, there are always formal means by which a complaint or concern can be addressed. See your university's policies for resolving complaints and concerns for more information.

Example of a Well-Written E-Mail Regarding a Concern/Complaint

Dear Professor Smith,

I am writing to inform you of something that happened during my exam today, and request that you assist me in resolving it.[a]

As you know, I am approved for a private room as an accommodation for my disability. During my exam, there was an active construction project outside the window. I tried to inquire about relocating to a quieter space, but was unable to reach you.[b] There was consistent noise throughout my exam, which was particularly distracting due to my disability.[c]

I fear that my performance was significantly impacted by this noise. I would like to discuss this impact and determine what can be done to address this unfortunate situation. I believe that given the poor conditions of my exam room, I should be permitted to retake the exam under better conditions.[d]

In the future, I think it would be helpful if I were permitted to bring noise-cancelling headphones into the testing room. I plan to ask Student Disability Services about the availability and reasonableness of this as a formal accommodation.[e] It would also be helpful to ensure that the phone number I am provided to ask questions and address concerns during future exams is closely monitored so such concerns can be addressed in the moment.[f]

I have copied the Disability Services Director and the Disability Services liaison in the School of Nursing on this e-mail in the hopes that they may be able to assist us with addressing the situation.[g]

I'm looking forward to resolving this issue and putting preventative measures in place for future exams.[h]

Best,

[a] You solicit your professor's assistance with a neutral tone.
[b] You describe the situation clearly and objectively; you explain why you are informing the professor after the incident occurred.
[c] You explain why this situation is particularly problematic given your disability status and related needs.
[d] You explain how you were impacted by the circumstance, and propose a solution to the issue.
[e] You propose a reasonable solution going forward, and your plan to reach out to the DS office to explore this further.
[f] You note the expected arrangement (that you can contact the faculty during the exam with questions or concerns), and explain what changes you feel would address the circumstances you faced. This points out what went wrong without calling out the professor in a confrontational manner.
[g] By copying the DS director and your school liaison, you solicit their assistance in resolving the situation. The DS office and your liaison are key resources for you and your faculty to ensure that the situation is appropriately resolved.
[h] You maintain a professional, collaborative tone while stressing that the situation needs to be addressed.

Example of a Poorly Written E-Mail Regarding a Concern/Complaint

Dear Professor Smith,

I tried to call you during the exam but you didn't answer. There was so much noise that I couldn't concentrate, and I'm pretty sure I failed the exam. This noise kept me from using my accommodations so I think I should be allowed to retake the exam ASAP.[a]

Please respond to tell me what you'll do about this!!![b]

Sincerely,

[a] In this version, you are expressing your frustration, but not including key details. You don't orient the professor to the exam you are referring to, and do not paint a full picture of the situation you experienced.

[b] This statement is confrontational and demanding; it doesn't convey a collaborative tone. The DS office and/or your school liaison are not included on the e-mail to solicit their assistance in resolving the situation.

IV. COMMUNICATING ABOUT A CHRONIC HEALTH CONDITION

If you have a disability with symptoms that ebb and flow over time and find it difficult to attend an essential activity, or find that an exacerbation of symptoms impacts your ability to complete an assignment by a set due date, you should request consideration of flexible attendance and deadlines as an accommodation from the DS office. You should speak with your DS provider to determine if and when flexibility is warranted.

If you have an approved accommodation that allows for flexibility, communication is essential. It is best to work with your DS provider to establish concrete expectations for attendance per the approved accommodation, along with a clear understanding of the consequences or actions that may result for absences beyond the agreed-upon change to course policy.

As a general rule, when such an accommodation is approved, a reasonable number of absences and/or instances of tardiness beyond the standard course policy will be predetermined as a reasonable accommodation. The number approved will depend on the course structure and requirements, and will be predetermined in an interactive discussion among you, the DS provider, faculty, and the school.

When possible, you are encouraged to attend your classes. Flares in symptoms and other unexpected exacerbations can contribute to unexpected tardiness. Although some adjustment period is anticipated, you should adjust your schedule to reflect the need for additional time to ensure an on-time arrival for class and other obligations, generally within a 1- to 2-day period.

Although the amount of flexibility that will be provided as an accommodation is normally predetermined by the DS office in consultation with the school, it is your responsibility, along with your faculty member, to set the expectations regarding notification. *You must determine, in advance, a protocol for notifying faculty when the accommodation needs to be activated* (i.e., when you experience an exacerbation of symptoms). There are several key points that you should discuss with your faculty. This discussion should occur in a meeting or by e-mail, and you should follow up to confirm faculty members' understanding of the process in writing. The following are examples of key points for consideration:

1. Whom should I notify if I am going to be late or absent from a required activity?
2. What is the best way to notify someone (e.g., phone, e-mail)?
3. If I am going to be absent from a required activity, what are my options for making up work?
4. If I am going to be late or absent for an exam, is the process any different?
5. Are there other instructors who should be notified about this plan (e.g., small-group leaders, co-instructors, preceptors, clinical instructors); if so, who will notify them?

You should write two e-mails: one that alerts the faculty to the potential for this need and the afforded accommodation, and a second for when a flare-up happens. Determining a protocol at the beginning of the course shows respect and consideration for faculty and reduces the need to negotiate accommodations in the middle of a potentially debilitating flare-up of symptoms.

A. Notification of the potential need for flexibility
Example of a Well-Written E-Mail: Attendance Flexibility Accommodation

Dear Professor Smith,

I am a student in your XXX course. I am also registered with Student Disability Services (please see my attached accommodation letter).[a]

As part of my approved disability accommodations, I am afforded some flexibility around attendance should I experience an exacerbation of my symptoms. I cannot always predict the need for the accommodation in advance of an event. I'm writing to ask that we meet to discuss an agreed-upon protocol for communicating my absence/tardiness and the need to use my approved accommodation.[b] An ideal protocol would include the best method of contacting you, and any alternative participatory method that might be available to me (e.g., remote attendance, weekend hours, research). I would also need to know how to proceed if I were to experience an exacerbation on the day of an exam.

(continued)

Example of a Well-Written E-Mail: Attendance Flexibility Accommodation (*continued*)

> Please let me know when we might be able to meet. Once we determine the protocol I will e-mail you a confirmation to ensure that I understand what is expected. My hope is that I will not experience any exacerbations during this course, but I find it best to be prepared just in case.[c]
>
> Best regards,
>
> [a] You introduce yourself as a student first to provide context to your e-mail, and provide the letter confirming approved accommodations that the faculty will expect in any discussion about accommodations.
> [b] You take early action to schedule a time to discuss the protocol should you need to activate the accommodation.
> [c] You communicate your desire to be prepared in the event that you require the approved accommodation, which in turn communicates your professionalism.

Example of a Poorly Written E-Mail: Attendance Flexibility Accommodation

> Dear Professor Smith,
>
> As part of my accommodations I am allowed to miss class. If I can't make it to class I'll let you know and will plan to make up the work.[a]
>
> Thank you!
>
> Best,
>
> [a] Although it is friendly, this message does not have sufficient specificity. You have not included the verification of your approved accommodation. You have not communicated that you would like to understand the expectations should you need to exercise the accommodation. Your description of the accommodation is ambiguous and does not clearly communicate the approved accommodation, which is a reasonable level of flexibility. It may communicate instead that you are permitted to never attend class.

B. Notifying faculty that you will need to use the flexibility accommodation

An e-mail regarding a missed activity should remind your faculty members about the circumstances, inform them that you will be or were absent (be specific about what you missed), and communicate how you would like to resolve the incident, per your previous discussions.

Example of a Well-Written E-Mail Regarding the Need for Flexibility

Dear Professor Smith,

I'm writing to inform you that I am experiencing a significant exacerbation of my disability today, and as such will not be able to attend the lab session.[a] Per our predetermined protocol I am e-mailing you with a potential solution/make-up scenario.[b] I understand that Group B will perform the same lab on Friday. I would like to request that I be permitted to attend the lab session on Friday to make up for missing today's lab.[c]

Thank you in advance for your consideration.[d]

Best,

[a] You inform the faculty about the situation without including specific details of your condition—this is good, as it is not necessary to share specific medical information in these communications.
[b] You remind the professor about your previous conversations, which orients the professor to the agreement you made at the beginning of the quarter.
[c] You provide a reasonable make-up scenario that presumably was discussed in your initial conversation.
[d] You close with a professional statement of gratitude.

Example of a Poorly Written E-Mail Regarding the Need for Flexibility

Dear Professor Smith,

I'm sick today and can't go to lab.[a] I'm SO, SO sorry!!![b] I don't really know what to do.[c] I feel horrible. Is there anything I can do to make up the lab?[d]

Thanks,

[a] Stating that you are "sick" does not alert professors that the issue is related to your disability. Faculty often have specific policies regarding illness, which are separate from your accommodation, and often require students to provide a note from a doctor. An accommodation of flexibility due to disability does not require the student to provide a doctor's note. Flexibility as an accommodation supersedes most attendance policies.
[b] It is not necessary to apologize for your disability or condition. Further, the format of this apology is not professional.
[c] You should have discussed the protocol for such circumstances prior to your need to access it. Stating that you don't know what to do can appear that you are helpless and unprepared. In fact, most students do have an idea of what they should or could do, and should communicate that.
[d] Again, this communicates that you have not previously discussed the accommodation and related need with the faculty, is informal, and relays a feeling that you are incapable of managing your circumstances.

Example of a Well-Written E-Mail Regarding Absence

Dear Professor Ali,

I was absent from lecture today.[a] Unfortunately, it was necessary for me to use 1 of my 4 preapproved absences to attend to a flare-up in symptoms.[b] As discussed previously, I will get the notes from a classmate and view the lecture capture to catch up on the material missed.[c]

Please let me know if there is anything else I should do.

Best,

[a] You send an e-mail on the day of the absence to notify the faculty member.
[b] You reference your prior conversation and protocol—indicating that you have used one of the agreed-upon absences. You note that it is a disability-related issue without providing unnecessary details.
[c] You note the steps you will take to make up the work missed, as per your previous conversation.

Example of a Poorly Written E-Mail Regarding Absence

Dear Professor Ali,

I was out of class today. Can you please provide me the information that I missed? I was sick, and as you recall, I am allowed to miss class because of my disability.[a]

Thanks,

[a] Indicates no proactive protocol was established regarding absences. Saying you are "allowed to miss class because of your disability" is misleading.

Example of a Well-Written E-Mail Regarding Tardiness

Dear Professor Garcia,

I woke up today with a significant flare-up of symptoms related to my disability.[a] Per our previous discussion, I'm writing to let you know that I will be late for my small group today.[b] I have copied my small-group leader for the day to ensure that she is aware.[c]

I am working out how to best manage my symptoms so I am able to be on time going forward. Please let me know if you have any questions.[d]

Best,

[a] You reference the sudden onset of a flare-up, and that it is related to your disability. You don't provide unnecessary details about the nature of the flare-up.
[b] You reference your previous discussion, and provide timely notice of your need to be late.
[c] You copy any other parties who should be aware of the circumstances.
[d] You note that you are working to manage your symptoms going forward.

Example of a Poorly Written E-Mail Regarding Tardiness

Professor Garcia,

I'm so sorry I was late to small group today.[a] My symptoms are terrible and I had to take medicine in the middle of the night, which made me sleep in late, and it was really hard to get up in time.[b] I hope no one is mad at me.[c] Can you let my leader know so she doesn't think I am just lazy?[d]

Sorry again.[e]

Thanks,

[a] It is not necessary to apologize for your disability-related need.
[b] It is not necessary to provide details of your disability, or the nature of your flare-up of symptoms.
[c] This statement reflects a fear of stigma and judgment due to disability-related needs rather than the approved academic accommodations.
[d] You should copy your small-group leader if it is relevant for her to know of the circumstances. Suggesting that someone might think you are lazy is an emotionally loaded statement and is less than professional.
[e] It is not necessary to apologize.

V. DISCUSSING CLINICAL ACCOMMODATIONS

Our guidance regarding communication thus far also applies to communicating about accommodations in the clinical setting. E-mailing a professor about your needs, however, can be quite different from the face-to-face communication that occurs when working with an attending physician or preceptor. In these situations you may need to communicate about your disability-related accommodations on a daily basis.

It is important that you follow your school or program's procedures for accessing accommodations in the clinical setting; check your student or program handbook for guidance. Most programs follow a "top-down" approach, whereby you are responsible for notifying a lead faculty member, sometimes referred to as a block director, faculty of record, or clinical supervisor, of your approved accommodations. Together, you and the lead faculty member identify who else in the clinical setting needs to be notified of your accommodations.

If you will work with a single team during your rotation, the most effective communication may be to notify the team members as a group in advance. This is easily achieved via e-mail communication following the communication guidelines from previous sections.

However, sometimes a large and relatively unpredictable group of individuals (e.g., faculty, residents, and other team members) work with students. In these cases, *it is essential that you have the initial conversation with your lead faculty member.* This follows the top-down approach and ensures that the people in charge are aware of your accommodations and can assist you with addressing concerns that arise. It is best to take direction from these individuals regarding who needs to be aware of your accommodations, and when. For example, if during a 4-hour surgery you need to take breaks every hour, you may need to notify the operating room charge nurse several days in advance to ensure pertinent members of the team are aware, and to set a protocol for leaving and reentering a sterile space. Your DS provider can consult with you and your lead faculty member to help determine who on the team needs be notified.

In any of these circumstances, it is helpful, and may be necessary, to remind faculty and pertinent team members of your accommodations.

A. Initial notification of clinical faculty

Example of a Well-Communicated Initial Notification of Clinical Faculty

"Hello Dr. Lee, my name is XXXX, and I am registered with Student Disability Services.[a] You may have heard about me from Dr. Jordon. Due to my disability, I will need to take a 10-minute break every 2 hours.[b] I plan to take these breaks in the breakroom.[c] I will plan my breaks around my patients' needs to ensure that they are met before I take my break."[d]

[a] You remind the supervisor of a previous notification of your circumstances.
[b] You explain the accommodation you need in a direct manner, without extraneous details.
[c] You notify the supervisor about how you plan to implement the accommodation.
[d] You assure the supervisor that your accommodation will not interfere with your ability to provide patient care.

Example of a Poorly Communicated Initial Notification to Clinical Faculty

"Hello Dr. Lee. I'm a disabled student so I need to take breaks during the day. Is that okay?"[a]

[a] You don't remind the faculty member of any previous notification of your circumstances. You don't explain the specifics of your approved accommodation, so the need appears ambiguous. Asking permission to access your accommodation is not necessary. The accommodation has already been reviewed and approved by the DS office and your school or program. Making a request instead of informing the faculty member opens the door for an unaware faculty member to try to negotiate the accommodation with you.

B. Clinical scenario where a reminder of your accommodations is necessary

Example of a Well-Constructed Response

Your clinical preceptor asks you to take a medication to the emergency room (ER), but is not facing you when she provides the instructions. You read lips, and need her to face you to ensure that you can understand the instructions.

"I'm sorry, but I didn't understand you. Remember, I need you to face me when you give me instructions so I can read your lips."[a]

[a] A short, polite, and succinct reminder of your disability-related need.

Example of a Poorly Constructed Response

Your clinical preceptor asks you to take a medication to the ER, but is not facing you when she provides the instructions. You read lips, and need her to face you to ensure that you can understand the instructions.

"Huh? I didn't catch that."[a,b]

[a] In this example you don't seize a teachable moment to remind your preceptor of what you need in order to effectively function as a student. You may appear inattentive instead of reminding the faculty member of your needs.
[b] Another poor response would be to try to guess what the preceptor said, and act on a poorly informed assumption. It is also not wise to ask another student what was said. In order to get the most out of your experience, and endeavor to improve the situation going forward, you need to be able to effectively communicate with your preceptor.

VI. CONCLUSION

We hope this guide helps to clarify the "hidden curriculum" of communicating with professors regarding your disability and related accommodations. We have assembled some key take-away points from this guide.

We wish you success in your journey through graduate and professional school!

DOS AND DON'TS FOR WRITING EXCELLENT E-MAILS TO PROFESSORS

Do take a neutral, objective, and assertive tone in your communication.
Don't use emotionally loaded language, blame, or attribute emotions to others in your communication.

Do communicate early and follow up if you don't hear back. Elicit support from your campus DS office when you run into difficulties.

Don't wait until the last minute, or you are in danger of failure to self-identify at the DS office or inform your faculty of your approved accommodations.

Do use formal language in your e-mails to professors.

Don't use "Internet speak" or emoticons to convey your message.

Do share the approved accommodations you need to use in a course or rotation with your faculty.

Don't feel obligated to share your diagnosis, medical history, details, or other information with your faculty.

Do learn and follow the procedures set forth by your school for requesting and accessing accommodations.

Don't assume that you can get what you need outside of a formal process, or that the procedures will be the same as those at your previous academic institution.

Do take a collaborative approach to resolving concerns and complaints. Follow the formal process for grieving a complaint when necessary. Use campus resources to support you.

Don't become combative and try to resolve a difficult situation independently.

Do be proactive in planning for possible changes in your health status, and need for nuanced supports.

Don't assume that this time things will work out fine, and be caught off guard if they do not.

Do use positive and empowered language when discussing your disability and related accommodations.

Don't apologize for your need for accommodations.

Problem Solving Difficult Cases

Neera R. Jain, Barbara L. Hammer, and Shelby Acteson

INTRODUCTION

Despite the best intentions and preparations of disability services (DS) providers, difficult situations with students do arise. These can include late disclosure of disability (after the student is in academic jeopardy), faculty providing inappropriate accommodations without input from the DS provider, new staff inheriting complex and poorly documented cases, and claims of discrimination or threats of legal action during a dismissal process. This chapter will provide guidance regarding steps DS providers and administrators can take to unravel a difficult situation and determine the best way forward, with a focus on both student success and campus legal liability.

Despite the best of intentions, and in some cases because of them, complicated situations do arise in the course of working with students with disabilities in the health professions. When this happens, it is incumbent upon the DS provider to step back and view the "big picture"—hear all sides of the story, consider the best outcome for all parties, and work toward a resolution. During this time, DS professionals are required to walk a delicate line between serving as an advocate for the student and serving as an advocate for the institution—including upholding the integrity of the academic program.

    This chapter identifies some common pathways to complication, outlines what must be considered when dealing with particular problems, and then provides concrete steps for resolving them in partnership with the student and other university officials. Inherent in this process is resolving the current issue and taking steps to prevent the issue from happening again (see Best Practice 8.1). Following this approach cannot eliminate all future problems, but it will give the DS provider a solid foundation for addressing future issues.

BEST PRACTICE 8.1
Goals for the DS Provider in Complicated Situations

1. **Resolve the current issue**
   - Determine the nature of the issue.
   - Determine next steps and follow them to a resolution.

2. **Prevent the issue from recurring**
   - Determine what went wrong and develop a strategy to address it.
     - Review, create, or revise related policies and procedures.
     - Provide training or targeted intervention on the relevant policies and procedures to students, faculty, and/or staff.
     - Ensure policies and procedures can be found and easily followed in the future.

PATHWAYS FOR COMPLICATION

There are a multitude of potential pathways for complication when working with students with disabilities, but they generally originate from one of three places: the faculty/school/program, the student, and the DS office. Regardless of the origin, such situations can become particularly complex, requiring DS providers to tease out the facts of the situation, explore historical practices, review current case law, and mediate an appropriate resolution.

ISSUES THAT ORIGINATE WITH THE FACULTY/SCHOOL/PROGRAM

As discussed in previous chapters (in particular, Chapters 3, 4, and 7), faculty and school/program administration have a critical role to play in referring students with disabilities to the DS office, in engaging in the interactive process to determine appropriate accommodations, and in implementing the accommodations recommended by the DS office. The dos and don'ts for working with students with disabilities noted in Chapter 10 also provide guidance for faculty and school/program administrators.

Issue: Faculty Provided Accommodations to a Student Who Is Not Registered With DS

Students who are not familiar with the DS process sometimes request disability accommodations directly from faculty, such as adjustments of time, deadlines, or other considerations, without a formal recommendation by the DS office. Although a faculty member might provide informal accommodations for students for a variety of reasons not necessarily tied to disability (e.g., temporary illness, death in the family, car accident), providing informal accommodations for a disability-related issue can create confusion in the long run, especially when a student who has been informally accommodated in the past encounters a faculty member who refuses an informal disability accommodation request, instead referring the student to the DS office to establish formal accommodations. Such students can often feel frustrated and shocked that they must "prove" they have a disability—especially when disability accommodations have been provided informally in the past.

Further complicating this scenario are cases in which a faculty member extends informal accommodations that are not supported by a student's disability documentation, or are in direct conflict with the official determination of the DS office (see Table 8.1). It is important that both students and faculty are aware of the role of the DS office and the appropriate steps for seeking disability services. Chapters 2 and 3 outline the process for determining disability status, granting approval for accommodations, and determining individual accommodations for a student's specific academic program.

• **TABLE 8.1 Process When Faculty Provide Disability Accommodations Not Approved by the DS Office**

Considerations

- When did the student bring forward the concerns? In what stage of the program is the student? What prompted the issue?
- Was the student informed of student rights and responsibilities regarding disability disclosure and accessing services? If so, when, how (e.g., e-mail, syllabus statement, in person), and by whom?
- Is the issue related to a newly identified disability? If so, what steps were taken to ensure that the student was aware of disability services (DS)? What are the circumstances around the newly identified disability?
- Is the faculty member new or an adjunct?
- What training has been provided to faculty members about their responsibilities to refer students to the DS office and only implement approved accommodations?
- Is there a liaison in the school/program who assists with these issues?
- What is the standard policy for approving accommodations?
- How long has the student been receiving the unapproved accommodations?
- How has the issue been brought to your attention?

(continued)

• **TABLE 8.1 Process When Faculty Provide Disability Accommodations Not Approved by the DS Office (continued)**

How to Resolve

- Listen to each party's version of events.
- Determine if the accommodation was provided in relation to a disability or for another reason (e.g., student had the flu, death in the family, etc.).
- Explain the standard policy for registering with the DS office and determining accommodations; point to the places where this policy is outlined (e.g., website, student handbook, orientation materials).
- Require that the student submit disability documentation and complete formal registration.
- Determine and implement accommodations, if appropriate, or explain to the student why any requested accommodations are not warranted.
- Document what was done, including all e-mail communication and notes from phone conversations and meetings.

Prevention Strategy

- Review policy for registering with the DS office and requesting accommodations—is it in writing and clear?
- Ensure written policy is easy to find by making it available in multiple places (e.g., DS office, school, and program websites; admissions information links to DS office page; course websites; student handbook; syllabus statement; acceptance letter; reminder e-mails to all students annually; etc.).
- Ensure the DS office is on the agenda for orientation programming, and that DS providers are able to introduce DS services and the process for registering to all incoming students.
- Review the current model for faculty training. Ensure that all new faculty, including adjuncts, are informed of their responsibilities. Consider an online training module that can be provided to faculty to complete independently (see Chapter 10 for an outline of dos and don'ts that can be used as a basis for faculty training).
- If a school/program liaison is in place, work with that person to improve notification to faculty and students about DS-related procedures in a format that works with the culture of that school. If no liaison is in place, consider implementing one (see Chapter 3 for more information about liaisons).

Issue: Faculty/Program Attitudes

Faculty and administrators' attitudes and knowledge of disability (or lack thereof) can contribute to complicated situations, often resulting in inappropriate comments or expectations regarding students with disabilities (see Table 8.2). In the health sciences, there is often an institutional expectation of excellence that is not easily translated to qualified students who happen to also have a disability. Attitudes based on previous negative experiences with the disability accommodations process (e.g., experiences with

• **TABLE 8.2 Process When Encountering Negative Attitudes From Faculty/Staff**

Considerations

- What is the faculty member's prior experience with disability?
- Has the faculty member worked with students who have disability accommodations before?
- What were those experiences? Positive? Negative?
- What is the general culture of the school/program toward students with disabilities?
- Is the student being held to the same standards as other students (higher or lower)?
- How does the faculty member perceive the role of the disability services (DS) office? Adversarial or collaborative?

How to Resolve

- Talk to the student, faculty, and others involved to fully understand the situation and identify (if possible) the source of attitudinal issues.
- Coach the student about how to self-advocate in situations involving inappropriate treatment; ensure that the student is aware of grievance procedures.
- Ensure that faculty understand that accommodations are intended to "level the playing field," not provide a crutch, minimize program performance standards, or subject students to greater scrutiny.
- Provide faculty with strategies for working with students with disabilities to ensure student privacy, respect, etc.

Prevention Strategy

- Provide training to faculty, including awareness of how students with disabilities might present in the academic environment, with strategies regarding how to provide a supportive environment for all students (see Chapter 8 on communication).
- Ensure that faculty and administrators understand the rights of students to privacy and confidentiality.
- Partner with employee disability services to educate faculty on employment accommodations versus academic accommodations to clarify expectations of students, especially in the clinical environment.
- Share examples of students with disabilities thriving in similar programs, and successful professionals with disabilities in the health sciences.

students, patients, staff, DS office) can also present challenges in terms of how complex situations are approached by faculty and administrators. It is difficult to undo perceptions of working with students with disabilities that are grounded in real-life negative experiences; however, a good start is to ensure that all parties clearly understand the DS process and their role therein and that all parties are equipped with communication tools for navigating complicated situations.

Conversely, a faculty member or administrator who has a family member with a disability may wish to become an ally for students with disabilities. Although well intentioned, there is always a risk that faculty might have preconceived notions about a student's ability, and as a result have unnecessarily low (or high) expectations based on his or her limited and personal understanding of what it means to be a person with a disability. Such faculty members or administrators may even have an unconscious tendency to "protect" students based on their close emotional connection to people "like them." When this happens, these allies become additional barriers. It is prudent to tread carefully when working with a faculty ally, to ensure everyone shares the same goals for supporting students with disabilities.

Issue: Student Perceived a Faculty Action as Discriminatory

Complications often stem from a perceived or actual incidence of discrimination (see Table 8.3). A student may claim that a faculty member discriminated against him or her or disclosed a disability without permission. This sometimes happens inadvertently, for example, when an accommodation letter is accidentally left sitting open on a computer, or intentionally, for example, if a faculty member mentions a student's disability when chastising the student in clinic for a delayed response to questions or poor attendance. Perceived discrimination can also result from a faculty member who expresses exasperation or frustration each time a student presents a letter of accommodation, or who makes derogatory statements about disability in general.

Discrimination also may take the form of faculty or administrators discouraging students from disclosing their disability because they believe it will be difficult to get a job in the future if their disability status is known.[1] In other cases, students may perceive discriminatory behavior from faculty who lack understanding of disability (e.g., only understand and recognize "visible" disabilities), doubt that a disability exists altogether, or have fundamental concerns about the concept of accommodations. As agents of the university, faculty have an obligation to behave in a nondiscriminatory manner and to make appropriate referrals to the DS office (see Chapters 1, 2, and 3) if a student discloses.

Claims of discrimination can be detrimental to the relationships between the student and fellow students, members of faculty, and department administrators. Even when issues are successfully resolved, relations can be so impaired that it negatively affects a student's performance. Most institutions have clearly defined procedures, points of contact, and processes to handle such complaints (see discussion in Chapter 1 on grievances and formal complaints). The DS provider and program administrators should be familiar with these offices and make appropriate referrals when necessary.

---

[1] North v. Widener University, 869 F. Supp. 2d 630 (E.D. Penn. 2012).

• **TABLE 8.3 Process When Student Claims Faculty Discrimination**

Considerations

- Who displayed the alleged discriminatory behavior (e.g., student, staff, or faculty)?
- What policies and procedures exist on campus regarding discrimination and harassment? Who is responsible for the policy/procedure?
- What channels exist for the student to pursue a complaint and/or mediation/resolution?
- Does the student want to pursue a formal complaint or merely resolve the immediate accommodation-related issues?
- Has the student already filed a formal complaint—if so, is it internal or external (e.g., with the Office for Civil Rights [OCR])?
- What steps have been taken to investigate the allegation thus far? What more investigation needs to be done? Who should undertake it?
- Who else should be involved in the resolution of the issue (e.g., faculty, other student support offices, administrators, other students)?

How to Resolve

- In writing, inform the student of the right to file a formal complaint (see Chapter 1).
- Make the student aware of all other channels for resolving concerns available on campus.
- Determine if the described incident must be reported to the office responsible for claims of discrimination, even if the student chooses not to report it (discuss with your supervisor, legal department, ombudsperson).
- Address any accommodation-related concerns that are within the DS office's purview.
- Refer the student to any other campus supports that may be of assistance (see Chapter 1).
- Document all discussions and actions in writing.

Prevention Strategy

- Suggest training for faculty regarding disability issues to avoid future problems (see Chapter 10's list of dos and don'ts, and Chapter 7, Tip 7.3, Ensuring Confidentiality of Student Information).
- Ensure a clear guide for addressing problems is available on the DS office website, including all available channels for informal and formal appeals and grievances.

Issue: Student Claims Implementation of Accommodations Was Inappropriate

Disagreements about how approved accommodations are implemented are not uncommon (see Table 8.4; see also Chapters 3 and 7 for further discussion of implementation of accommodations). When implementation is handled

- **TABLE 8.4 Process When Student Claims Implementation of Accommodations Was Inappropriate**

Considerations

- What is the student's perspective on the issue, and the perspective of others involved?
- What is the standard process that should have been followed? Where is that documented? Were all parties aware of it, and was it followed?
- Did the student complain to others, and if so, to whom and when? Was the DS office involved? What actions were taken to resolve the issues?
- Were communications and interactions related to the situation (e.g., accommodation requests and response to such requests) adequately documented?
- In addition to the responsible faculty member, is there a liaison who should be contacted first to discuss the issue?
- How well does the DS provider know the involved parties? What approaches have worked with them in the past?
- Has the student filed a formal complaint about the issue?
- Has there been an academic consequence resulting from the situation (e.g., has the student failed an exam or course, or been brought before an academic or professional standing committee as a result of the incident)?
- Is there legal precedent to provide guidance?

How to Resolve

- Discuss the concern with the student, faculty member(s), and school/program liaison to hear all perspectives on what happened.
- Review any documentation related to the situation (e.g., e-mail communication or other).
- Determine the appropriate resolution based on the facts of the situation:
  - If the student followed appropriate processes but faculty/school/program did not, the student should, in all likelihood, be given a second opportunity to attempt the requirement with appropriate accommodation.
  - If the student did not follow appropriate procedures, discuss with faculty/school whether a second attempt is warranted. This may be governed by factors such as how new the student is to the accommodation process or other mitigating factors.
  - Discuss with legal counsel and colleagues if unsure about how to proceed or if culpability is unclear.
- Implement the appropriate solution.
- Document the process, information, and resolution.
- Discuss the appropriate procedure and actions to be followed in the future with the faculty/school and student. Encourage all parties to contact the DS office (or school/program liaison if available) immediately with any concerns that arise.

(continued)

• **TABLE 8.4 Process When Student Claims Implementation of Accommodations Was Inappropriate (*continued*)**

Prevention Strategy

- Review policy and procedures for students and faculty/school for accessing accommodations. Are they clear, in writing, and available to students?
- Ensure all students who register with the DS office are given clear information about the processes for accessing accommodations.
- Ensure information for faculty and related FAQs about accommodations are clear and available on the web.
- Ensure adequate, ongoing training occurs with faculty members regarding their responsibilities for providing appropriate accommodations.
- If a school/program liaison is in place, work with the liaison to improve knowledge of providing appropriate accommodations to faculty. If no liaison is in place, consider implementing one (see Chapter 3 for more information about liaisons).

poorly, it can lead to accusations of unfair treatment, informal complaints, and even grievances. For example, a student may complain that the accommodation provided for testing was inadequate (e.g., noise in the environment, extended time not provided, lack of access to faculty to ask questions, computer system failure, etc.). In these situations, DS providers should assess the circumstances from the viewpoint of each party involved when determining an appropriate solution. If the accommodation was improperly implemented, a "retake" of the exam may be appropriate. The school or department's practices with respect to exam accommodations may need to be modified to avoid future issues. DS providers should take these opportunities to further educate faculty and staff on how to appropriately implement accommodations.

ISSUES THAT ORIGINATE WITH THE STUDENT

Many students experience challenges in the health sciences environment due to the large volume of new information, the variety of complex settings, and the competitive nature of the field. For the student with a disability, this transition is further complicated by the adjustments needed to navigate this new and complex environment, such as when and how to disclose a disability, navigate the school's DS system, and deal with faculty or program staff who may not understand the scope of their responsibilities to students with disabilities. It is important to make sure that students understand *their* role and responsibilities in the DS process and develop strong skills to advocate for their own needs.

Students invest an enormous amount of time and resources to get to this point in their education. For many students, admission to the program fulfills their hopes and dreams of becoming a doctor, nurse, physical therapist, or other health sciences professional, and completing the program successfully is paramount to their sense of self. When a student with a disability experiences academic difficulty, it may exacerbate fears about "inability" deeply seated in the student's disability identity. Thoughts of this nature can disrupt the student's new identity formation—that of budding health professional—and stall the student's ability to succeed, which can further complicate situations. It is helpful to remember these factors when seeking to understand the emotions and actions of students experiencing difficulty.

Issue: Late Disclosure of Disability

Disclosure of disability can be complicated (see Table 8.5; see also discussion in Chapter 3 on an individualized analysis of student needs, and discussion in Chapter 7 on effective disclosure). Students may hesitate to disclose a disability, given the stigma of disability in our society. As such, disclosure may only occur once a student experiences failure in a program. Hesitation to self-identify can delay critical conversations about accommodations, preplanning, and available supports. The resulting situation is particularly complicated because universities are not obligated to accommodate a student until the student formally self-discloses a disability and requests accommodation,[2] nor are they obligated to readmit a dismissed student if the student fails to do so.[3] Although it is not legally required, some students are given second chances—for example, when a previously high-performing student sustains a traumatic injury or receives a new diagnosis. Decisions about second chances are not so clear, however, in situations where the student's past performance was average, or for students who struggled academically and in the clinical environment until a formal diagnosis was made. Further, it may be difficult to assess whether remediation or a second chance is appropriate for students whose conditions result in periods of complicated symptoms or who exhibit unprofessional behavior. The role of the DS provider is to ensure that an *objective and consistent approach* is taken when evaluating each situation.

---

[2] Shamonsky v. Saint Luke's School of Nursing, 2008 U.S. Dist. LEXIS 20426 (E.D. Pa. 2008). College of Saint Rose, Case No. 02-00-2055 (OCR Region II 2001); Texas Woman's University, Case No. 06-00-2038 (OCR Region VI 2000); Western Michigan University, Case No. 15-99-2016 (OCR Region XV 2000); A.T. Still University, Case No. 07-09-2017 (OCR Region VII 2009).
[3] Leacock v. Temple University School of Medicine, 1998 U.S. Dist. LEXIS 18871 (E.D. Pa. 1998).

- **TABLE 8.5 Process When Student Makes a Late Disclosure of Disability**

Considerations

- When did the student first disclose a disability? What prompted the disclosure?
- What stage of the program is the student in?
- Was the student informed of the rights and responsibilities regarding disability disclosure and accessing services? If so, when, how (e.g., e-mail, syllabus statement, in person), and by whom?
- Is this a newly identified disability? If so, what steps were taken to ensure that the student was aware of disability services (DS)? What are the circumstances regarding the newly identified disability?
- Is this a situation that would benefit from involving legal counsel (e.g., is the student about to be dismissed or receive academic sanctions; has the student indicated he or she plans to take legal action)?
- How entrenched are the relationships between the parties involved?
- Were communications and interactions related to the situation adequately documented (e.g., disclosure of disability, referral to DS office, notification and warnings of poor performance, accommodation requests and response to such requests)?
- If the student has been dismissed (or dismissal is imminent), were there opportunities prior to dismissal for the student and program officials to resolve the issues? If yes, how were these addressed?

How to Resolve

- Determine the circumstances surrounding the disclosure to identify the best course of action.
- If the student has not yet been dismissed:
  - Direct the student to follow the standard DS registration process—submit documentation, request accommodations, and determine accommodations (see Chapters 2 and 3 for a full description).
  - Implement approved accommodations.
  - Manage any ancillary issues, such as helping faculty and staff to understand the sometimes fluid nature of disability and the reasons students may disclose late in the program, assisting in repairing the relationship between student and faculty, and identifying possible needs, such as offering the student a new clinical setting instead of returning to a place where things went badly and relationships are irreparable.
  - Educate the student about the accommodations process and the need to come forward immediately to request further accommodations. Explain that accommodations are not retroactive.
  - If any issues regarding a failure to refer the student to the DS office promptly for consideration of accommodations were identified, educate faculty and staff about their obligation to do so.
- If the student has been dismissed (or dismissal is imminent):
  - Educate the student about the standard DS registration and accommodation request process. Explain that the school is not required to provide retroactive accommodations.

(continued)

• **TABLE 8.5 Process When Student Makes a Late Disclosure of Disability** (*continued*)

How to Resolve

- Direct the student to follow the standard DS registration process if the student would like to formalize his or her disability status.
- If requested, provide information to the academic standing committee or others regarding the standard DS registration process, and principles regarding the lack of obligation to provide retroactive accommodations.
- If any issues were identified with the student not being referred to the DS office immediately for consideration of accommodations, ensure that academic standing or review committees are aware of this breach of policy and that it should be duly considered before taking adverse action against the student.
- Direct the student to any applicable appeal or grievance procedures.
- Document all conversations and actions carefully.

Prevention Strategy

- Ensure faculty and staff of the university (including support offices such as health and mental health services, learning and writing support, multicultural affairs, etc.) are aware of DS services, understand their obligation to refer students who disclose a disability to the DS office immediately, and understand the need to document the referral in writing.
- Ensure all students are notified early and often about DS services, and how to contact the DS office to register and request accommodations.
- Be open to meeting with students to discuss registration processes and requirements. Document all discussions and information provided.

Issue: A Student Who Is Successful in the Didactic Environment Experiences Difficulty With Transitioning to the Clinical Environment

For some students, the unique demands of the clinical environment often reveal disability-related issues that were unexpected, disabilities not formally disclosed or diagnosed, or issues that did not require accommodation in the past (see Table 8.6). For example, a student with autism spectrum disorder who performed well in the didactic environment suddenly begins having difficulties in the clinical environment, failing to understand the "unwritten rules" of professionalism and interpersonal interactions; or, a pharmacy student with a visual/spatial disability who has significant difficulty navigating the complex physical environment of a large city hospital is therefore continuously late for rounds and patient meetings as a result of getting lost. Another example might be a nursing student with a learning disability who relied on the ability to proofread writing assignments for class, but has significant difficulty writing accurate, understandable, and timely case notes and is in danger of failing a rotation.

Clinical demands often reveal time management issues that were easily resolved in the didactic setting with well-developed compensatory skills. New or unexpected demands can also exacerbate preexisting conditions in the context of the clinical environment. For example, a student with mild hearing difficulties who compensated well for lectures may encounter major barriers in a busy and noisy hospital environment such as an emergency room, where the failure to accurately hear directives can put patient care in jeopardy.

These concerns, when addressed immediately and appropriately accommodated, can represent a simple bump in the road. However, in the worst cases, these situations fester, the student's performance suffers, relationships with faculty and peers break down, and the DS office is not alerted to the issue until the student's standing in the program is at risk. DS providers can avoid these situations by attending orientations and presenting a thorough overview of DS services, along with some examples of how DS works to support students in the didactic and clinical environments. Faculty and clinical staff members should be made aware that accommodations are subject to change as the student encounters different environments and that they need to be flexible and work closely with the DS provider to implement accommodations. Students should be encouraged to disclose early to minimize bumps in the road and ensure a smooth transition from the didactic to the clinical setting.

• **TABLE 8.6 Process When Student Experiences Difficulty in the Transition to the Clinical Environment**

Considerations
<ul><li>What prompted the issue?</li><li>Was the student informed of student rights and responsibilities regarding disability disclosure and accessing services? If so, when, how (e.g., e-mail, syllabus statement, in person), and by whom?</li><li>Did the student notify any others of the difficulty experienced, and if so, to whom and when? Was the disability services (DS) office involved? What actions were taken to resolve the issues thus far?</li><li>Did the school follow due process in addressing issues of performance (e.g., a transparent process of progressive remediation, informed of the right to appeal a dismissal)? Are these processes in writing online and in the student handbook?</li><li>Is this issue related to a newly identified disability? If so, what steps were taken to ensure that the student was aware of DS services? What are the circumstances regarding the newly identified disability?</li><li>Is this primarily a disability issue, or is disability secondary to the concern?</li><li>Who are the parties involved, and how well does the DS provider know them? Is there a program or school liaison who should be contacted first?</li><li>How entrenched is the relationship between the parties involved? Would it be helpful to involve other people?</li></ul>

(continued)

• TABLE 8.6 Process When Student Experiences Difficulty in the Transition to the Clinical Environment (*continued*)

How to Resolve

- Listen to each party's version of events.
- If the student has not yet registered with the DS office, explain the process, collect documentation of disability, and determine appropriate accommodations (see Chapters 2, 3, and 4).
- If the student is registered with the DS office, explore additional accommodations that may help in the clinical environment (see Chapters 3 and 4).
- Address any ancillary concerns, such as misunderstandings and frustrations surrounding the situation. Determine if relationships at the clinical site are irreparable or if education and support are needed with staff at the site to ensure the student is able to reintegrate.
- Determine if time away from clinical work is needed to build skills, develop compensatory strategies, receive treatment, or obtain equipment, and work with the student and school to organize this, if possible.

Prevention Strategy

- Begin discussions about clinical accommodations with all registered students early. Send a reminder with a suggested timeline for discussions to all registered students before clinical placements are made.
- Organize shadowing or informational opportunities for students to get a better sense of what is required in the clinic, to determine what barriers may exist and what accommodations would be needed.
- Ensure students know to come to the DS office to discuss disability-related difficulties (or changes in status) early to determine if additional accommodations are needed, before academic difficulty occurs.
- Ensure all students, clinical coordinators, and clinical faculty are aware of DS services and related services, and know to consult with the DS provider if they suspect a disability-related concern is present.
- Include information about DS services and the need to register and request accommodations in clinical handbooks.

Issue: Student Needs Time Off Due to Disability

In the health sciences, the "lock-step" nature of the curriculum may create further barriers and stressors. Students often feel unable to take time off to tend to disability-related health issues and may fear that leaving the program means losing health care coverage when they need it most. At the same time, staying in a demanding program and not performing well can lead to dismissal and exacerbated health issues. Taking time off often causes a student to become 1 year behind the initial cohort, lose a spot in a program, or have to reapply for admission to the program. These undesirable options often drive students to stay in a program, even while their performance and health are slipping.

Additionally, faculty and administrators may experience increased levels of frustration in attempting to support these students, particularly if the students are not communicating with the program about their circumstances. DS providers should talk with program leadership to develop methods of supporting short- or long-term leaves of absence, when warranted by a disability- or health-related issue. Often, the no-leave policy (or waiting 1 year) is not based on curriculum or essential requirements of the program, but on "the way it has always been done." If well planned, students, administrators, and DS providers can work to extend—or expand—a student's program in a way that works with the student's disability-related needs (see Table 8.7).

• **TABLE 8.7 Process When a Student Needs Time Off Due to Disability**

Considerations

- What is the standard policy for medical leaves of absence?
- What is the nature of the curriculum? Is there room for flexibility, or for adjusting expectations with respect to "time to completion"? If not, why not?
- At what point in the program is the student requesting time away? Does this make a difference in terms of how easily the request can be granted?
- Is the student already registered with the disability services (DS) office? Does the student (and the program) understand that a leave-of-absence request could be a reasonable accommodation?
- What impact will the absence have on the student's learning progress?
- Are there client/patient relationships that could be impacted by the student's absence?
- What impact will the student's absence have on the progress of other students (e.g., does the program use a patient-based, collaborative learning approach)?
- Is there any precedent for this having been granted before, perhaps for nondisability-related reasons?
- Who will have final "say" in granting the student's request? Is there a formalized process for reviewing such requests, and is DS involved if it is a disability-related reason?
- What will the student need to do to resume studies following an absence? Is there a reapplication process? If so, why?
- Has the student's performance already been negatively impacted? Is it salvageable?

How to Resolve

- Identify the standard leave-of-absence policy, and whether the student's request is addressed by that policy.
- Determine how much flexibility the program can allow. If it cannot allow flexibility, be prepared with substantive reasons why it would fundamentally alter the program to change it in the way requested.
- Where there is room for flexibility, be clear as to how much flexibility is possible, what the limits are, and why.

(continued)

• **TABLE 8.7 Process When a Student Needs Time Off Due to Disability** (*continued*)

How to Resolve

• Involve faculty members, with the student's knowledge and consent, to develop a plan for reentry following an approved absence.
• Work with the student to develop a plan going forward: Is there potential for future requests for leave of absence? How can this be prevented (or can it)? Develop a clear agreement as to expectations for both the student and the program that are reasonable and fair.

Prevention Strategy

• Evaluate all policies and procedures with respect to leaves of absence, time-to-degree expectations, and program structure with the program to determine what, if any, changes can be made to allow for program flexibility.
• Ensure students are informed, early and routinely, of their rights and options with respect to program flexibility.
• Include information about policies related to leave of absence and program resumption in the program materials/clinical handbooks.
• Discuss policies regarding student health insurance plans and provisions for coverage during medical leaves of absence with relevant administrators. Explain the effect on students with disabilities (particularly chronic health conditions). Suggest consideration of a reasonable period for continuing health insurance at the same rate during that time (i.e., not at COBRA insurance rates).

Issue: Student Exhibits Unprofessional or Unsafe Behavior, Attributes It to a Disability

Professionalism is a core competency in most health sciences programs (see Chapter 7 for more information). Claims of disability do not negate reasonable expectations of professional behavior; students with disabilities are expected to adhere to the same standards of professionalism as their nondisabled peers (see Case Example 8.1).

CASE EXAMPLE 8.1 • *Halpern v. Wake Forest University Health Sciences*[4]

A student with attention deficit hyperactivity disorder (ADHD) and an anxiety disorder was dismissed from medical school for unprofessional behavior, including rudeness, inability to accept criticism, multiple unexcused absences and tardiness, consistent failure to meet deadlines, and

(continued)

---

[4] Halpern v. Wake Forest University Health Sciences, 669 F.3d 454 (4th Cir. 2012).

CASE EXAMPLE 8.1 • *Halpern v. Wake Forest University Health Sciences (continued)*

belligerence. During the dismissal process, he claimed that his behavior was attributable to his disability and associated medication, and that the university had not adequately accommodated him.

The court ruled that because professionalism was an essential requirement of the program, the student must be able to meet the professionalism standards. If he is unable to do so, the court held, he is not otherwise qualified to be in the program, and dismissal was proper.

Inconsistent, vague, or subjectively defined standards of professionalism complicate the assessment of when and how a disability contributes to a student's failure to meet standards. Standards of professional conduct should include clear, objective statements with respect to confidentiality, interpersonal skill, responsibility, integrity, and, in the case of clinical/health-related programs, patient care and safety.

With respect to patient care and safety, programs should have established procedures that address situations when a student's behavior is found to be so extreme as to constitute a threat to the safety and health of others. As long as the determination of student behavior is based on an assessment of actual risk (using reasonable judgment) and not driven by stereotypes or perceptions, and as long as the risk cannot be mitigated by "modification of policies, practices or procedures, or by the provision of auxiliary aids and services,"[5] the program or institution can take steps to remove a student from the setting or take other appropriate measures to protect patient safety (see Table 8.8).

ISSUES THAT ORIGINATE WITH THE DISABILITY SERVICES OFFICE

Issue: Historical DS Records Are Incomplete, and a Student Is Facing Dismissal and Claiming a Complication Related to Disability Accommodation

It is not unusual for DS providers to join a university and inherit inadequately documented case files, unclear policies and procedures, and, at times, poorly managed issues. A student may claim a history of being supported in a way that is not well documented in the student's file. Or the accommodations granted may have been documented, but ill advised, leaving the new DS provider in a sticky situation. Alternatively, the DS office may

[5] 28 C.F.R. § 35.130; 28 C.F.R. § 36.208.

• **TABLE 8.8 Process When Student Exhibits Unprofessional Behavior**

Considerations

- Are there clear, objectively defined statements for what constitutes professional conduct? Are these included as core competencies in the technical standards?
- What is the culture within the institution or program? Does it model the standards as they are defined? What consequences are there for faculty members who do not uphold the standards of professionalism expected of the students?
- Are the expectations for student behavior consistently applied throughout the program?
- What are the consequences for students for unprofessional conduct? How is this defined? Is it clear and is it stated in objective terms?
- Does the program follow due process in addressing issues of performance (e.g., a transparent process of progressive remediation, informed of the right to appeal a dismissal)? Are these processes in writing (e.g., online and in the student handbook)? Have they been followed?
- Has communication to the student about unprofessional conduct (notifications and warnings regarding unacceptable performance) been adequately documented?
- Is the unprofessional conduct putting at risk the safety and/or health of others (patients, fellow students)? If so, what steps need to be taken?

How to Resolve

- Determine if due process has been followed in addressing the student's performance/lack of professionalism.
- Ensure that the student understands the expectations: What the standards are, why they exist, and what consequences are likely when the standards are ignored.
- Determine if there is any relationship between the nature of the disability and the observed actions. If there is, assess how this may impact the student's participation in the program going forward.
- Determine if the student's behavior is placing patient care/safety at risk. If so, be prepared to take appropriate measures to protect patient care and safety.
- Ensure that all communication with the student regarding assessment of performance, feedback, and actions taken is thoroughly documented.

Prevention Strategy

- Within the program technical standards, include clear, objective statements regarding professional conduct with respect to confidentiality, interpersonal skills, responsibility, integrity, and patient care and safety (when appropriate).
- Ensure that application of the standards is consistent and unambiguous throughout the program.
- Ensure that students are provided with consistent, clear feedback regarding their performance, and document all feedback thoroughly.
- Ensure that adequate, ongoing training occurs for faculty members on the importance of objective, consistent feedback regarding performance.

be contacted because a student is about to be dismissed, and it is clear that the student has a complicated history with the DS office that is not well documented and possibly mismanaged. In some cases there may be a gap in the records available from the student's faculty/program and the DS office regarding how accommodations were determined and implemented. This creates even more challenges for a new DS provider charged with deciphering complex cases.

In these cases, DS providers should collect any and all documentation, including documentation submitted by the student. Then, the provider should do a thorough interview with all parties and begin to document the respective accounts of history and any specific or current issues. It is also wise to include the school's legal counsel and possibly the risk management office, if there is one, in the process of resolution. See Table 8.9 for more details on this process.

• TABLE 8.9 Process When DS Records Are Incomplete and Student Is Facing Dismissal

Considerations

- What records are available?
- Does any other office or university official have copies of communication regarding the situation (e.g., a school/program liaison), or does the student? Can historical e-mail records be recovered?
- Who was involved? Can the parties be contacted/interviewed for additional insight?
- What are the program policies around dismissal? Were they adhered to, including proper notification to the student?
- Prior to dismissal, was the student provided with appropriate notification? If applicable, was remediation offered?

How to Resolve

- Gather all available notes, files, and correspondence.
- Meet with all parties to gather additional details about the student's accommodations and their implementation.
- Ask the student for a timeline of events, to add to information gathered internally.
- Assess whether the disability services (DS) office and the program followed policies and procedures.
- If policies and procedures were not followed, consult with program leaders and/or consult the school's legal counsel to determine if additional accommodations can be made to provide the student with an equal chance to demonstrate the knowledge/skills in question (leading up to dismissal).

(continued)

• TABLE 8.9 Process When DS Records Are Incomplete and Student
Is Facing Dismissal (*continued*)

Prevention Strategy

- Keep good-quality records of communication with students, and any communications about the student with liaisons, faculty, and so on.
- Maintain records of meetings with students who inquire about DS services but do not register.
- When staff leave the university, maintain access to their e-mail records regarding students and accommodations.
- Consider utilizing a database system that keeps records of all communications and determinations of student accommodations in one place and is easily searchable.
- Ensure that administration, faculty, staff, and others involved understand the institution's responsibilities to students with disabilities and that they know what the process is for DS and implementation of accommodations.

WHEN TO INVOLVE THE "HIGHER-UPs"

Before complex situations arise, it is important to have a good idea of who should be involved in resolving them. Resolving issues on a low level is ideal, and at times the best strategy is a preventative one, which requires ongoing consultation with campus partners when complexities begin to arise. However, when things get difficult, it is important to partner with the appropriate offices (e.g., campus legal counsel, Americans with Disabilities Act [ADA] coordinator, risk management) to consult on cases and help to push for early resolution.

Understanding Campus Policies and Practices

It is essential that the DS provider understand campus policies regarding resources for resolving situations and associated complaint procedures. There may be multiple avenues to resolution that are department- or school-specific, in addition to university-wide grievance procedures. Policies should be clear, easily found on the university website, and known to key personnel. If policies are unclear or unavailable, DS providers should work with the respective schools to develop and disseminate them (refer to Chapter 1, Know Your Campus Resources, for more information about key partners on campus). See Best Practice 8.2 for key policies DS providers should be familiar with.

BEST PRACTICE 8.2
Key Policies Disability Services (DS) Offices Should Know

- Appeals of disability accommodation requests
- Complaints of discrimination
- Complaints about access

When a situation does arise, it can be helpful to give campus partners, particularly campus legal counsel, a "head's up." Although DS professionals are employed to serve as campus experts on inclusion of students with disabilities, they should not be asked (or tempted) to resolve complex and potentially litigious situations on their own. Consulting with the legal department, ADA coordinator, or other relevant office on campus early helps ensure campus guidelines are followed (see Best Practice 8.3 and Case Example 8.2). Legal counsel can also be helpful in reviewing correspondence to students or staff/faculty regarding contentious or high-stakes issues. Support from the legal office can more forcefully address staff or faculty members who are blocking access through discriminatory behavior or actions. At times, a call from the legal office may be the most effective means for getting everyone on the same page.

BEST PRACTICE 8.3
Notifying Supervisors and Legal Counsel

Disability services (DS) providers should notify their supervisor and legal counsel immediately when:

- There is a claim of discrimination.
- A faculty or staff member has refused to provide standard accommodations.
- A student threatens legal action.

CASE EXAMPLE 8.2 • Student Concern Requires Bringing in "Higher-Ups"

Scenario:
A student with a well-documented history of attention deficit hyperactivity disorder (ADHD) is eligible for exam accommodations including the provision of quiet, separate space for exams. After taking a final exam in an environment that allegedly does not meet the need for a "quiet, separate space," the student approaches the disability services (DS) provider with an informal complaint.

The student's complaint is about the environment in which the exam was administered, but also includes frustration about the lack of sincerity shown by faculty members toward the student's disability and need for accommodations. The student believes that certain members of faculty are dismissive of the student's claim of disability, noting that they have violated the student's right to privacy through their communications and voiced their opinions that the accommodations result in an unfair advantage.

(continued)

CASE EXAMPLE 8.2 • Student Concern Requires Bringing in "Higher-Ups" (continued)

The student also notes that a department committee meeting is being convened to address "failure to progress," pointing out that one member of the committee is the faculty member who administered the exam. The student raises concern of discrimination.

The response of one of the faculty members, when informed of the student's complaint, is to describe the student as "abrasive and challenging of authority." The faculty member also expresses concerns about the student's potential as a future health professional, alleging problems with professional conduct.

Considerations:
The student's complaint reflects problems with faculty attitudes, implementation of accommodations, *and* a potential claim of discrimination, while at the same time at least one faculty member has identified concerns about the student's behavior with respect to professional conduct. By the time the complaint has been brought forward, the degree to which the involved parties have become entrenched in their respective positions makes a positive outcome unlikely using an informal process.

Resolution:
Ensure the student is aware of rights to file a formal complaint, as well as other avenues for resolving concerns on campus. Ensure that all parties are included in discussions and that all perspectives are heard. Bring in the appropriate campus partners (e.g., equal employment opportunity [EEO] coordinator and/or Americans with Disabilities Act [ADA] coordinator, legal counsel) to assist in responding to the claim of discrimination. Determine what happened (e.g., who followed appropriate procedures?) and propose solutions. Tease out distinctions between concrete situations (failure to implement accommodation, clear evidence of substandard conduct) and perceived actions (attitudes). If an accommodation was inappropriately handled, a retake of an exam may, in fact, be a reasonable solution. If the student's behavior does not meet professional standards, clear communication regarding the consequence of such behavior must occur.

Challenging Historical Practices

If the historical chain of command for consultation and resolution of issues does not seem to be well structured, it may be appropriate for the DS provider to develop a new, tightly structured chain of command for resolving complex issues (see Case Example 8.3). For example, if there is a history of complex situations that have not gone well, including a history of litigation with clear patterns regarding how situations have been managed, it would be important to bring the related offices together to discuss how a different structure and procedure might help to better resolve situations in the future.

CASE EXAMPLE 8.3 • Historical Procedures Need Reevaluation

Scenario:
A newly hired disability services (DS) provider is identified as the person on campus responsible for managing services and accommodations for students with disabilities. In her first month on campus, she is faced with multiple difficult situations regarding students with disabilities who have recently been dismissed.

Considerations:
She comes to understand that the previous DS manager was told to bring concerns to the vice chancellor for student affairs, who had overseen the DS office for some time. It was not common practice to include campus counsel at an early stage. When she looks into the situations surrounding dismissals, it becomes clear that key information was often not evaluated early in the process, which led to hasty dismissals, and subsequent complaints from students.

Resolution:
The DS provider brings together key campus partners—campus counsel, the vice chancellor, liaisons from the relevant schools, the Americans with Disabilities Act (ADA) coordinator, and a representative from risk management and the ombudsperson's office to discuss the pattern of circumstances and to jointly determine a more suitable practice for managing situations going forward.

ESTABLISHING GOOD PARTNERSHIPS

It pays to develop good relationships with partners on campus. Collaborative approaches to complex or complicated cases ensure that resolutions are well informed. DS providers should begin cultivating a network of liaisons across schools or academic programs (see Chapter 3 for further discussion of liaisons). The identified liaison can provide invaluable insight into specific programs and students in addition to serving as a champion for students with disabilities, especially when situations present challenges.

In addition to maintaining relationships with liaisons, it is helpful to meet with campus partners from key offices such as the equal employment opportunity (EEO) office, ombudsperson's office, ADA coordinator, campus counsel, risk management, and so forth to learn more about their roles, their historical relationship with the DS office, their responsibility in complex disability-related cases, whether they have a standard role in managing complaints, and if they have any history of complaints related to students with disabilities. This will provide a sense of what to expect when a complicated situation arises, and will help to solidify a strong team approach to sorting out difficult cases (see Case Example 8.4).

CASE EXAMPLE 8.4 • Whose Responsibility Is It?

Scenario:
A student who requires double time for exams, who is also Sabbath observant, comes to the disability services (DS) office because a 6-hour take-home exam is scheduled for a Friday. Given the extra time, the student has 12 hours to take the exam.

Although students are required to return the exam before Monday morning, the allotted extra time, in conjunction with the student duties as an observer of the Sabbath (no work from sundown Friday to sundown Saturday), does not allow for the accommodated time.

The student spoke to the professor, who stated that there are no exceptions.

Considerations:
The student views this as a disability-related concern; however, in reality it may be more clearly framed as a religious discrimination issue that is compounded by the inability to access the allotted accommodation (extra time). Layered situations like this are often new to schools and require a team approach.

Collaboration:
It may be helpful to gather the responsible person on campus for issues of religious discrimination as well as the responsible person for exam-structuring policies (it may be the professor or another member of the school's administration), to make clear that a conflict exists.

Resolution:
Have a group discussion to clarify the reasoning of the established time frame. Determine a compromise that allows the student equal access to the exam, without compromising his need for religious observance, short-changing the exam time allotted, or creating an unreasonably exhausting time frame for completion of a long exam.

Working collaboratively on these issues provides an opportunity to challenge the tight structure of the schedule and propose a universal design solution (flexible schedule to accommodate disability, family circumstances, etc.) so that future conflicts are more easily addressed.

CONCLUSION

This chapter mentions some of the most recurrent problems that originate with faculty, students, and DS offices. It provides a framework of questions that need to be considered as diverse problems emerge, and offers strategies designed to prevent ongoing complications in the future. Table 8.10 notes the five guiding principles of this chapter, and the principles DS offices should follow to ensure best practice during difficult situations:

• **TABLE 8.10 Tips for Disability Services (DS) Providers**

1. Develop clear policies and procedures	Ensure that policies and procedures for registering with the DS office and accessing approved accommodations are clear and well documented (see Chapters 2 and 3, and Table 3.1, for more information).
	Ensure policies and procedures related to DS are provided in writing, explained, and signed off by students to acknowledge receipt when they register with the DS office. Make sure that these materials are accessible to all students.
	Review policies and procedures annually to ensure they are up to date. Consider having liaisons, faculty, and students provide feedback to ensure they are clear and concise.
	Ensure that information about the DS office, and associated policies and procedures, can be easily found on the university website and are referenced in student handbooks, admissions pages, acceptance letters, and other formats.
	DS providers should make themselves aware of specific course/program competencies, technical standards of the program, and applicable college-wide policies.
2. Maintain a balanced approach	Before taking action, first get a clear picture of the situation by taking the time to understand and empathize with each party's experience and report of the events, including the student's.
3. Document carefully	To ensure accountability and transparency, send summaries of conversations and meetings to everyone involved to confirm that records are accurate.
	Keep notes of meetings with students, and discussions about student cases with faculty and administrators.
4. Differentiate between disability issues and other student concerns	When problem solving, separate disability concerns from other standard student concerns, and refer students to the appropriate university official to address nondisability-related situations.
	Where a disability-related issue is enmeshed with a standard student concern, work in partnership with the other campus official to address the situation (see Case Example 8.4).
	Consult with legal counsel, risk management, and central administration to clearly define the role of the DS office and communicate this to the participants in the disability services process.

(continued)

• **TABLE 8.10 Tips for Disability Services (DS) Providers (*continued*)**

5. Collaborate with peer institutions and organizations	Actively engage in listservs, forums, and professional organizations to expand your scope of knowledge to better address issues as they arise (see Appendix 9.1 in Chapter 9 for a list of resources available).
	When new or complex situations present themselves, reach out to these supports and colleagues for advice and guidance.
	Use professional relationships with peer institutions to establish regional alliances and policy precedents.
	Run difficult cases by peers in order to support or check actions toward resolution.

Debunking Myths and Addressing Legitimate Concerns

Timothy Montgomery, Lisa M. Meeks,
and Elisa Laird-Metke

INTRODUCTION

This chapter focuses on some prevailing myths regarding students with disabilities in health sciences and medical education programs. It addresses five of the most common myths, exposing them as "false notions," while discussing the legitimate concerns that underlie them, and how disability accommodations can be created that will provide access without diminishing the outcomes for students or patients.

WHAT IS A MYTH?

Myths and misconceptions about disability are common. In this context, *myth* refers to inaccurate assumptions about disability that are often triggered by fear, lack of understanding, or prejudice. Those working in higher education, and in particular health sciences and medical education, are not immune to these beliefs—in fact, all individuals carry their own set of biases that may be hidden even to themselves (Ross, 2014). Although they are incorrect, myths may nevertheless inform work with students with disabilities and beliefs about ability or disability accommodations; therefore, it is important to confront myths to ensure that decisions about accommodations are grounded in the facts about a student's abilities and disability-related needs, and the university's legal obligations.

MYTH #1: STUDENTS WITH DISABILITIES CANNOT FULFILL THE RIGOROUS REQUIREMENTS OF HEALTH SCIENCES PROGRAMS

Meeting the program requirements in the health sciences is an expectation for all students, with or without disabilities. When determining accommodations, it is critical for both students and disability services (DS) providers to review the academic and technical standards for each program. In fact, many programs require students to sign a form indicating they have read, understand, and can meet these requirements before they begin their education. As discussed previously, well-crafted academic and technical standards focus on the behavior or competency a student must exhibit (see the section "Technical Standards" in Chapter 3). *How* a student meets the technical standards is where the accommodation discussion begins.

Often, the initial response from faculty is that a requested disability accommodation simply cannot be made. However, a denial of a requested accommodation is appropriate only after a careful review has determined that creating an accommodation would have the effect of excusing a student from an essential requirement of the program.[1] If told that a particular activity or standard cannot be accommodated, it is critical for DS providers to respectfully inquire about the reasoning, to open up a dialogue about *why* an activity or standard is essential, and how the desired educational outcome might be measured another way. Often, it turns out that a requirement is in place solely because it has traditionally been done that way, and when opened up for discussion, the parties come to realize that the same skill could be acquired by another method (see Example 9.1 and Best Practice 9.1).

EXAMPLE 9.1 • Release From Overnight Call

> **Concern:** Students who must maintain good sleep hygiene due to their disability may request a waiver of overnight call duties. Students released from overnight rotations are not getting the same educational experience as their peers.
> **Educational Objective:** Medical students are required to do overnight call because it is part of the medical school experience, and because it trains students on how the medical facility operates when there are fewer personnel on staff (e.g., when a physician must follow a patient from admission through release, and limited specialists are on hand).
> **Response:** Disability services (DS) providers should explore whether the same essential learning objective can be met by having the student do call at another time when staffing levels are similar to those overnight, such as during a weekend day.

---

[1] Zukle v. Regents of the University of California, 166 F.3d 1041 (9th Cir. 1999).

BEST PRACTICE 9.1
The Interactive Process

The interactive process to determine whether a disability accommodation can be created must take place even if the decision makers suspect that an accommodation is likely not possible. The parties involved in the interactive process need to:

1. Determine the essential learning objectives of the practice for which accommodations are sought
2. Determine whether those objectives can be achieved in an alternate, but equally effective way that would provide disability access
3. Explore and discuss all possible options
4. Make determinations as to whether particular accommodations are reasonable
5. Document, in writing, the options that were considered and why they were rejected

(See also the section "Key Considerations in Accommodation Determinations" in Chapter 3.)

MYTH #2: PROVIDING ACCOMMODATIONS TO STUDENTS WITH DISABILITIES COMPROMISES PATIENT SAFETY

Patient safety is one of the most fundamental aspects of health care, and accommodations for students with disabilities should *never* compromise patient safety. However, patient safety concerns must be legitimate—they cannot be based on conjecture or worst-case scenarios.[2] The Americans with Disabilities Act (ADA) regulations provide very specific guidance for creating accommodations where patient safety is involved:

> In determining whether an individual poses a direct threat to the health or safety of others, a public accommodation must make an individualized assessment, based on reasonable judgment that relies on current medical knowledge or on the best available objective evidence, to ascertain: the nature, duration, and severity of the risk; the probability that the potential injury will actually occur; and whether reasonable modifications of policies, practices, or procedures or the provision of auxiliary aids or services will mitigate the risk.[3]

Technical standards can be used to determine whether a genuine safety risk exists; well-written technical standards will focus on the behavior or

---

[2] 28 C.F.R. 35.130(h).
[3] 28 C.F.R. 36.208.

competency that each student must demonstrate, as well as practices to ensure the safety and wellness of each patient. (See Example 9.2; see also the section "Technical Standards" in Chapter 3.)

EXAMPLE 9.2 • Technical Standards

An example of a well-written technical standard from Georgetown University's School of Nursing & Health Studies (n.d.) for its Nurse Anesthesia Program, which unambiguously defines what is required of all students—including those with disabilities—and sets a clearly measurable standard for the skill that must be demonstrated is as follows:

Possessing sufficient motor strength to mask, ventilate, intubate, and conduct manual ventilation to provide for sufficient oxygenation of the patient. (n.d., section 4)

As long as a student can perform the described tasks effectively, even with a disability accommodation (e.g., a stool for a person of short stature to reach the patient), safety will not be compromised.

Established safety protocols, processes, checks, and procedures are in place for all students in medical and health sciences programs, regardless of whether they have a disability or need accommodations. As long as these are followed consistently, providing disability accommodations will not endanger patients. See Examples 9.3, 9.4, and 9.5.

EXAMPLE 9.3 • A Deaf Student in Surgical Clerkship

Concern: A student who cannot hear will not be able to receive communication from supervisors in the operating room (OR). Much of the communication is oral, and masks cover the surgical team's mouths. A student who cannot hear directions in the OR cannot assist with surgery, because it will endanger the patient if the student cannot be guided throughout the procedure.

Educational Objective: The student must be able to receive instructions while the surgery is occurring.

Response: Disability services (DS) providers must determine whether the student can get access to spoken communication in the OR. Brainstorm ideas with faculty for facilitating communication in the OR environment, and investigate alternative communication options, such as using sign language interpreters or using communication access real-time translation (CART) to provide a transcript of the spoken communication on a tablet computer or projected onto a wall in the room. Include the student in the discussions to get feedback on what ideas will provide the most effective access.

EXAMPLE 9.4 • Medical Student With Seizure Disorder in Surgical Clerkship

Concern: A medical student with a seizure disorder could have a seizure during a surgical procedure, endangering the patient.

Educational Objective: The student must be able to observe and assist during the surgical clerkship.

Response: Any student or staff member, even one with no disability, could become suddenly ill or black out during a procedure. The established safety precautions and procedures already in place to address sudden incapacitations for medical personnel in surgical settings should apply to a student with a seizure disorder. An institution may inquire about how often a student experiences seizures, and make safety determinations based on this information. The school may not be required to allow a student who, for example, experiences grand mal seizures every hour to participate in a surgical rotation. However, the fear that a student with a well-managed seizure disorder *might* have a seizure while in surgery is an insufficient basis on which to prevent the student from participating in a surgical rotation.

EXAMPLE 9.5 • Pharmacy Student With Dyslexia

Concern: Pharmacy students with learning disabilities that affect how they read and write language and numbers might dose or dispense medication incorrectly.

Educational Objective: The student must be able to accurately dispense medication and adjust doses as necessary.

Response: There are safeguards and procedures in place for *all* medical professionals who handle medication to ensure that the medication and dosage are correct and that potential interactions are identified. The National Patient Safety Foundation (2014) states, the pharmacist and pharmacy technicians must understand the physician's order, enter the order accurately into the computer record, identify potential problems with the prescription that the physician may have missed, pick the correct drug and strength from their supply, and place the drug in a container that has been correctly labeled for the drug. Most pharmacies use a system of checks and double checks designed to help optimize the safety of patients. (para. 1)

These safeguards, designed for all pharmacists, will also protect against any possible errors caused by a learning disability. Further, an additional layer of checks and balances can be instituted for the student with dyslexia to follow. The preceptor, student, and faculty should work together to develop additional safeguards, as needed.

MYTH #3: ACCOMMODATIONS IN THE CLINICAL SETTING DO NOT PREPARE STUDENTS FOR THE "REAL WORLD"

Faculty and administrators may be concerned that the accommodations provided in the educational setting will not be available to a student after graduation, and, that they are setting up students to fail once they encounter the "real world" of the workplace. However, accommodations are also available in the workplace, and are determined in a manner similar to accommodations in the academic and clinical settings. The abundance of professional associations for individuals with disabilities in the health sciences attests to the ability of those with disabilities to do the work and the willingness of health care facilities to hire them (see Appendix 9.1). It is critical that decisions about accommodations and technical standards are grounded in the reality of the current world of work, and not on historical assumptions, as shown in Case Example 9.1.

CASE EXAMPLE 9.1 • *Palmer College of Chiropractic v. Davenport Civil Rights Commission*[4]

A blind student in a graduate chiropractic program requested a sighted assistant to describe the radiographs verbally, to assist with making a diagnosis. The school had recently adopted technical standards that required students to have sufficient vision to review radiographs. The school asserted that the standards were based on the standards of the national accreditation body for chiropractic schools. The student requested that the school modify the standard, but the school refused, saying that interpreting radiographic images is an essential part of both the program and the job of a chiropractor. The court, however, disagreed, noting that 20% of chiropractors do not maintain the equipment to take radiographic pictures in their offices, and often outsource this task as needed, so the ability to read them is not an essential part of chiropractic practice. The court went on to discuss the increasing numbers of blind students who have completed medical school as well as chiropractic programs, saying that these real-world examples support the court's decision that allowing the requested reader was not a fundamental alteration of the educational program.

Some skills and standards that students are required to master are very much directly related to "real-world" employment. Comprehensive discussions about whether a skill is truly essential should take place within the

---

[4] Palmer College of Chiropractic v. Davenport Civil Rights Commission, 850 N.W.2d 326 (2014).

school, and those skills determined to be essential should be included in the school's technical standards (see Example 9.6; see also the section "Technical Standards" in Chapter 3).

EXAMPLE 9.6 • Dental Student With Visual or Fine Motor Disability

Concern: A dental student with visual or fine motor disabilities may not be able to complete that program, as employment in the dental field requires the use of a drill (referred to in dentistry as "direct impact") to perform the vast majority of the duties and responsibilities. Direct impact on the tooth is necessary in nearly all dental settings. As such, related skills are considered a critical component of dental programs, and all students must be able to perform them. There are few, if any, employment opportunities in the dental field that do not require "direct impact" on the tooth with instruments.

Educational Objective: The student must be able to demonstrate mastery of skills required when working with a direct impact on teeth.

Response: Due to the immediate and direct effect of the drill on the teeth, there is no margin for error and dentists (and students) must be correct in every instance. In collaboration with dental professionals, disability services providers, and the student, it is critical to address the specific levels of visual acuity and motor skills that will be required to continue and meet the standards in the dental school program. This should be done as early and as transparently as possible, in order for the student to be able to make well-informed and appropriate decisions moving forward. Reasonable alternatives and adjustments should be explored and considered, but, ultimately, some students will be unable to meet the technical standards and will not be suitable for the program.

MYTH #4: ACCOMMODATIONS LOWER PROGRAM STANDARDS SUCH THAT STUDENTS WITH DISABILITIES ARE LESS QUALIFIED AFTER GRADUATION

The ADA requires that disability accommodations must not fundamentally alter the requirements and standards of a health sciences program such that essential components of the program are changed. This ensures that students with disabilities are required to meet the same academic and technical standards as their peers. No accommodations should ever be granted that would result in a student with a disability completing a program with lesser skills than the other students (see Example 9.7; see also discussion in Chapter 3 on avoiding a fundamental alteration of the educational program).

EXAMPLE 9.7 • A PhD Student With a Tremor Using Lab Instruments

Concern: A PhD student in a genetics lab has an essential tremor, which poses difficulty when using lab instruments (e.g., pipettes, needles). Students working in the lab are required to use instruments to extract genetic materials or transfer chemicals within the lab or DNA from laboratory animals to petri dishes, which requires fine motor skills.

Educational Objective: The student must be able to demonstrate the ability to critically analyze the data, develop ideas, and understand relationships between components in the lab.

Response: Because the goal of the lab work completed by a PhD student is cognitively based, the ability to use a pipette is not an essential learning component. When viewed in this manner, the idea of having an intermediary or a lab assistant complete these tasks is not a "fundamental alteration" because the standard has not been changed, merely the manner in which the student collected the data (see "Accommodations in the Laboratory Setting" in Chapter 4).

MYTH #5: STUDENTS WITH DISABILITIES CANNOT HANDLE THE INTENSITY OF HEALTH SCIENCES PROGRAMS

Navigating health sciences programs with a disability can be challenging; however, the myth that students with disabilities are unable to handle the rigors of a health science curriculum is false. All students face life challenges at various points in their academic careers, and experience periods of greater and lesser functioning due to these natural life stressors, such as divorce or financial difficulties. Many students with disabilities will say they believe they are more resilient and have developed better compensatory skills for working through challenging situations, based on their historical experiences with managing their disabilities in the academic setting.

However, awareness that others may subscribe to this myth can have negative repercussions for students. It can, for example, lead them to delay disclosure of their disabilities in the educational setting, as they wait to see how they are received within the school before requesting accommodations. Students often fear that disclosing a disability will result in reduced professional opportunities because faculty's knowledge about a disability will prevent the student from entering a particular clerkship, clinical experience, preceptorship, rotation, or residency. They fear it may cause faculty to decide not to provide a recommendation for residency or employment.

Rather than addressing Myth #5 through specific accommodations, responding to it adequately requires a coordinated campus effort to educate faculty and staff, and build awareness among students, about the value and unique perspectives that people with disabilities bring to health sciences campuses. It requires building a community that is supportive of their contributions, and that sends the message to students that they are welcome and expected to attend health sciences programs. The decision to seek accommodations often depends on the attitude displayed within the school about students with disabilities.

CONCLUSION

The inclusion of students with disabilities in the health sciences fields can provide valuable insight and understanding to research and practice that is unique from that of their peers. Appendix 9.1 highlights a number of professional associations for individuals with disabilities in the health sciences. These organizations evidence the many health sciences professionals successfully working in the field today.

REFERENCES

Georgetown University School of Nursing & Health Studies. (n.d.). *Technical standards.* Retrieved from http://nhs.georgetown.edu/nursing/resources/technical

National Patient Safety Foundation. (2014). *What you should expect. For patients and families: Pharmacy safety.* Retrieved from https://npsf.site-ym.com/?page=pharmacysafety

Ross, H. J. (2014). *Everyday bias: Identifying and navigating unconscious judgments in our daily lives.* Lanham, MD: Rowman & Littlefield.

Organizations Supporting Health Sciences Professionals With Disabilities

Association	Contact Info
Association of Medical Professionals With Hearing Losses	www.amphl.org
Canadian Association of Physicians with Disabilities	www.capd.ca
Coalition for Disability Access in Health Science and Medical Education	sds.ucsf.edu/coalition
Council on Access, Prevention and Inter-professional Relations (American Dental Association)	altdentalcareers@ada.org
Exceptional Nurse	www.exceptionalnurse.com
National Organization of Nurses with Disabilities	www.nond.org
Society of Healthcare Professionals with Disabilities	www.disabilitysociety.org
Society of Pharmacists with Disabilities	www.pharmacistswithdisabilities.org
Society of Physicians with Disabilities	www.physicianswithdisabilities.org

Dos and Don'ts for Working With Students With Disabilities

Elisa Laird-Metke, Lisa M. Meeks, and Grace C. Clifford

INTRODUCTION

University personnel uniformly want to do the right thing when it comes to students with disabilities, but are often uncertain what that is. This chapter offers concrete steps for steering students toward effective campus supports, and flags potential "land mines" for faculty and administrators, such as inappropriate boundaries or potential legal liability for the school.

Disability services (DS) offices on every campus work in partnership with the faculty and students to ensure that both stakeholders are well served, and that their respective interests are protected. Faculty and administrators, particularly those new to working with students with disabilities, frequently ask disability providers for guidance concerning best practices and common pitfalls. This chapter summarizes this guidance and can be used by disability providers to conduct short trainings for administration and faculty.

DO PROVIDE THE ACCOMMODATIONS APPROVED BY THE DS OFFICE, AND CONTACT THE DS OFFICE WITH ANY QUESTIONS

Don't provide disability accommodations beyond those approved by the DS office

Formal notification of approved accommodations is usually communicated via a letter from the DS office (see Chapter 3, The Process for Determining Disability Accommodations). Faculty and administrators should carry out the accommodations exactly as written in the letter. Any questions or concerns should go directly to the DS provider, who can provide clarification or address concerns.

In the absence of a formal letter or notice, faculty should *not* provide disability-related accommodations (e.g., a student requests more time to complete a paper, citing a chronic health condition that prevents him from working as fast as other students). Providing informal accommodations undermines the legally mandated process followed by the DS office (see Chapter 2, Disability Law and the Process for Determining Whether a Student Has a Disability, and Chapter 3, The Process for Determining Disability Accommodations), and makes it difficult to defend a school if accusations of discrimination or arbitrary and capricious treatment of students are levied.

Legally, disability determinations must include personnel who are trained in disability needs, and cannot be made by faculty alone.[1] DS providers weigh the decision about whether to accommodate a student very carefully, and have specialized training regarding the school's legal obligations based on best practices informed by case law. They also have access to information about the school's history of accommodating students in similar circumstances.

The law also requires that accommodations decisions be made only after thoughtful deliberation.[2] When faculty make quick decisions about when and how to accommodate students, the school fails to meet this legal mandate. Offering students accommodations without going through the process required by law may result in students receiving accommodations to which they are not entitled, or for which they have previously been denied through a formal review. Alternatively, a student might not receive a necessary accommodation, resulting in a failure to provide reasonable accommodation for the student's disability-related needs.

If a student's request to faculty for consideration is not disability related—for example, a student got the flu and asked for a few extra days to complete an assignment—this should be considered according to school or faculty discretion, as it would for any other student. However, if a student's request for accommodation is grounded in any long-term medical condition or injury, the student should be directed to the DS office for formal evaluation. By referring a student to the proper office, faculty avoid potential liability ramifications of failing to follow the legally mandated processes for considering disability accommodation requests. Following this process also offers the student assurance that accommodation decisions are made in a confidential, objective, and consistent manner.

---

[1] University of California, Santa Cruz, Case No. 09-97-2169 (OCR Region IX 1999).
[2] Wong v. Regents of the University of California, 192 F.3d 807 (9th Cir. 1999); Wynne v. Tufts University School of Medicine, 932 F.2d 19 (1st Cir. 1991).

DO REFER STUDENTS WHO YOU LEARN OR SUSPECT OF HAVING A DISABILITY TO THE APPROPRIATE CAMPUS OFFICE

Don't make disability determinations yourself

Occasionally, students may disclose a disability to an advisor or other trusted faculty member. A disability-related reason might also be offered to a faculty member as an explanation for poor performance or as the reason for failing to meet a requirement or deadline. This disclosure often takes the form of a simple statement, or a student may even provide a note from a doctor, test results, or some other documentation to "prove" that a medical condition is real. Faculty *should not accept* any medical documentation offered in a request for accommodations (aside from nondisability-related circumstances, as noted earlier), and instead should direct students to the DS office.

If a student discloses a disability to a university employee (i.e., faculty, staff member, administrator), it is imperative that the employee refer the student to disability services. This may be done verbally, but university staff should also refer the student to disability services in writing. This is due to the fact that once a student has disclosed a disability to a school official, the institution as a whole is deemed to be aware of the disability and is obligated to respond appropriately. As such, a student must be referred to the appropriate place to discuss disability-related needs and request accommodations (see Chapter 2).

Faculty should follow any verbal referrals with a confirmation e-mail. Sending the student an e-mail containing the DS office contact information serves as a reminder, ensures that the student has the correct information, and provides a written record showing that the student was encouraged to seek accommodations through the appropriate channels. The latter can become important if the student does not seek accommodations and later experiences academic difficulty and pursues a formal complaint or litigation.

Even if a student does not mention having a disability, a faculty member may come to suspect that a student has a disability after getting to know and observing the student in the educational setting. Faculty members should resist the urge to suggest that a student has, or shows signs of, a particular disability—*even if they are clinically qualified to do so*. Suggesting that a student has a disability is problematic because the student might feel that the instructor views him or her as less capable than peers. It also may lead to a charge of discrimination if the student believes a particular grade was low, or that he or she was otherwise mistreated, due to the faculty member's perception of the student as a person with a disability.

The more prudent approach for faculty who suspect a disability is to suggest that the student seek support from the relevant campus resources, such as the counseling center, student health center, tutoring program, learning specialist, or academic support. These offices are staffed by individuals trained to recognize the signs of a learning or psychological disability, and

• **FIGURE 10.1 Referring Students to the Appropriate Supports**

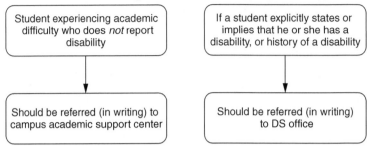

can refer students for testing as appropriate (see "Suspected Disability" in Chapter 7). See Figure 10.1 for direction on appropriate student referrals.

DO WORK TO ENSURE THAT DOCUMENTS AND COMMUNICATION PERTAINING TO ACCOMMODATIONS ARE KEPT CONFIDENTIAL

Don't discuss a student's disability or accommodations unless there is a clear "need to know"

Confidentiality of a student's disability-related information and need for accommodations is important. When there is a need to share disability-related information in order to implement accommodations, faculty and administrators should *only* discuss the relevant accommodation(s), not the disability. For example, instructors should not forward e-mails containing a student's entire list of accommodations to a teaching assistant who only needs to schedule testing. When implementing accommodations, avoid sharing the name of the student receiving them where it is not necessary (see Chapter 7's tips for faculty and administrators to ensure confidentiality of student information).

DO LISTEN TO STUDENTS AND OFFER SUPPORT AS APPROPRIATE

Don't ask students for specifics about their disability, or why they need certain accommodations

Students are not prohibited from sharing disability-related information with faculty, and may choose to do so. Faculty may respond however they are most comfortable: listen supportively or explain that you prefer not to cross such personal boundaries in professional settings. If faculty engage in discussions about disabilities, it is important to let students disclose, without feeling pressured, to an appropriate level; however, oversharing of personal information should be discouraged (see "Faculty and Student Boundaries in Communication" in Chapter 7).

Although it is often perfectly appropriate to ask how a student is coping, faculty should exercise some caution when making inquiries about a student's well-being. Health sciences faculty, due to their expertise, can have difficulty separating their roles as health practitioners and teachers. Faculty and administrators with medical expertise often find that the instinct to ask follow-up questions about a student's health, treatment regimen, and prognosis—combined with the student's instinct to want to please an instructor and history of responding to such questions as a patient—can quickly lead to an inappropriate and awkward patient–health provider role replacing the student–faculty role. Further, knowing a student's diagnosis may cause a faculty member, even subconsciously, to view the student differently from other students.

DO CREATE MATERIALS AND ASSIGNMENTS THAT EMBRACE PRINCIPLES OF UNIVERSAL DESIGN BY BEING INHERENTLY ACCESSIBLE TO ALL STUDENTS, WITH OR WITHOUT DISABILITIES

Don't cause students with disabilities to be singled out in your classroom

For an instructor, implementing multiple accommodations for a variety of students in each class might seem like a challenge to manage. One way to streamline this process is to adopt a universal design model for teaching, wherein course content and materials are presented in a manner that is accessible to all individuals, regardless of disability, age, or learning style. The emphasis is placed on removing any potential barriers to accessing information, and it does not challenge academic rigor. Rather, those who use universal design often feel it enhances the delivery of the material to all students while simultaneously providing the necessary accommodations to the students who need them.

Universal design can be accomplished by using a variety of delivery methods and materials. For example, an instructor may use the Socratic method of lecture to disseminate course material but add an interactive and hands-on component, provide visual graphs/charts to reinforce information, invite guest speakers, or provide supplemental videos. Another way to create a universally designed curriculum is to offer students options regarding how to complete an assignment. For example, allowing all students to choose whether to write a paper, do an oral presentation, or present the material in a visual manner permits students with or without disabilities to choose the method that best showcases their abilities. This practice also avoids singling out, for example, a student with a communication disorder, who may need an alternative assessment when an oral presentation is required.

Many faculty members who have adopted a universal design approach choose to provide lecture slides, outlines, or study guides to all students prior to the class, not just those who need notes as a disability accommodation. Access to the material before the lecture increases the likelihood that all students will be able to participate in a meaningful way by allowing students to prepare for class discussion in a way that works best for their learning. For post-class learning, providing both video and audio recordings of the lecture allows students to review the material covered during class, and to pause and review any concepts they found confusing on first exposure. Access to the aforementioned materials before and after class reduces the need for students to divide their attention during class and allows students to learn and review the material at their own pace.

A universal design approach to providing notes can eliminate the need to provide note takers specifically for students with disabilities, and meet the learning needs of all students. In this arrangement, a comprehensive set of notes would be provided to all students in the class, allowing them to process the information as it is being presented, and encouraging richer classroom discussion, as students are not concentrating on writing down every word. In some iterations of this arrangement, a note taker is selected from the class or the role rotates between several classmates who share their notes with all students. In other cases, a teaching assistant or professor provides the notes.

Helpful resources, such as the University of Washington's DO-IT program, are available to learn more about and successfully implement universal design principles in the classroom (www.washington.edu/doit). Additional examples of universal design are provided in Table 10.1.

Syllabi statements that alert students with disabilities to services (e.g., the DS office, related contact information, and the process for obtaining accommodations in the classroom and clinic) suggest that students with disabilities are welcome and approved accommodations will be honored. This also normalizes disability for the other students in the classroom, who may not be aware that their classmates include students with disabilities (see "Syllabus Statements" in Chapter 7).

When creating classroom restrictions, it is also important to keep students with disabilities in mind. An example is a ban on electronics (usually laptops and tablets) during a class, to minimize distractions. Although faculty might think that making an exception for a student who needs electronics as an accommodation (e.g., textbooks in e-format, the ability to type instead of handwrite notes) will be sufficient, the reality is that students using electronics in a class where they are otherwise prohibited allows other students to easily identify which students have disabilities, and may even cause resentment from other students. When placed in this situation, students with disabilities frequently choose not to use their approved accommodations to avoid being labeled "different," or "outed" to their peers, which negatively impacts their education. An alternative approach might be to ask that electronics be put into "airplane mode" while in class, instead of requiring that they be put away altogether.

• TABLE 10.1 Universal Design for Learning

Universal Design for Learning Practice	How Students Benefit
Posting lecture outlines prior to class	Allows students to review and create context for lecture material. Aids students in structuring and organizing their notes.
Posting lecture slides	Allows students to review the material prior to class, creating context for the lecture. Enables students to review the lecture as needed.
Posting supplemental course materials	Allows students to interact and process the material in the way that best matches their learning style.
Posting discussion questions prior to the lecture	Allows students to prepare for the discussion, increasing the likelihood of a meaningful discussion.
Cooperative learning strategies for in-class discussions (e.g., think, pair, share)	Allow students time to process and draft a response. Offer a nonthreatening environment for students to share their thoughts in a small-group environment. Assist students in gaining multiple perspectives on the topic.
Online reading responses	Allow students to read and respond in a low-pressure forum. Enable students who may have missed class an opportunity to contribute to the class discussion. Assist students in gaining multiple perspectives on the topic.
Recording and posting of lectures (podcasts)	Allows students to review the lecture as needed for further processing of the presented material. Enables students to catch up on missed material. Offers the student the opportunity to review and add to their class notes.
Graphic organizers (charts and graphs that represent information visually)	Provide a quick, clear reference for students.
Guest lecturers	Offer a tangible approach to the material, which may further the students' understanding of the content.

CONCLUSION

Although this chapter touched on a few prominent "dos and don'ts," faculty should make use of the expertise in the DS office when working with students with disabilities. By asking questions and staying in touch with the campus DS specialists, instructors can ensure that students with disabilities receive appropriate accommodations and support, and feel welcomed in the academic environment.

Afterword

People with disabilities were traditionally excluded from school, left in the back wards of institutions, and abandoned by society. Even today, across the world, there are still young people with disabilities left behind by the educational system. Many are expressly forbidden from attending school, whereas others are excluded by inadequate funding of the accommodations and supports that would allow them full access to education.

In the contemporary United States things are gradually improving, but stereotype threat remains a pressing issue in higher education. This concept has long been used to explain underperformance among students in situations and environments where it was traditionally believed they did not belong, usually due to a socially stigmatized aspect of their identity. The stress of operating in an environment that sends implicit and explicit messages that one is "out of place" leads students to bear the additional weight of continuously fighting against a presumption of their inability (Steele, 2010).

The legal mechanisms established in the United States are one of the key factors that have generated change and enabled people to exercise their right to an inclusive and accessible educational environment. Although many argue that the use of lawsuits and complaints to enforce disability law is heavy handed, it is precisely these cases that have been instrumental in generating real change and improving access to education. And although change often feels glacially slow, the past 25 years have gradually opened up new possibilities for people with disabilities.

In the preface, we describe a significant growth in the number of students with disabilities in professional health sciences programs. There are many reasons for this, but the power of strong legislation, evolving understandings of the importance of inclusion, and case law that clarifies the meaning of access have undoubtedly pushed us to reevaluate our expectations for people with disabilities, and our image of the health professional.

It feels like an important and exciting time to be doing this work. Lisa and I have discussed the recent decisions by the National Board of Medical Examiners, the National Board of Osteopathic Medical Examiners, and the Association of American Medical Colleges to stop flagging the scores of students who take their exams with accommodations. We agreed that this one small change—the removal of an asterisk next to a score—is akin to the fall of the Berlin Wall for budding health professionals with disabilities. Often I sat with students as they endlessly deliberated whether to seek accommodations for entrance and licensing exams, considering the very real implications of "outing" themselves as having a disability. *Would they still be considered if it was known? Could they succeed sufficiently without the accommodation they required? Was taking the chance that they might be discriminated against worth the more accurate score? Would the financial expense and time of obtaining the necessary documentation even result in approved accommodations?* To entirely eliminate the "how will the asterisk be interpreted" question is a triumphant win for these students. Finally, the principle that accommodations *level the playing field* has been realized in this context. There is still much change to be made, but with every crack in the wall, and the strong wedge of organizations like the Coalition for Disability Access in Health Science and Medical Education working to pry these cracks further open, it feels as if the dam is starting to break.

We are all fortunate to be doing this work at a time of significant advancement in the field. We are called upon to support students with disabilities in the health professions, and to work within institutions to ensure that these students are given equal access to the educational environment. Schools are now recognizing the important contributions and power of students with disabilities, who, like other diverse populations, bring unique perspectives to the academic environment and the professional field. Meanwhile, evolving case law, early intervention, and accommodation have resulted in capable students with disabilities achieving at levels that allow them to gain entrance into health sciences institutions. Universities must be ready, willing, and able to include these students fully into their educational programs. And, if they are resistant, or lack thoroughness in their attempts to provide access, students and strong advocacy groups need to push back (sometimes to the tune of thousands and millions of dollars in lawsuits).

Although the law is a powerful tool to further the accessibility agenda, being a successful advocate for equal access within an institution necessitates working *with* others. It requires developing partnerships with key institutional players and striving to create a network of "champions" willing to pursue the accessibility cause. If disability services (DS) providers attempt to work alone as agents of change, they run the risk of finding themselves burnt out well before anything substantive has been accomplished. Bringing about change requires thoughtful attention to message delivery. Providers must skillfully educate their colleagues about the legal and ethical motivations for providing an accessible environment. This requires providers to use case law as a scalpel instead of a hammer, avoid scare tactics, and know when to use the potential for a lawsuit to further progress in a way that is not seen as threatening, but raises sufficient concern to push change.

Students in high-stakes health sciences programs are at risk for increased feelings of isolation and exhaustion when they have to fight for basic access to rights, on top of the existing stress and expectations of being a student. Students rely heavily on their professors, whose influence can make or break their careers. As a result, small injustices often go unreported and unresolved because students simply do not have the energy to fight and do not want to be viewed as troublemakers. Microaggressions (subtle or unconscious forms of discrimination) are also experienced by students with disabilities on a daily basis. The buildup of these everyday stressors fuels existing feelings of isolation and marginalization, threatening the ability of students to learn and thrive in their studies.

To address these circumstances effectively, DS providers must educate themselves to be able to take on the nuanced situations that arise in health sciences environments. They must also attend to the climate and everyday culture in which students operate. This can be pursued through promoting educational initiatives, heightening awareness of social justice issues related to disability, and implementing universal design principles. Working with faculty and administration through thoughtful collaboration, developing a keen understanding of the clinical and professional aspects of education, and carefully handling complex incidents solidifies the DS provider as the expert on campus while building the trust of colleagues. Most important, perhaps, the culture can shift by identifying the implicit messages that students receive when operating in the university environment and ensuring that those messages are not ableist in nature. If stereotype threats are weakened and students feel they are valued community members, the ongoing struggle for inclusion will begin to subside.

As DS providers, then, there are key principles that should inform our practice. First, become an agent of change on your campus—work to bring people on board, build allies, and support students to become leaders and outspoken voices on campus (or respect their decision to be silent partners). Second, use your position of privilege and power to push for equal access, instead of acting as a gatekeeper: As L. Scott Lissner often reminds us, "Say yes when you can, and no when you have to." Third, collaborate across campuses, reach out to colleagues in the field, and work together to bring about systemic change—the burden is reduced when carried on the shoulders of many. Fourth, when faced with challenges, "get curious, not furious." Identify the underlying problem, and develop a plan for change. Finally, and most important, listen to your students. Hear and understand their struggles, appreciate their perspective, and ensure that they have a fair chance to succeed, while honoring the standards of the professions they have chosen to enter.

Students with disabilities have such great promise to change the face of health care or, if they are not so interested in changing the world, simply be excellent clinicians. We must support them to realize this potential. In short, go forth, and do good work.

Neera R. Jain

REFERENCE

Steele, C. (2010). *Whistling Vivaldi: And other clues to how stereotypes affect us.* New York, NY: W. W. Norton & Company.

Index

National Board of Osteopathic Medical
Examiners (NBOME), 90
National Institutes of Health, 14
New York Medical College, OCR
complaint, 49
nonstandard accommodation, 41
North v. Widener University, 148, 192

objective structured clinical examinations
(OSCEs), 79–80
obligations, student and school
accommodation request process, 23
disability, notification of, 23, 25
readmission, requirements and
limitations, 27–28
students' documentation,
confidentiality of, 25–27
obstetrics and gynecology (OB/GYN)
clerkship, 77–78
Office for Civil Rights (OCR), 12–13, 17, 23,
27–28, 34, 47, 119
OSCE accommodations
for student with low vision, 79–80
for student with multiple
disabilities, 80

*Palmer College of Chiropractic v. Davenport
Civil Rights Commission,* 218
patient interaction, 79
"pimping," medical education, 76–77
portable document format (PDF), 124
posttraumatic stress disorder (PTSD), 51
practical lab exams, 68–69
private litigation, 13–14
private-room exams, ADHD and, 62
professionalism, 142–143, 166
in communication, 165–185
graduate schools and, 165
students with disabilities and, 166–167
program modifications, 44, 75

reduced-distraction environment, ADHD
and, 62
Rehabilitation Act of 1973, 4, 12, 14, 16, 72
requesting accommodations process, certification and licensing exams
appointments, with licensed
professionals, 103
cost, for assessment, 103
current (updated) documentation and,
102–103

disability, historical evidence of, 104
disability services or academic program
letter of support, 107–109
discussions of, 102
DS provider, assisting, 103
letters of support, for academic
performance, 107–109
limited free time, for assessment, 103
necessary elements, gathering, 102
personal statement, of disability and,
105–106
transcripts and, 104–105
rights and responsibilities, for faculty and
school, 51, 53
rights and responsibilities, for students,
51–52
risk management office, 5

School of Nursing, accommodations, 57
screen-enlarging software, 135
screen readers, 135
Section 504 of the Rehabilitation Act of
1973, 4, 14, 16, 72
simulation labs (SIM labs), 69–70
smartpens, 133
social model, of disability, 15
standard accommodations, 41
"stop-the-clock" breaks, 61
student accommodation requests,
timing of, 50
student support, for academic
difficulties, 7, 9
academic standing and, 10–11
disability claims and, 11
issue, identifying, 9
teamwork and, 9–10
student support offices
on campus, 5–7, 8–9
campus counseling center, student
referral and, 6
ensuring effective support,
students, 7
multioffice collaboration, for supporting
students, 6
multiple, diverse identities, students
with, 7

technical standards, 38–40
creation of, 39–40
disseminating, 38
Tecza v. University of San Francisco, 26